"The Long Road to the Sky"
Night Fighter over Germany

A group of 85 Squadron aircrew perched on 'shambles', A.K.A. 'Chalky's Chariot', outside the squadron crew hut at Tangmere in 1946. The author is sitting on the roof. The others, from left to right, are Andy, my navigator at the time, Roy Southern, Albert (see 'Death in the Afternoon') and Larry, later to succeed Andy in my navigator's seat. (see chapters twenty-six and twenty-seven).

"The Long Road to the Sky"
Night Fighter over Germany

Graham White

Pen & Sword
AVIATION

First published in Great Britain in 2006 by
Pen & Sword Aviation
an imprint of
Pen & Sword Books Ltd
47 Church Street
Barnsley
South Yorkshire
S70 2AS

ISBN 1 84415 471 8
978 1 84415 471 5

A CIP catalogue record for this book is
available from the British Library.

Typeset in Palatino by
Phoenix Typesetting, Auldgirth, Dumfriesshire

Printed and bound in England by
CPI UK

Pen & Sword Books Ltd incorporates the imprints of Pen & Sword Aviation, Pen &
Sword Maritime, Pen & Sword Military, Wharncliffe Local History,
Pen & Sword Select, Pen & Sword Military Classics and Leo Cooper.

For a complete list of Pen & Sword titles please contact
PEN & SWORD BOOKS LIMITED
47 Church Street, Barnsley, South Yorkshire, S70 2AS, England
E-mail: enquiries@pen-and-sword.co.uk
Website: www.pen-and-sword.co.uk

Contents

TO THE MANY WHO SHARED THE SAME SKY WITH
ME, AND TO THE BRAVE FEW WHO SHARED THE
SAME COCKPIT WITH ME; BUT ESPECIALLY TO THE
ONE WHO SHARED A WHOLE LIFE WITH ME,
AND WAS ALWAYS THERE WHEN I
CAME BACK DOWN TO EARTH.

Acknowledgements

My thanks to those who helped to shine a light in a few darkened corners of memory, in particular to John (Dagwood) Wooding, to date still enjoying life; Johnny (Wacker) Wakefield, a great mate who sadly died just as this book was completed; and Doug Wilkinson who moved on to that Last Great Stalag in the sky some years ago.

And to those others – like Mike, Duncan, Terry and Marian – who dragged me, kicking and screaming, out of the Amstrad and Brownie camera era, to which I intend returning without delay.

Foreword

Some twenty or more years ago, during one of my more serious attacks of nostalgia, I suddenly felt a desire to see some of my old pals again. People like Butch, Ben, Jamie, Bob, anybody, just to chat over old times while I could still dredge up the faded images from an ageing brain.

I found that the squadron association held a reunion each year, so I contacted the association secretary (a man, I felt, whose sense of humour had died young as a result of a severe attack of pomposity) and ordered a ticket.

'Sorry, all sold out', he told me.

Ah well, it had been a good idea. But he came back at the last moment with news of a cancellation.

I found myself in a hotel room in London, packed with noise and people I didn't know. I wandered vaguely through the massed chatterers without seeing a recognisable face, and wishing I was home. Then a lady came over: I looked lost, did I want someone to chat to? It seemed that her husband had been unable to attend due to illness – hence the availability of my ticket. She told me he had not been on our squadron but an auxiliary squadron, weekend flyers at the same 'drome. I recalled only one name from that lot, Freddy Butcher, a flight sergeant who had been on a 'drome with me (but a different squadron) during the war. He was known as a 'Pat', or a Pleasantly Amiable Twit.

After the war he had wangled a commission with the weekend flyers, and I'd seen him there as a flight lieutenant. The last I'd heard of him, there had been a rumour of trouble over some missing petrol, but I never learned the details of it.

The kind lady was Mrs Butcher, and I joined her group at the meal. Thanks to her the evening wasn't a complete disaster, but I didn't repeat the experience, although I continued to receive the newsletters for a while. In one of them was a comment by a Squadron Leader Butcher DFC, now manager of a prestigious branch of a well-known bank, modestly suggesting that all references to rank in the squadron association should be dropped as no longer relevant.

Squadron Leader? And DFC? Surely not! I could only recall him at the war's end as a flight sergeant, and DFCs could only be won in action and by officers – NCOs were given the DFM. Did he, perhaps stretch the truth to boost his peacetime prospects at the bank? I don't know.

Butcher wasn't his real name, but even though both Freddy and his kind wife are long dead I wouldn't dream of revealing it. If the bank chose to judge a man's fitness for a job by counting the rings on his sleeve or the ribbons on his chest, that was up to them. It is not my place to comment on it. Nor have I the right to judge the behaviour of anyone mentioned in this book, alive or not. I simply record it. So where there's any chance of my causing embarrassment I've either not given the name or I've changed it. And in one or two cases events have also been altered sufficiently to prevent recognition.

But make no mistake, it all happened.

CHAPTER ONE

The Way War Broke Out

It's odd how casually you can make decisions that are going totally to alter your life. Take me, for example. I was crossing Derby Market Place one Saturday afternoon early in July 1941, and I noticed that the Assembly Rooms had become a recruiting centre for the RAF. This didn't take any great powers of deduction on my part because there was a notice outside that said,'JOIN THE ROYAL AIR FORCE'. It didn't say, 'PLEASE', but on the other hand it didn't say, 'OR ELSE'. So there was obviously quite a choice in the matter. On the spur of the moment I decided to drop in and see what they had to offer. I wasn't all that serious, I was just browsing, really. For one thing, I was in a reserved occupation, which meant that I couldn't be called up because my work was designated as vital for the war effort.

Mind you, even for me that took a bit of believing. Fresh out of school a few weeks before the start of the war, I was a newly hired dogsbody in the drawing-office of a large engineering company, where I was kept busy sharpening pencils, fetching and filing drawings and taking messages. Nominally I was an apprentice draughtsman, a title that meant they could get away with paying me as little as twelve shillings and sixpence per week. That's sixty-two and a half pence in present-day coin of the realm. Of this vast sum I kept the two shillings and sixpence and gave my mother the remaining ten shillings, or fifty pence, for my week's keep. At twenty-one I would become a fully-fledged draughtsman at around three pounds a week. And that was my life all set out ahead of me for the next forty-five years or so. While Britain's armed forces fought desperate rearguard battles on the continent to stem the steamroller onslaught of an all-conquering enemy, I was fated to wield nothing more lethal than a sharpened HB at a drawing-board. The prospect didn't exactly thrill me.

But while the war was on regulations were very strict. You couldn't change your job without permission, and you could even be dragged into court and fined for persistently turning up late for work. It seemed as if I was chained to a boring and inconsequential job in my home town while tremendous battles that would decide the fate of the Free World were being fought out elsewhere. The only way that I could get out of my present job was by climbing into an aeroplane.

Just joining the Brylcreem Boys in any other capacity wouldn't do: you had specifically to be a member of aircrew. For some reason, if you volunteered to fly, no matter how vital your civilian work, they would happily clap you on the shoulder and say, 'Well done, lad! Off you go and get yourself up into that there sky and shoot things down, or drop bombs on things.'

Of course, if I'd had any sense this should have told me something, but it didn't.

I should have realised that if they were that desperate for people to fly then the life expectancy of a birdman elect left something greatly to be desired, and they weren't expecting to pay out all that many old-age pensions to folk who scudded round the sky for a living.

Still, the prospect of exchanging my drawing-board for an instrument panel, my HB pencil for a 20 mm cannon, and my old grey flannels and Harris tweed jacket for a sky-blue uniform adorned with the famous 'wings' was an alluring one for a lad of my age. OK, I could dream, couldn't I! So I'd just pop into the RAF recruiting office and have a quick browse through the Sits Vac. column on the notice board, and then have a long Walter Mitty daydream about it for a year or two.

I was pretty vague about what sort of reception I might receive. Should I, perhaps, break the ice with a merry little quip? 'I saw your notice outside – "JOIN THE ROYAL AIR FORCE". I didn't know it had come apart!' No, too flippant, I'd just play it by ear.

I fondly imagined a friendly chat with some clean-cut young Adonis on temporary rest from combing the clouds for planes with evil-looking black swastikas on them. He'd have a slight limp, of course, from where a German bullet had nicked his ankle – all heroes did. That's what made them sexy. And over a cup of tea and a cream bun he would casually float various ideas in my direction. Like, 'There's a squadron leader's job going, down in Kent, that might interest you, old boy. Just the thing for a clean-living young chap like yourself. It's a nine-to-five shift, fairly light work – a couple of Messerschmitt 109s a day for starters, with the chance of a good bit of overtime when Hitler starts his invasion. Everything found – pilot's badge, VC ribbon, a bucket of Brylcreem a week, admiring female to hang on each arm. Oh, and free accommodation in one small Spitfire at thirty thousand feet, fitted with all mod cons.' Then he'd elaborate a bit and explain that when he said all mod cons there were actually nine of them, eight large machine-guns and one rather small pee-tube, so a good aim in a restricted space could be a definite asset in both cases.

And I'd modestly mention the cut-glass bowl I'd won on a dart stall at Ilkeston Fair and taken home to my mum, and I reckoned that would just about clinch the deal.

Instead, the recruiting sergeant turned out to be a tough old bird with a beaky nose, a face like a sunburnt window leather and a voice reminiscent of a steel rasp. 'Aircrew? Sign here, son.'

Hang on! I corrected him carefully, not aircrew. Well, not exactly. I just came in to ask about becoming a pilot. And the emphasis was on the words 'just' and 'ask'.

'A pilot's aircrew, in' 'e! Sign 'ere, son!'

I told myself it was just an application form for further information to be sent to my home and airily scrawled my name. He inspected the signature carefully, to make sure that in a light-hearted moment I hadn't scribbled Hermann P. Goering, Benito Abercrombie Mussolini, or something equally daft, and found it all legally binding. Got the little sod!, his cold blue eyes said.

'Right. Report to Derby Railway Station termorrer morning, nine o' clock. You'll be going dahn to the Assessment Centre in Birmingham for a test and a medical.' Tomorrow morning? Whoa! I hadn't even told my mother yet, or my boss, or anybody else, come to that. And you can't rush these things, they take time.

'Nine o' clock termorrer mornin',' he repeated tersely. 'Be there!'

Really, this had all started back in my schooldays, in the sixth form at Bemrose School. That's where things first began to go awry with my life-plan.

You didn't do much in the Sixth. It was more a sort of sanatorium where you convalesced after taking your School Certificate exam. You just sort of faffed around amiably all day, playing at being prefects. One or two of you – no more – made a stab at getting to university, but such a thing was considered beyond the scope of the normal lad. For one thing, people like that were expected to be fluent in Classical languages, and that was all Greek to most of us.

So it was quite a shock when one morning we were each handed a slip of paper and told to write down what sort of job we wanted to spend the next fifty years of our lives doing, and we had five minutes to think about it. The shock was compounded when we were reminded that we would be finishing school in a couple of weeks' time and from that moment on we would be expected to start actually working for a living. That is if we were planning on eating regularly. The thought was mind numbing, and I desperately cudgelled my brain for an occupation that I fancied.

For as long as I could remember I had been scribbling cartoons – in fact I had actually sold one to the *Sheffield Telegraph* at the tender age of fourteen, for the princely sum of five shillings, shortly followed by a second one to the man's magazine, *Men Only*, for quite a bit more. Dazzled by the prospect of such potential riches, without hesitation I confidently wrote down the word 'Artist' on the slip of paper.

It was just as promptly crossed out again by a bad-tempered form master (by the name of 'Nunky' Norville, a man who seemed to have washed in olive oil and spent his life trying to wipe his hands clean of it). I was told not to be so stupid and to go back and put down something sensible. Deflated, I could think of nothing else that I wanted to do, so the teacher, on the basis that both artists and draughtsmen used pencils, wrote down 'Draughtsman' on my form for me. Which is why I ended up as an apprentice draughtsman in a large drawing-office in an engineering company that made pipes.

Fat pipes, thin pipes, long pipes, short pipes, straight pipes, bent pipes, pipes like petrified concertinas, you name them, they made them. However, there is no way that drawing a metal pipe could ever be described as creative or straining the brain cells to any great extent. And just in case you had any fancy ideas of your own, like making a square pipe for sending bricks along, or bending a tube round so that it disappeared up its own fundamental orifice with its contents doomed never again to see the light of day, you were constrained by being given strict standards to follow. It was all written down on pieces of stiff card – what size hole to specify for what size flange, and what diameter bend for what diameter pipe. Fresh thinking was firmly discouraged.

I hope my erstwhile fellow draughtsmen in that drawing-office – as good a bunch of blokes as you would wish to work with – will forgive me for appearing to denigrate the work that they did, but frankly it bored me stiff. And as in wartime you couldn't change jobs without permission, there was no way out. Indeed, you were expected to spend your spare time attending night school several times a week There you were taught such esoteric mysteries as how to calculate the size and number of rivets in a boiler and how to work out the horsepower required to drive a machine. It looked as if there was going to be a very long and very uneventful working life ahead of me

Not that I actually got around to drawing a pipe for a long time. My first job in the drawing office, as war clouds gathered ominously, was to cut up old tracings into long thin strips and glue them, criss-cross fashion, across the office windows. The idea of this was that it would prevent flying glass from slicing off vital parts of your anatomy if a bomb happened to drop nearby during an air raid.

I must have made a half-decent job of my window reinforcement, because almost as soon as I had finished the Government felt confident enough to call Adolf Hitler's bluff. I can still recall quite clearly Neville Chamberlain's thin, piping voice on the radio at eleven o'clock on that still Sunday morning, announcing that '. . . I must tell you now that no such assurance has been received, and that consequently we are at war with Germany.'

Of course, I hadn't the slightest idea what war would involve, nor I suppose had anyone else who hadn't lived through the muddy horror of trench warfare in the previous conflict. In my youthful innocence I felt a mixture of apprehension and excitement at the news. At last we'd stopped retreating and drawn a line in the sand. (How were we to know that Hitler would pinch the sand?) Now, surely, things would change.

And change they did. The moment war broke out the BBC demonstrated the new steely determination of the British nation by coldly referring to the German Chancellor, not as Herr Hitler, as before, but as plain 'Hitler'. Personally, I thought that was going a bit far. Such withering contempt was rather ill mannered, and quite possibly against the Geneva Convention. Certainly it wouldn't have been tolerated in these days of political correctness, but this was war, dammit.

At once the newspapers and cinema newsreels began airily to explain how Germany couldn't possibly win any war, and it would all be over by Christmas, saving parents from having to answer awkward questions about how Santa Claus got past anti-aircraft fire and balloon barrages and the like. Of course, when Germany promptly started winning, they began equally airy explanations that the enemy wasn't really beating us, he was being lured into a clever trap.

After all, God was an Englishman, albeit an honorary and recently naturalised one. We had the world's largest navy and the atlas blushed a warm, patriotic pink on every page. We had an Empire (most towns had a Gaumont and an Odeon as well), and that comic little Charlie Chaplin lookalike had to be mad to think of taking us on. And the reason for our belief was that those self-same newsreels came jammed in between our weekly fix of celluloid dreams. Films showed a world where everyone talked down their noses, and the message blaring forth down those nostrils was the same as the one they told us every Sunday at Sunday School. The hero always ended up with the girl (though in those days he never seemed to have much clue about what to do with her) and invariably triumphed. The villain got his come-uppance in the last reel, at which point the hero routinely beat seven kinds of donkey droppings out of him before we stood respectfully for the National Anthem, God-Saving-The-King heartily before we ran for the last bus with a warm feeling that once again justice had been done. We were conditioned from puberty to expect good to come out on top, and that meant us. End of story. Our confidence was total.

Unfortunately, Hitler didn't watch our films or our newsreels, he watched his own, and they showed him winning. Suddenly, that last reel began to look a long way off. The Germans not only didn't get out of Poland when they were told, they began to get into lots of other places with consummate ease. As when we (quite illegally) mined Norwegian coastal waters to stop Swedish steel being stealthily slipped into Germany, and they showed what cunning, low-down swine they were by leap-frogging the world's biggest navy and invading Norway by air. They even took their military bands with them, and oompahed us out of the place on our arses.

My mother was usually the announcer of any such bad news, relaying it hot from early morning bulletins on the wireless, when calling urgently up the stairs just after eight o'clock of a morning: 'Graham! It's ten minutes to eight, you'll be late for work and Hitler's gone into Norway!' The implication being that if I didn't get a move on, I was going to have quite a long wait at the corner of Stores Road for all those Panzer columns to pass.

However, our rulers remained unperturbed. 'Hitler has missed the bus!' Chamberlain quavered, in that piping voice of his. But Hitler wasn't going by bus, he was travelling by private Panzer column. Mind you, that bus came in handy to get us out of Narvik in a hurry.

And it didn't stop there. The derided little Austrian ex-corporal not only ignored all the rules of warfare, he just wasn't a gentleman. France had gone to enormous trouble and expense to build a line of fortifications along their common border, called the Maginot Line. And what happened? While they were busy trying to find a plumber to fix one or two small problems (they had built their bunkers lower than their sewers and were having trouble trying to get their effluent to flow uphill), the Nazi hordes nipped round the top end of the fortifications, and through Belgium and Holland, without so much as a by-your-leave in a most under-handed way. In fact, it was not only under-handed, it was against international law (the same international law that we'd ignored in the Norwegian minelaying, though, of course, that was different).

Then, before we knew it, things suddenly went from bad to desperate. Hitler's tanks cut their way, like a cold knife through hot horse-shit, through the French lines to the Channel coast. And the French, like the Dutch and the Belgians before them, collapsed. It's a good job there was no Channel Tunnel in those days, or the only thing that could have stopped the *Wehrmacht* from charging straight on through it like a dose of salts was the Dover Customs, and then only if the Germans had been carrying too many cigarettes with them.

We were alone. Hurriedly, we clawed the remnants of a gunless army back from the sands of Dunkirk on anything that would float. Then we grinned at each other a little nervously, and said, 'Well, we're in the final!' All of which goes a long way towards explaining why it began to look more and more to me that what this country needed rather desperately to help turn the tide was me. In fact, I didn't fancy its chances much without me.

For a while I staved off my patriotic pangs by joining the Home Guard, the hurriedly formed rag-taggle army of the hedgerows. It was known as Dad's Army, but really it was dads and lads. I had gingerly dipped a first youthful toe into the war.

For a long time none of us were quite sure what we were supposed to do, but that didn't matter too much because we had nothing to do it with, anyway. In the case of invasion, we stood ready to ring church bells and light warning beacons across the country if we spotted any Tiger tanks being paddled in our direction, but beyond that we weren't altogether clear as to what our purpose was. Much thought was given to ways of slowing down the invader, should he come. One favoured idea was to turn signposts round the wrong way to confuse them, though probably all this would have done was confuse men drivers but allow women drivers to find their way round the country without having to turn their road-maps upside down. The trouble was, the cunning Nazi swine would have probably countered this by using female drivers in their tanks, a move calculated to completely unnerve any defensive troops. We'd seen newsreel pictures of lusty *Frauleins* doing press-ups for Hitler. Not only did they have a lot more to press up in the first place, but they managed to press it all up a damn sight further than we ever could. So the plan was quietly dropped and we contented ourselves with removing the signposts altogether.

This almost led to us losing the Battle of Britain, because the RAF fighter pilots' favourite method of navigation was to follow a railway line to the nearest station and read the name on the platform. Luckily someone invented radar just in time, which allowed other people to tell them where to go.

In the end, all our particular platoon of Dad's Army did – twice a week – was patrol the grounds of our headquarters, each man armed with an ancient Lee-Enfield rifle and five rounds of ammunition, which we carefully handed on to the next man on patrol. We were a mixture of innocent young lads and superannuated World War One veterans, and our bloodthirsty little sergeant would exhort us, should the balloon go up, to 'take a German with you when you go!' This we found rather worrying, because several of us, especially the nervous ones, needed to go quite a lot, and some of those big blonde Germans looked distinctly dodgy. It was even rumoured that they used perfumed aftershave, which just goes to show how vicious propaganda can be in wartime.

But the real stroke of genius lay in the choice of our headquarters. We were stationed at the Kingsway Mental Hospital on the edge of Derby, and we patrolled its grounds to the bone-chilling shrieks of the unfortunate inhabitants. Presumably, it was considered that the Boche would have great difficulty in distinguishing Home Guard private from hospital patient. We must admit that sometimes we got a bit confused ourselves.

One of the inmates, a gentle giant of a man, cleaned our room and kept us company throughout the long night. He always wore a small, round, woollen hat on his head, rather like a very tiny tea cosy on a very large teapot, and we were told he was quite harmless, providing no-one tried to take his hat off him Then he was liable to go berserk. We planned, should the Germans ever turn up, to tell them that he was hiding our secret defence plans under there, thinking this was a master-stroke that could shorten the war. Certainly it could have shortened any Gestapo man who tried it. But we changed our minds later when our giant friend won all our Home Guard pay off us one night, at pontoon. After that, we decided that the better plan would be to get him to play the Germans at cards for their rifles.

Recognising the invaders when they came our way was always going to be the big problem. There were garish tales of the various disguises adopted by German assault troops in their lightning attack on the Low Countries, but generally speaking, we were given to understand that any six-foot tall nun with hairy legs coming down by parachute and wearing hobnailed boots, a Schmeisser machine-pistol and a three-day growth of chin bristle should be considered as fairly high on the list of suspects. Of course, these days Women's Lib would never have let them get away with that description without a big argument.

What good did we do? Probably not a great deal, except provide the inspiration for a favourite post-war situation comedy. But at least we did *something*. If nothing else, we kept the Mental Hospital safe from the Panzers. We manned the walls with our old empty Lee-Enfields and our home-made and murderously dangerous Molotov Cocktails, and not a single Tiger tank got as far as Stenson Bubble. In some small way, and with a little help from the Army, Navy, and RAF we helped hold the gate against the Nazi hordes and their threat to our freedom. Today, our political masters seem determined to hand over the key to those self-same enemies who admired us for not giving in to them, and the so-called friends who hated us for the same reason. Maybe it's time to form a new Home Guard.

In between defending Britain all night and drawing pipes all day, life carried on pretty well as normal. The only apparent difference was that England was now prevented from sinking into the North Sea by being suspended from the dangling cables of a few thousand barrage balloons. There was a total blackout, of course, and anyone lighting a fag after dark was liable to be accused of signalling to enemy aircraft. Exactly what message they were supposed to be transmitting by waving one small glowing Woodbine, heaven only knows. I can hardly imagine they were trying to signal 'Drop zer bomben on zis tiny liddel red glow-vorm – I am standink next to Vinston Churchill!'

One shop in town that left a light blazing out into the night got an ugly mob threatening to stove in its plate-glass windows. But while the blackout covered any gently nefarious activities – you could get away with any number of minor sins under its dark cloak – it could also be a mixed blessing. Chatting up a bumped-into female hid the shy blushes of a young would-be Romeo, but equally, the lack of illumination prevented you from seeing whether the young lady you were eagerly trying to impress was a ravishing beauty or a real dog. The solution, when arranging a second encounter, was to 'meet them inside' some place of entertainment. There, you could give her a stealthy once-over before revealing your identity. And it was a lot cheaper that way.

The favoured spot to meet was in the local dance hall, just inside the door at the top of a long flight of stairs. Several girls were usually waiting there, so you were never really certain which one was yours. Repeating your original bump was discouraged by the proprietor, so you had to hang about waiting for all the ugly ones to be claimed before you approached the final dazzling survivor. If you didn't fancy any of them, you slid off to the bar, disguising yourself with a slight limp, and sought fresh conquests there.

We still went to the cinema. I was in the local 'flicks' soon after the declaration of war when there was a sudden muffled rumble from outside and all the lights went out. So the German bombers were already striking at the heart of civilisation as we knew it – the Gaumont cinema in London Road! No one moved – the British do not panic easily – not for us the terrified scramble for the shelters of lesser nations. Not before the manager had offered us a full refund, anyway. We sat there, waiting stoically for the bombs of the *Luftwaffe* to come tearing through that ornate ceiling, and when the cinema organ rose gracefully from its pit, thundering out great chords of defiance at the unseen raiders, we half expected to see a gun turret swinging round menacingly on the top of it, ready to take on the massed Messerschmitts and the Stukas while the organist pounded out 'There'll always be an England' on the mighty tubes.

It later turned out that the noise came from a thunderstorm. A barrage balloon somehow broke free from its moorings and the steel cable shorted across the electricity supply lines, causing a blacker blackout than usual. The cable then wrapped itself round one of the cathedral tower's stone pinnacles, sending it crashing harmlessly to the ground. So besides increasingly severe shortages of food and threatened attacks from the air it looked as if we were going to have to take on the enemy short of one of our pinnacles. War can be hell, sometimes.

Of course the bombers did come our way occasionally. Then we would scuttle down our long garden to the corrugated iron shelter, a far flimsier structure than the house we'd just vacated, as the sirens howled and the throb of unsynchronised engines droned overhead. 'Don't worry, that's one of ours!' we would declare confidently at the sound, before the crash of bombs, usually aimed at the Rolls-Royce works at the far end of town, proved our technical knowledge to be somewhat unreliable.

But most of the time we were protected from the overhead raiders by the mists of Bronchitis Valley. And when the River Derwent refused to provide us with such clammy cover, the authorities created an artificial substitute of their own. It was called the smoke screen, an evil, black, all-enveloping fug that hid the city. I don't know what fuel was used – burning oil rags, dead dogs, buckets of tripe – but you could taste it for days afterwards. The daft thing was, had the Germans dropped stuff like that on us it would have been against the Geneva Convention and we would have been awarded the war on a foul.

Our Saturday nights were usually spent at a dancing school in the town centre. It was known as a 'Social Evening', when we would try out the dance steps that we had learned in the mid-week session. The dancing school was located in a long room over a small printing works. There we clodhopped our way through the strict ballroom routines of the waltz and the quickstep, and even the occasional contortions of the tango, training that later gave us a head's start on our marching and drilling skills on numerous parade grounds. Week after week we would trundle pale young girls with damp hands up and down the long room, trying our hardest to tread on their toes in strict tempo to the superannuated recordings of Victor Sylvester. We thought it the height of sophistication.

But finally such an existence began to pall and I could stand it no longer. I was beginning to feel as if I was travelling through life down one of those pipe-lines that I daily drew out at work, unable to get out and forced to go in one direction. I made up my mind that I would have to take a more active part in the conflict. And right from the start there was little doubt about what my choice of service would be. True, I had never flown in my life up until then, but pre-war I had been on a school trip, by boat, to Norway, and I had been violently seasick. So the Navy was out. I had worn the khaki of the Home Guard, and gone on route marches – which had crucified my corns – and fired a rifle, which had bruised my skinny shoulder. So the Army, too, was in no danger of my joining their ranks. On the other hand, my parents had once taken us to an exhibition at Tollerton aerodrome, in Nottingham, where some mad moron called Clem Sohn had jumped out of a plane at a very great height and flown like a bird. He did this by means of elementary wings formed by stretching a diaphragm between his arms and legs, making him look like a sparrow with alopecia.

True, he carried a sneaky parachute, because he couldn't actually land with wings like a bedsheet for incontinents, and he carried a second one in case the first one didn't work. This made him so heavy that he had to open his chute at a height that made him look no bigger than a tiny black spider squashed against a windscreen, so he carried a smoke plume to let you know where he was. So what we had actually paid to see was a long, thin streak of smoke, high in the sky, followed by some nutter landing by parachute. And the only way we knew he had flown with the birds was because they said he had. No, not the birds – the people we'd paid the money to.

What did this have to do with me joining the RAF? Not a lot, except that after seeing a nutter like him jump out of a plane like that and live, I had no fear about my own ability to stay alive up there. And, anyway, the RAF was the only service I was allowed to join.

The day after my rather furtive signing-on, I travelled down to Birmingham, along with five other hopefuls, including, I recall, a policeman in civvies. There we reported to the RAF Aircrew Assessment Centre, where they tested our suitability to fly, both physically and mentally.

Physically they checked that you had two of everything important (well, all right, nearly everything, two heads were not exactly encouraged), could hold your breath for two minutes, stand on one leg with your eyes closed, without falling over, and saw the same colours that everyone else did. For this, you looked in a book at pictures made up of different-coloured dots. They could have easily got the same result by watching us play each other at snooker.

Then came the aptitude and reaction tests. There was a machine with a small lever on the top that could move four ways, each way cancelling a certain event. The machine rang a bell, flashed a light, sounded a buzzer or blew a horn in a totally random order, and you had to turn it off as quickly as you could by moving the lever the right way. It was simple but effective, as it tested your speed of recognition of a stimulus and your reaction to it.

Finally came the Bartlett test, a half-hour written exam that checked your intelligence and education. It was heavily weighted towards grammar and public school types.

The only question I recall involved a farmer who had a rectangular field 48 yards long by 36 yards wide. If the farmer went from one corner to the opposite one how far did he walk? Well, you could work it out by Pythagoras or you could realise that it was a 3, 4, 5 triangle (three times twelve and four times twelve gave you a five times twelve diagonal, or sixty yards.) It was that kind of gimmicky test. I completed it in about ten minutes and spent another five trying to find out where I'd gone wrong, it seemed so easy.

Finally, we were interviewed by a board of three officers – a group captain, a wing commander, and a squadron leader, all of them resplendent with a chestful of pilot's wings and a blazing display of 'fruit salad', as we called medal ribbons. They beamed at me, told me I'd done very well, and said they were happy to recommend me for aircrew. But in those days I hadn't learned when to keep my big mouth shut. I still haven't. I shook my head firmly. Not aircrew, I said, pilot!

Ah yes, they agreed amiably, pilot, if possible; but should I fail pilot training, then as navigator, wireless operator, air gunner . . .

That wasn't the deal, I told them loftily (I still blush at the thought of my outrageous impudence). I was in a reserved occupation and if I couldn't make pilot I'd return to it – it was up to them.

Their faces went as black as thunder. 'We don't like your attitude', the group captain said, icily, 'We need people who want to fight for their country in whatever capacity they are fit for, not someone who just wants to learn to fly.'

'I want to do both,' I said firmly, 'it's pilot or nothing.'

'All right, that's all!' said the wing commander, distantly. 'I must say that we are very disappointed in you.'

I walked out thinking, 'You great prat! You've gone and blown it!' We were told our fate just before we left. It was a very quiet journey home. I was the only one who had passed. I'm sure there's a moral in there, somewhere. My own guess is that when I'd left the room they'd grinned at each other evilly and said, 'Oh, we must get that cocky little smart-arse in the service! It's going to be a pleasure teaching him to keep his big mouth shut and do as he's ordered!'

I told my mother that night that I had joined up. I had to. I was under age at barely seventeen, and she had to sign her agreement. She threatened not to, but secretly she was pleased. She was of a generation to which patriotism was not yet a dirty word.

Telling my boss the next day wasn't nearly as easy. 'Now what did you want to go and join the RAF for?' he complained, in such an aggrieved tone of voice that I was startled. It seemed such an odd thing to say. What was wrong with joining the

RAF, it's what you did in wartime, wasn't it? Surely he didn't think I'd volunteer for the *Luftwaffe*?

I attempted to console him. It's all right, I won't be going for at least three months yet. But this seemed in no way to mollify him; in fact, quite the reverse. Then I realised: he wasn't bothered whether I was joining the Crusades or the Cosa Nostra, all he wanted me to volunteer for was overtime. He was worried in case I started a rush to volunteer among the rest of the staff. And the thought of me hanging around for three months, spreading the poison of patriotism round the office, only made things worse. From that moment on he started working towards getting me out of the place.

It wasn't going to be easy. Just as an employee was forced to remain in his job, an employer couldn't get rid of a worker without permission and a very good reason. He began finding fault with everything I did, personally raging at me for the slightest errors I made, errors that normally would barely rate a quizzically raised eyebrow from my section leader.

And it worked. At that tender age I could never take injustice, real or imagined, in silence. I answered back, strongly and indignantly. My angry retorts gave him a golden opportunity to apply to dismiss me. Without informing me in any way he obtained permission, and planned to dismiss me at his favourite time, midday Saturday, as people were going home for the weekend and least expecting trouble.

But among my ex-schoolfriends was one who worked at the Employment Exchange, and I was quietly warned. I gave in my notice at a quarter to twelve. His fat smile of satisfaction faded when he realised this meant I had to work a week's notice, giving me a week longer than I would have got had I been summarily sacked for insubordination.

The next week passed quietly and uneventfully. I was given nothing to do and my making-out of my timesheets at the end was my first experience in writing fiction. On the following Saturday, an hour before going-home time, I followed the custom of going round the office, saying goodbye to each of them in turn, spending a couple of minutes at each board. All of the men, more or less ostentatiously, depending on how much they quailed at the boss's black looks, wished me good luck. After half an hour he could stand it no longer. He sent for me, and curtly informed me that I had my wages and my cards and I could go at once.

'As soon as I've said goodbye to everyone', I told him.

His irritation suddenly exploded into rage. 'Get out or I'll have you thrown out!'

'I'm paid until twelve,' I said, stubbornly, 'I'll stay until twelve.'

And I did. He watched in baffled fury, uncertain of the union's reaction if he attempted to carry out his threat. I walked away to a new life, realising that I had cut my last connection to the old one.

CHAPTER TWO

Arsy-Tarsy

Most aircrew began their wartime service in London.

I was given a travel warrant and told to report to Lord's Cricket Ground. It seemed an odd place to go. Were we expected to send stumps flying before we could take an aircraft flying? If so, then they had chosen the wrong man. I was no cricketer, I couldn't catch a cold on a wet day. But no, it was simply a place where I and a couple of hundred other hopefuls could sit patiently in the empty main stand in our civilian clothes, clutching half-empty suitcases, waiting to be led away to our new life. In RAF language this was an ACRC – Air Crew Receiving Centre – but known far and wide to all aircrew as Arsy-Tarsy.

Eventually, a ramrod-stiff drill corporal sorted out a group of us, loudly demanded to know from some anonymous but vengeful God why he should be lumbered with such a shower, then shambled us away – that is, shambled as in a mixture of shuffled and ambled, you couldn't call it marching – to one of a group of empty high-rise flats at St John's Wood, close to Regent's Park Zoo. In fact, we made use of the half-evacuated zoo. Three times a day from then on we were marched along to eat at the Zoo restaurant, giving the animals a chance to watch somebody else being fed, for a change.

The days that followed were spent drawing kitbags full of blue uniforms with the texture of sandpaper and mind-baffling flying gear from stores, getting jabbed and stabbed full of unknown antidotes to unmentionable or unheard-of diseases, and pounding the London streets flat with our marching feet.

But the nights made up for it. This was November 1941, there was little or no bombing at that time, and for all the blackout, the city was alive with people from exotic corners of the earth, in strange uniforms. There were several service clubs for overseas troops that we were allowed to use – such as the Beaver Club for Canadians, and the Fern Leaf Club for New Zealanders – which had superb facilities for entertainment and relaxation. We could buy a red, white and blue Services Travel ticket, costing one shilling and sixpence (15p), that you stuck in your hat and that would get you anywhere on London transport for the whole weekend, and there were plenty of shows and cinemas open, albeit behind darkened fronts.

It was all new and fascinating to a lad up from the provinces, and they even paid us! Every two weeks they handed over the princely sum of one pound seventeen and sixpence, or one pound eighty-seven and a half pence. (All right, he wasn't a very well off prince!) I recall, on the first pay parade, feeling a little embarrassed. They already clothed and fed us, now they were giving us money as well? I couldn't see that we had done anything to earn it.

Meanwhile, our drill corporals bullied us into shape from morning to early evening, and took us for the gullible greenhorns we undoubtedly were.

One day, our own two-striper stood us at ease, and spoke to us in a sad and troubled voice. He was ashamed to tell us, he confessed, that a cadet in the next block of flats, Stockleigh Hall, had had all his money stolen by some unknown and despicable thief. It was a slur on the honour of the RAF, and all the drill corporals had agreed to chip in to help compensate the victim. He was sure we would all wish to contribute, say a shilling each, so that nobody would feel embarrassed. We rushed to dig deep in our pockets.

Months later, after we had moved on, we met up with a cadet from Stockleigh Hall, scene of the Great Training Robbery, and we asked whether our contribution fully repaid what had been stolen.

'No, no!' he said, earnestly, that wasn't in Stockleigh Hall. They, too, had given generously – to the victim in St James's Court.

We didn't tell him that we had been in St James's Court, and that the only light-fingered humans around there must have been the ones with two stripes on their arm. With a constant flow of new recruits, still flush with civilian wages, ACRC must have been a conman's paradise. Certainly it was inhabited by the richest gang of drill corporals in the RAF. We had all paid a shilling to learn a salutary lesson.

But I didn't move on with the others when they were due to be posted to the next destination in the training chain. It was a time when the importance of the Rhesus factor in the blood supply was just beginning to be recognised, and one or two of us were found to be Rhesus positive. The medics' eyes lit up with joy at the discovery. It was my first experience of a well-known command in the services: 'You, you and you will volunteer to give a pint of blood apiece. And that's an order!'

So as the others entrained for pastures new, we few were held back while they attempted to empty my abnormally tiny veins with an enormous syringe that felt like a petrol-pump nozzle. But as a blood donor, I seemed peculiarly determined to hang on to every drop. As 'Ancock might have said, many years later, monkey blood it might be but it was life and death to me, and I intended keeping it. Finally, before the frustrated quacks could resort to a swift punch up the bracket to get the full quota they were after, I was moved on. We left our luxury flats in the Big City for the sea air of Brighton.

I've never been back to St John's Wood so I don't know if those tower blocks we lived in are still there, but if I they are I should be able to identify our particular block of flats quite easily. On the third morning of our life in the RAF the drill corporal had gone round the rooms in the early morning to rouse us all for the march to breakfast. He found the rooms strangely empty, and thought he had a wholesale desertion on his hands. He must have thought, 'Was it something I said?'

Eventually he located his lost underlings. They were crowded at the windows on one side of the building. Opposite, in the neighbouring flats, a young and nubile young lady was in the habit of getting dressed at a high, but uncurtained, window. As I said, the building shouldn't be difficult to identify, it probably bears a remarkable resemblance to the Leaning Tower of Pisa.

But the small delay I had suffered before leaving London had been the first little nudge of fate to ensure that, some two years later, I would meet up with the man destined to share a cockpit with me. Because as I left, unbeknown to me, a certain John David Wooding (later to gain the nickname of 'Dagwood', as I was to be re-christened 'Chalky') was just arriving at ACRC from Manchester University.

The two of us had begun our life in the RAF almost at the same time and in the same place, but subsequently moved half a world apart to do our training. Yet whatever we did, Fate seemed determined that we should end up flying together. But right now Dagwood was to begin his RAF career by achieving a spectacular first. He recalls his introduction to RAF life with wry disbelief:

At the age of 18 I was at Manchester University, courtesy of the Royal Air Force under its University Air Squadron Scheme.

These schemes were set up by a slightly miffed RAF when it realised that the Army and Navy were snaffling all the best graduates. So in return for studying aeronautical subjects in the appropriate University Air Squadron, undergrads were lured into aircrew by guaranteeing them a commission on completion of their training, always providing, of course, that they passed the training courses.

Accordingly, when my turn for call-up came, I was ordered to report to Arsy-Tarsy in London. There, I found most of the new cadets had arrived in civilian clothes, and were immediately sent for kitting out, whereas I had already drawn a uniform at the University Air Squadron, leaving me with little to do but hang around for the rest of the day. I lived in London, and so got permission to slope off for the afternoon. I rang my girlfriend, Joy, and we went to a cinema for the evening, parting at around 11.15 p.m., when I went to catch the underground back to St John's Wood. There were not many trains running at that hour, so by the time I wandered unhurriedly into the orderly room and tendered a pleasant 'Good evening!' to the corporal it was a minute or so past midnight. His reaction, to say the least, was startling. Before I could tell him I thought it was nice of him to wait up, he shook me warmly by the throat, pointed at the clock, and in a little scream of fury observed that 'You should have been here by 23.59 hours!'

I resisted the temptation to ask 'Why – what happened?' It was an old joke even then, and somehow he didn't seem in the mood to appreciate old jokes.

But he did appear to me to be rather splitting hairs. I mean, what was a couple of minutes between friends? In fact, I was in two minds whether or not to drop a heavy hint that I still hadn't actually turned down that very good offer from the Navy. But he said 'Shaddap!' before I could say anything, so I decided against it. He then took a deep breath and went on, 'You are absent without leave, and I am putting you on a charge!'

What, on my first day? And absent from what? I hadn't been anywhere yet to be absent from, apart from the main stand of Lord's Cricket Ground! And on that basis, they could have put the whole England cricket team on a fizzer each time they went in to bat and were out for a duck.

But it was no good. Next day, I was paraded before the Duty Officer and found guilty as charged, awarded three days Confined to Camp, and presented with a large pile of spuds to peel. It was not exactly a hero's welcome, I thought. The way I saw it, until I got there I wasn't even in the bloody RAF so I couldn't be absent from it. And the moment I did arrive, I was no longer absent without leave, so what was the problem?

But I wasn't the only one to fall foul of the corporal. On the first morning he attempted to get us all out on parade in the half darkness of 7 a.m. But what with stiff new buttons on shiny new uniforms, and tight new boots, it wasn't an easy task. And someone was missing. As the corporal turned in frustration to seek him out, a splendid vision of brilliant colour appeared in the doorway. It was a scarlet silk dressing-gown, bearing a large jade-green dragon motif on it, and it was wrapped round the sleepily elegant form of the missing cadet.

'I say, Corporal!' he called affably, 'Where's the jolly old bathroom?'

Why he wasn't skewered on a broom handle on the spot and fed to the lions as we marched past their cage to breakfast, I shall never know. But within a couple of weeks, looking a little more like airmen and a little less like members of the Typhoo Chimps' Tea Party, we were climbing aboard the train for our new destination, a large hotel on the seafront at Brighton.

Brighton was showing a bedraggled border of barbed wire along its seafront like the lace edge to a grubby petticoat. I suppose I must have passed Dagwood a hundred times along the promenade of that Edwardian tart of a seaside resort, but I had no reason to remember him, because there were a thousand others just like him. Brighton was a holding unit, a place to park unwanted Air Force cadets until the lot in front had moved on. They filled the beds left by a long-gone peacetime crowd of holidaymakers, and they marched up and down the barbed-wire entanglements along the foreshore, grim reminders of the threat of would-be invaders lurking just across the Channel.

A bunch of us shared a room on the top floor of the Grand Hotel, but it was a hotel stripped bare of any of its pre-war comforts. Not that the place was allowed to go to rack and ruin. When we weren't marching through the streets of Brighton, we were kept busy cleaning the rooms, and especially polishing all the brass fittings in the place – the light switches, the door handles and plates, the taps, even the drain pipes under the sink were inspected each day with a powerful torch, to see that they were highly polished. What really got up our noses was the fact that we had to buy the metal polish to keep these rooms gleaming bright out of our own meagre pay.

The RAF permanent staff who checked everything so remorselessly seemed to be a special breed of *Homo sapiens*. They were heavily muscled, especially between the ears, with loud voices, the skin scraped off their knuckles by the pavement, shiny black boots and a knife-edged crease to their trousers – an effect obtained by rubbing the inside of the cloth with soap before a night's pressing under the mattress. You could have shaved with the resulting knife-edge.

In our long training we often seemed to end up billeted in hotels belonging to one particular hotel chain. The story going the rounds – I don't know the truth of it – was that the chairman, an ex-World War One Army officer of high rank, had devised a training schedule for aircrew that utilised most of the group's currently empty hotels throughout the country, and was rewarded by being put in charge of the scheme with an appropriately high RAF rank. He was also said to be connected with the racing world. Perhaps this explained the zeal with which the buildings were cared for, and why so many of the officers in these places seemed to look, and sound, like ex-tictac men and pensioned-off bookies' runners.

But Brighton was best suffered in silence and forgotten. The next step we took – remember we hadn't even seen an aircraft yet, let alone sat in one! – was back to school at an ITW, or Initial Training Wing. Mine was in Stratford-upon-Avon, where we were lodged in a Dickensian rabbit warren of a hotel, the Washington Irving. Presumably to attract pre-war American tourists, it had been named after the Yankee author of *Rip Van Winkle*, a favourite folk-tale of theirs.

Stratford was now empty of tourists, and the decrepit old hotel was freezing in the bitter early spring. No heating of any kind was allowed in the rooms, and we had to break the ice in the washbowl each morning before shaving in freezing-cold water.

There were five of us crammed into one tiny room, so we had to take it in turns to shiver, as we studied the theory of aeronautics, navigation, aircraft recognition, meteorology and Morse code. Each man in the room was a stranger to the others, the only reason for our being closeted together being that our names were alphabetically adjacent. Thus we had a Taylor, two Whites, a Wheeler and a Valentine. We were lucky, at that. There had been a sixth cadet, but he seemed to suffer from intermittent blinding headaches and mysterious rages. God knows what would have happened had he actually got in a plane; possibly he would have crash-landed on Buckingham Palace to ease his throbbing temples, but anyway he quietly disappeared

Each week our dirty washing went out to a local laundry, and on its return it was not unknown for the garments to bear little notes from the laundry ladies. One day Bill Taylor's newly washed underpants came back with a note pinned to the flies, inviting a reply, so we decided to send them one that would get their mangles whirring that little bit faster.

We would invent a hero.

We set to and composed a letter worthy of the Bard himself – it could well have become one of the masterpieces of English literature. We changed Bill's name to Jan Van der Rolyat (Taylor spelled backwards) of the Royal Dutch Air Force, and we made up a hair-raising tale of his escape from the German invasion of his country that could have come straight out of Biggles, the pre-war James Bond. It was written in an appalling mix of pidgin English and pseudo-Dutch. ('I mis vary mutch mein groote liebling back home en Amsterdam. Please to make meet me for an nacht of grate plezzure soon . . .') And so it went on. It was so bad it was good, and we just hoped the Soap Queens wouldn't fall into their dolly tubs, laughing.

''oo the 'ell', asked Big Tone, the beetle-browed drill corporal, a few days later as he handed out the post, 'is Jan Van der Roly-bluddy-poly?'

A pink-faced Bill collected it, along with a funny look from the corporal, and that evening we gathered in our room to read it. We planned to draw lots for who would play the gallant Dutchman, and the other four would chip in to pay for his night out, though on the strict understanding that we would all share a blow-by-blow story of the encounter.

From somewhere we had 'won' a small but illegal electric fire, and we cooked a tin of soup over it as we settled down to an evening of forbidden warmth and hot conspiracy. The corny jokes flew round the room. 'Whoever goes, remember she works in a laundry, so keep it clean!' Then Bill read out the reply, and the wicked grins faded from our faces. The lady had swallowed our yarn completely. She was, she wrote, a young widow – her husband had died at Dunkirk – and life hadn't been too kind to her for a long time. But she was so looking forward to her night out with the gallant young Flying Dutchman.

Of course, after that we couldn't go through with it. All we could do was write back and confess everything, with our apologies, but, hardly surprisingly, we heard no more.

To cap it all, we had forgotten to lock the door, and Big Tone, the drill corporal, came in just as we were discussing what to do. He had convinced himself that the 'Jan' on the letter referred to some female called Janet or Janice that we planned to sneak into the small back room, and seemed disappointed not to have disturbed an orgy. (He needn't have worried, it would have taken Eskimo Nell's daughter to appreciate an orgy under those conditions.)

''ello – it's warm in 'ere!' he observed ominously. We offered him a cup of our hot soup as a bribe. He drank it noisily, thanked us, and then put us all on a charge. We did a week's extra duties for stealing electricity from His Majesty's Royal Air Force. In a way it was a penance.

But cold spring soon turned into warm summer, and in no time at all Stratford's surrounding countryside changed into a rich vista of trees and meadows such as the young Will Shakespeare must have enjoyed. It was near final exam time, and my mate Bert and I took a punt out on the Avon, upriver from the theatre. Out of the five in the room Bert and I seemed to get on best, and we planned to do our revision in peace and quiet. Bert poled us along while I sat in the bow, checking his answers. It was a warm and sultry day, and I soon dozed off, so to wake me up Bert nosed the boat under some overhanging branches on the bank, forgetting that those same branches would tangle with his long punt-pole. I awoke with a start, just in time to see him clinging desperately to the top of the pole while his feet slid away from him on the boat, before he was finally dumped unceremoniously into the water.

He slopped his way back to the Washington Irving Hotel and stood steadily dripping puddles of water on the orderly room lino while Big Tone frantically searched for a charge to put him on. But he failed. Apparently it was against King's Regulations to get warm but not to fall into a river and get wet.

Some years ago, I was on a narrow boat that tied up on the riverbank opposite to Stratford's theatre and I went into the town in search of the old Washington Irving and a large helping of nostalgia. I found myself standing in the middle of a bustling new Marks and Spencer store.

Never go back.

But now, surely, with our exams safely passed, we would get just a little nearer to seeing an aircraft? Well yes, we would, but not exactly in the way we expected.

During this particular pause in our training, someone somewhere up in Training Command had a bright idea. Petrol was scarce, each precious drop brought in by tanker from overseas. Yet it was still being wasted in some places. The RAF was training Army pilots for an airborne assault force. Following the loss of Crete to

German glider troops, Churchill decided that we also needed some glider troops, little realising that it had been a Pyrrhic victory and the German troops had been severely mauled. But the trouble with gliders is that once they have done a practice landing they have no engine to taxi back into position for the next take-off. Petrol was being wasted on tractors to haul gliders back to the starting line.

Yet here the RAF had hundreds of flying cadets sitting on their backsides doing nothing – young, eager, fit young men, dying to get their hands on an aircraft. So let them get their hands on one! We were sent to a small grass airfield deep in the heart of rural Gloucestershire, Number Two Glider Training School at Weston-on-the-Green. The gliders were little more than plywood boxes with wings, bearing more than a passing resemblance to roomy rounded coffins. Our first thoughts on seeing them was that if they crashed all the RAF needed to do was pile the earth over them and stick a headstone on top.

To pull them up into the sky they used ancient pre-war biplanes – Audaxes, as I recall – probably last used to shoot Afghans up the Khyber Pass on the edge of the Empire. The gliders were towed up to a couple of thousand feet and then cast adrift to hit Mother Earth once more somewhere within the boundaries of the 'drome.

Elegant it wasn't, and the Army pilots received absolutely basic training because they would end up with a one-way ticket to battle. They would be walking back or else they would be walking to a prisoner-of-war camp. That's if they were still walking at all.

It was high summer. We were young and fit, far from the temptations of the city and a healthy distance from the nearest tiny country tavern. We spent our days hauling those tarted-up orange crates back across the airfield at the end of a long towrope, and our nights slaking our thirst at the end of a long stroll. One or two of us even cadged a ride in the ancient Audaxes, which was like flying in a rather noisy vacuum cleaner.

But after a few days life began to pall. We felt cut off and forgotten, and it seemed as if we were going nowhere. We were even beginning to like the local beer, which was a dangerous sign. It was laughingly labelled 'home-brewed', but no one ever said home-brewed what.

Then the sergeant in charge of us handed out a bit of news. The bigwig from Command Headquarters who had dreamed up the bright idea of human dog-teams – an air commodore, no less – was coming down to see how the scheme was working.

This, we decided, was our chance to escape and get back on the training treadmill. What we had to do was convince him that the task was beyond human capability and we were all beginning to develop ingrowing hernias. Surely the prospect of future bomber pilots having to untangle their throttle nuts from their trusses in the middle of an air battle over Berlin was enough to make anyone think twice.

We laid our plans carefully, arranging with the Army lads to land their gliders as far over to the distant boundary fence as they could. Bang on time, the air commodore arrived with his attendant minions – a mixed bag of attendant toadies who had discovered the way to advancement in the service was to say 'Oh, jolly good show, sir!' every five minutes – and we put on a performance that would have turned Olivier green with envy.

Or so we thought. A gang of us seized the towrope and we heaved and strained and grunted and groaned our way slowly across that airfield with our burden, finally collapsing in a pitiful heap of humanity at the starting point.

But our performance must have been more Les Dawson than *Les Miserables* because the air commodore was not impressed. 'Doesn't look all that hard to me!' he declared loftily to his gang of hangers-on, taking off his jacket. 'Come on, you lot, let's give it a go!'

Our hearts sank. We'd been rumbled! In deep gloom we watched them fix the towrope to the next glider to land, and soon the big plywood craft was whistling back across the grass at breakneck speed as the officers bent their backs to the task. It looked as if we were condemned to many more weeks on the chain-gang. Then a strange thing happened. As they reached the start line, one by one the retinue sank to the grass, gasping for breath. They were knackered!

We couldn't believe it, it hadn't been that hard! But we suddenly realised – the first man to collapse in a scarlet-faced struggle for air had been the air commodore himself. In his rugby-playing youth in the service he had carried all before him, but now all before him was a tightening waist-band as his desk-days caught up with him.

And his youthful yes-men? They weren't going to show up their bluff boss as an old has-been and lose a soft job at headquarters. Used to agreeing with him, from sheer force of habit they followed him gasping gracefully down to the turf.

And that was it! The air commodore replaced the tractors and we were given a forty-eight-hour pass as a reward for our efforts. After that we were on our way to Anstey, near Leicester, to No. 9 Elementary Flying Training School. And we were actually going to fly aeroplanes ourselves! Not a lot, and not very big ones, but it was a start.

CHAPTER THREE

Moving On

There were a number of these elementary flying training schools scattered around the country. Most of them consisted of a large field with half a dozen Tiger Moth trainers. They were used as preliminary assessment centres. You were given ten hours' flying in the old Tiger Moth and you had to go solo within eight hours to stand any chance. Almost all the proper training was carried out overseas, and they wanted to be sure that you showed some promise before going to the expense of sending you out there.

It all depended on the instructor, of course, and for once in our lives both Bert and I were glad that our names began with a 'W'. Like others with the same initial, we had long suffered The Curse of the Ws.

Ws were always last in the queue for anything (all right, except for the Yeomans, the Youngs, the Zacharys and the Zapoticznyjs, if you want to be pedantic, but how many of those do you normally get to the pound?), be it pay or promotion, and in this case it ran true to form.

All the officer instructors were doled out to those alphabetically ahead of us, leaving us to the tender mercies of the one sergeant pilot. But we preferred this. A sergeant instructor was not such an aloof figure as an officer, and ours was a quiet, friendly chap from Dorset who took infinite pains to try and drum the basic essentials of flight into us, though he didn't hold back on the odd sardonic remark when you did something particularly stupid.

The Tiger Moth was an old fabric-covered biplane with an open cockpit (or rather two open cockpits), so safe that it took a genius to kill himself in one. The cadet sat in the back seat with the instructor in front, with the only communication between them being by a one-way speaking tube, rather like an elongated stethoscope. He could talk to you but you couldn't answer him back. Let me rephrase that. He couldn't hear you answer him back! Which was just as well, because some of the retorts that were shrieked into the wind at the back of the instructor's neck after a particularly acid comment about the cadet's total unfitness to go higher than the bottom rung of a step-ladder would have failed him on the spot. Our instructor had a quiet sense of humour, and one day, while I was in the middle of hurling a highly coloured description of his family antecedents into the slipstream, I suddenly realised that he was watching my contorted face in his tiny rear mirror. His voice came through the speaking tube. 'You do know I can lip-read, don't you, White!' Of course, he couldn't, but the shock was enough to silence me! After that I just thought those same unspoken words, mentally adding at the end, 'All right, let's see you mind-read, you clever bastard!'

Then suddenly, after days of clawing your way round the sky, with Mother Earth taking a terrible beating each time you tried to land, you saw the instructor climb out with his parachute. You were convinced that he was refusing to fly any longer with such a clueless clot, and you waited with dread to hear him give you the final thumbs down. But all that he said was, 'OK, White – you're on your own – off you go!'

There was a moment of sheer panic as you tried to digest the tremendous import of those few curt words. Your first thought was 'Me, take this wire-and-string thing up there! All on my own? Is the man completely bonkers?' Then you were suddenly so busy trying to recall everything he'd been trying to drum into you for days – and failing miserably – that your fear was forgotten. You turned into wind and opened the throttle, and for the first time there was no warning voice, no sarcastic comment, from that empty front cockpit.

There is no exhilaration on earth quite like your first solo flight. Somehow you scramble into the sky, and then, suddenly, you find yourself alone in the vast emptiness of a new dimension. There is a tremendous feeling of freedom. Above you is an infinite canopy of blue, ringed with towering white cloud-castles, below you the great green map of England unrolls as far as the eye can see and you look at it with a new awe. You are in the playground of the Gods!

But we still didn't know who had passed and who had failed. After our short stumble into the air we were moved on to Heaton Park, in Manchester, where hundreds of aircrew cadets were gathered in a holding unit. Most, but not all, slept in tents in the park, others were lodged out in various houses and B and B accommodation. There was little to do but wait.

The day after his arrival, one cadet reported in from his outside accommodation and asked to see the CO. He wished to make a strong complaint. The previous night he had gone upstairs to bed, and shortly after he heard his landlady lock up and retire for the night. To his astonishment she came upstairs, turned into his room

and got into the bed beside him. Did he have to put up with this sort of thing?

The landlady was sent for and the CO questioned her. 'Oh yes,' she agreed cheerfully, 'it saves washing two lots of sheets', adding as an afterthought that nobody had ever complained before. The aggrieved cadet was quickly posted before he could be tortured for the address, and soon afterwards we were all called together into a mass meeting in the open air.

An officer read out a long list of names, about a sixth of those present, and told them to stand to one side.

'You', he told them, 'will be navigators!'

Another long list: 'You will be bomb aimers!'

We listened with hearts in our mouths, desperately hoping against hope, as further groups were culled from the diminishing mass. 'You will be wireless operators!' 'You will be air gunners!'

The small bunch remaining watched anxiously, their hearts dropping from their mouths to their boots, as the officer packed his lists away. 'Oh,' he said, pretending to suddenly notice us, 'I'm afraid there's nothing left for you lot . . .' We groaned aloud. 'So', he added with great relish, 'you'll have to stay as pilots, won't you!' It was cruel, and we could have gladly strangled him. Instead we cheered with relief.

And now we began to make ready for dispersal to different parts of the world. Our particular group was told to label our kitbags, in large black lettering, with the word BATTS.

That sounded about right.

Meanwhile, all unknown to me, Dagwood was taking a somewhat different route through the RAF training system, though our paths had crossed fleetingly. Here he tells his own story:

From Brighton, we went on to Booker, which was near Marlow-on-Thames. It was simply a large grass field, without runways, that held a handful of Tiger Moth light trainers. We were soon to discover that not many would be kept on pilot training, because, with the big four-engined bombers that were starting to come through to launch attacks on Germany, there was an urgent and growing need for navigators, bomb aimers, wireless operators and air gunners to man them.

Which is how I came to be moved to the ground navigation school in Eastbourne. It was summertime, and I was billeted at the Mostyn Hotel, on the sea front. The only reminders of war were barbed-wire barricades along the beach against a possible invasion, and our nightly chore of manning machine guns on rooftops – German planes had already targeted the town.

I had just come off this sentry duty one morning and there was still an hour to wait until breakfast, so I strolled along to the small headland, where there was a Martello tower. These were relics of the nineteenth-century defences against a Napoleonic invasion, strung along the south coast and known at the time as Palmerston's Follies. There, I lay in the shrubbery, enjoying the sea view and listening to the sound of the waves gently breaking. Despite the symbols of warfare spanning the centuries it was a very peaceful spot and the idea of conflict seemed very far away.

Then I heard voices – thickly accented guttural ones – and I saw three fairly elderly civilians walking along the promenade. They stopped, produced a camera, and began taking pictures of the Martello tower. But right next to it was a modern concrete coastal gun emplacement. Momentarily uncertain of what to do, I slid backwards through the bushes, crossed the road, and made for the nearby RAF police post.

They were astonished to hear my story, but said, 'You've done the right thing. Leave it with us.' The next day I received notice of my posting to Heaton Park, Manchester, and packed my kit ready to leave. But I could not resist the urge to call at the police post.

'Any news, Corporal?'

'The three were arrested right away – they're being questioned by Special Branch now', I was told. 'The officers asked us to thank you for your alertness.'

I heard no more. But I've often wondered.

Apart from one Air Navigation School on the Isle of Man, all the others were in Canada, the USA, South Africa and Rhodesia (present-day Zimbabwe.) You were given no choice.

After two impatient weeks in the camp at Heaton Park, our group, which still included many friends from my university air squadron days, were ordered to pack both kitbags (one personal and the other full of flying kit) and be ready to move off. We weren't permitted to phone or write home for security reasons, as several troopships had been sunk at sea. By lunchtime the next day we were lined up on the quayside of the River Clyde, in Glasgow.

In front of us was the mighty ocean liner, *Queen Mary*, in drab warpaint. It had shuttled thousands of servicemen across the Atlantic, and at such a speed that it rarely needed a Navy escort or to go in convoy. In a week or so, we thought, we would be at a Canadian Air Force base near Winnipeg, on the prairies. Slowly but steadily we filed in alphabetical order towards

the gangway which led into the heart of the great ship. Soon I was on the gangway itself and could see the embarkation officer, clipboard in hand, calling off the names '. . . Walton P.C. 498, Winn R. 499, Winter B.N. 500'.

An arm was thrust across my path. 'That's all we're taking on this trip. Sorry, lads, back you go.' So Wooding J.D., Watson F., and Younger K. struggled to turn about with their kitbags and return to the dockside. We stood disconsolately as our friends waved down to us from the upper decks. The Curse of the Ws had struck again. If my name had been John Gooding I'd have been on my way to Canada. Back in Manchester once more, we complained bitterly.

'Why did you send us if there were insufficient places?'

'We needed reserves in case of illness, but you will be top of the next list. You won't have to wait long.'

We calculated it would be about two weeks, when the *Queen Mary* had returned to Britain again, and sure enough, two weeks later, our embarkation notice was duly posted up. But there was a surprise. The notice read, 'The undermentioned cadets will depart tomorrow. You will parade outside the main stores at 2 p.m. today for the issue of tropical kit.'

That ruled out Canada. It looked as if there was going to be plenty of sunshine ahead.

When I trudged up the gangway of RMS *Winchester Castle*, with a kitbag on each shoulder, I felt sure, despite all the secrecy, that we must be on our way to South Africa. This was a ship of the Union Castle Line, which boasted, in peacetime, that every Thursday afternoon at 4 p.m. a Castle ship sailed from Southampton for Capetown, carrying passengers and the Royal Mail. Going to South Africa on a troopship had a family precedent. My father had volunteered to join a Staffordshire regiment and made a similar journey to South Africa to fight in the Boer War at the turn of the century.

Most of the military personnel on board were soldiers journeying right round the African continent to the Suez Canal. They were reinforcements for the Eighth Army, which was shaping up to do battle against Rommel's *Afrika Korps* in the desert. German air supremacy over the Central Mediterranean meant that it was too risky to send large troopships between Gibraltar and and Alexandria. There was also a small contingent from the Royal Navy going out as replacements for the Mediterranean Fleet – during the voyage they were our source of information about much that went on – and a couple of dozen Wrens (Womens Royal Naval Service) destined for duties in the Navy headquarters at Alexandria. Being a few girls aboard a ship with hundreds of young men, they were highly cosseted and had a special area of upper deck reserved for their exclusive use. The RAF contingent consisted of about a hundred aircrew cadets going out to flying schools to train as pilots or navigators.

Shortly after leaving Liverpool, there was a carefully arranged rendezvous off the coast of Northern Ireland. Two large troopships, the *Britannia* and the *Winchester Castle*, joined forces with several cargo merchantmen to form a convoy. It was surrounded by a screen of naval destroyers, with, for a time, an aircraft-carrier. We moved out into the Atlantic at quite a pace – no old or slow vessels were included, the better to out-run the German submarines.

We never followed a straight line, to fox any shadowing aircraft trying to pass on details of our course. The Fw Condor long-range aircraft seldom attacked a heavily armed convoy; the danger came from U-boats. Every so often the leading destroyer would sound its hooter, either once or twice, and the ships in the convoy would acknowledge in the same fashion. Once meant turn left, about twenty degrees, and twice meant everyone turn right. Around us the destroyers maintained a high speed, restless patrol, carving out huge white wakes, anxiously scanning the depths with their sonar.

As we moved south into the tropics and reached safer waters, some of the grey ships of the naval escort left us. We began to feel quite relaxed, as the warm trade winds blew and the ship's speakers played records of the Tommy Dorsey orchestra as we marvelled at the glorious tropical sunsets, with their continuously changing colours. And we slept well, despite the rumble of the ship's engines and the creak of metal plates, the endless coughing and snoring, and the all-pervading body odours.

Then, suddenly, everything changed.

The music stopped, the ship's engines throbbed with extra power as we increased our speed, and twice we turned sharply left to the urging of the hooters. Then we made four turns to the right, and hurried away into the setting sun, turning our backs on Africa. Towers of cascading white water appeared behind two of our escorting destroyers as they dropped depth charges, and purple pennants fluttered from their mastheads, a sign that U-boats had been detected. We anxiously scanned the horizon until dark for any sign of a periscope, our white knuckles gripping the rail, then most of us opted to sleep on deck. For most of the night we continued to zigzag, and then our speed dropped, and the loudspeakers were switched back on for an announcement from the Captain.

The excitement, he said, was over, prompt action had proved effective but there was a problem. Many extra days at sea had caused a shortage of food stocks and low levels of fresh water. We would have to enter a port the next day to take on supplies. He didn't say where, but our guess after our westward dash across the South Atlantic was that it would be somewhere in Brazil.

But while Dagwood was being transported in the relative comfort of the *Winchester Castle*, albeit in its *alter ego* of wartime troopship, we had neither the *Queen Mary* nor the Union Castle Line to carry us across the Atlantic to Canada. Instead, we were crammed into the hold of an old and hurriedly converted freighter. There were rows of wooden trestle tables put up in the hold below deck. Twelve of you sat and ate your two meals a day at each table. You were given three loaves per day per table, chopped into quarters, so that you each got a three-inch-thick hunk of bread with little to put on it. Not that many people fancied a six-inch-thick sandwich, anyway.

For the main meal you queued through the kitchens, holding out your small round galvanised mess-tin while the cooks hurled every kind of food into it – meat, potatoes, gravy, custard, and pudding, all together in one glorious heap. Your only defence was to get your mashed potatoes in first and swiftly build them into a small coffer dam across the centre of the mess-tin. Then by a skilful twist of the wrist, you tried to keep the gravy on one side separate from the custard on the other. Of course you could still end up with your sausages in the custard and your jam roly-poly in the gravy, but it all ended up in the stomach anyway. The important thing was keeping it there, because the ship seemed to roll continuously, trying its best to tip it out of you again.

But if the food was crude, the facilities could only be described as rough and ready.

At night the mess-deck became a sea of hammocks, so tightly packed together that they swayed in unison as the ship rolled and creaked through the waves. Getting into them was like trying to wrestle a very wide, flat snake – and losing. But getting out in the middle of the night to visit the 'heads' and back in again was even more of a problem. The hammocks formed a solid low ceiling about five feet high, and the only thing to do was walk along like the Hunchback of Notre Dame, banging each hammock in turn. The one that didn't swear at you was yours.

Speaking of the heads – those necessary installations were simplicity itself. Each consisted of a long, metal-lined wooden box with a row of holes in the top, through which was pumped a continuous flow of seawater. There were no partitions round it, and consequently no privacy of any kind. However, what started out as embarrassed and furtive visits in the small hours quickly changed through a nonchalant indifference to become almost a social occasion, sometimes complete with philosophical discussion. Socrates himself would have been proud to have chaired our six-holer.

But there's always a comedian somewhere. And this one chose to take the furthest point upstream for his ablutions armed with a small paper boat that he surreptitiously lit with his cigarette lighter before launching it through the hole.

I reckon that man was the inventor of the Mexican Wave.

We landed at Halifax, in Nova Scotia, Canada, early one morning, and took the whole day to travel by train to our new holding unit in Moncton, New Brunswick. It was a large hutted camp, close to town, and I mainly remember it for two reasons, the way you went out and the way you came back in.

A wire-mesh fence, six feet high, ran round the entire camp, and long ago someone cut a hole in it to get back in after lights-out. The following day they detailed some spare aircrew – there were plenty around – to go and repair it. Which they did in a certain way. They threaded a new piece into place with a loose wire, so that you simply pulled it out to renew the hole. Everybody came back that way after a late night in town.

I have never been in any other place in the RAF where 'The Hole in the Fence' was an official bus stop. You boarded the bus and asked for 'a single to the Hole in the Fence'. Then out with the loose wire and happily into bed, while the service police vainly watched the main gate for latecomers. Each day they sent more aircrew to repair the hole and each night the hole was renewed. I thought it was a very civilised way to run an air force.

So why did people not go out the same way? Simply because at the main gate was a large notice board, which said, 'The following addresses are strictly out of bounds to all ranks: . . . Mme Dupré's Massage Parlour at 22 Main St., The Black Pussycat Saloon in 17th Avenue . . .' etc., etc. There was always a large crowd round it, taking down the addresses, and you had to wait quite a while for your turn to get near.

Soon it was time to move on to our new flying training camps. Some were going to camps on the Canadian prairies, but our group was destined for the United States.

Originally, RAF pilots trained with the US Army Air Corps, a division of the American Army. It was called the Arnold Scheme, after the American General Hap Arnold, who helped devise it. Even while America was still officially neutral, RAF flying cadets, clad in civilian clothes, were unofficially trained to fly alongside the United States Army flying cadets.

Initially, it was a great help to the RAF, for which they were duly grateful, but there were problems. Their system was very different. Being part of the Army they were trained as officers before being taught how to fly, and this involved being thrown off, or 'scrubbed', for minor disciplinary faults as they taught their raw recruits the unquestioning obedience the Army demanded. The RAF had already assessed its recruits' flying capabilities, and to fail them for not folding their blankets correctly or saluting in a proper manner after sending them thousands of miles abroad was both costly and frustrating. In any case the RAF didn't demand blind obedience, they needed pilots who could take instant decisions in an emergency in the lonely darkness over hostile territory.

So as an alternative, half a dozen 'dromes were set up across the southern United States under RAF control, but run by American firms with civilian instructors, and the BATTS label on our kitbags turned out to mean British All-Through Training Scheme. It was to one of these that we were bound.

Bert and I were determined to stay together, but there was a big problem, and basically, it was one of simple class snobbery. There is little doubt that, rather like Waterloo, the Battle of Britain was won on and over the playing fields of Eton. Most of the fighter pilots at that time were commissioned and from public schools, and the dashing public school spirit undoubtedly played a vital part in the victory. But the coming Battle of Germany was to be very different. Bomber Command was slowly turning into a grammar school force. But old prejudices died hard. A sergeant pilot might be competent to command a large and expensive bomber with half a dozen officers in his crew, in a night battle over Germany, but if he ate his peas off the wrong knife, he wasn't good enough to live in the officers' mess.

(The idiocy of the RAF's policy was later demonstrated when we finally won our wings. The man chosen as the so-called 'Honour Cadet' had nothing to commend him above all the others except that he had attended the 'right school' – I won't name him because he died in the Battle of Berlin in 1944, like so many others – but apparently one thing he didn't learn at 'the right school' was cleanliness. He was averse to water and washing – in fact he was the only person I'd ever known to wash and shave while fully dressed in coat, cap, shirt and tie, using so little water that it evaporated before reaching the plug hole. In desperation, in the hot Arizona climate, we finally introduced him to the shower by sticking him under it, fully clothed.)

So great care was taken at this initial sorting-out that cadets 'from the right (i.e. public) school' were spread evenly through the six RAF 'dromes. That way they could all take up one of the strictly limited commissions to be handed out at the end of the course. They did this by blatantly dividing us into two groups – public school and the rest – before asking us where we wanted to go. Bert had been to Dulwich College and so was placed in the 'potential officer material' group.

Desperately we signalled to each other across the big hangar, like the ex-tictac men of Brighton, trying to signal the school number, but we must have put up the wrong fingers. Bert and all my other pals ended up booked for Oklahoma, while I found myself heading for No. 4 BFTS in Arizona. And the choice was final, the Powers-That-Be would allow no swapping.

It was one of fate's major moves.

Our great journey to Arizona was made on the once-famous (in song, at least) Atcheson, Topeka and Santa Fé railroad, via Toronto, Chicago, Kansas City, St Louis and El Paso, passing through state after state. It took five days in all, and during this time we lived mainly on hamburgers-and-coke-style food, eaten where we sat, and you whiled away the endless hours either playing cards (I learned the art of poker playing on the way) or watching small-town America drift past the carriage windows. It was like sitting in the one-and-nines in the Odeon, back home, waiting for the big film to start. All that was missing was Jimmy Stewart or Clark Gable. Only they were both over in England, flying with the United States Army Air Corps.

We were given no beds on the train. Instead, we had a coach to ourselves, with two seats each, one to sit on and one to put your feet on. At night you simply took off your cap, tie and shoes, rolled up your damp towel to form a pillow, and closed your eyes, hoping the rattling train would rock you into unconsciousness. After a couple of sleepless nights we dismantled our seats and fashioned rough-and-ready beds out of the cushions in the central aisle. This infuriated the train 'conductor', who ran his train like a martinet. Never had he seen such vandalism in his forty years' service, he raged, and in petty retaliation he locked us in our coach so that we couldn't get to the club car.

This was no great loss. Ordering a drink on a train had turned out to be a complicated process. If you were crossing a 'dry' state, where alcoholic licquor was illegal, they wouldn't serve you, and if you were crossing into a 'dry' state from a 'wet' one they even took the drink you had away from you, half consumed. But we had a further problem when we asked for a rum and coke. The American bartender demanded to know our age.

'Eighteen', we said, truthfully.

'No alcohol for any Army guys under twenty!'

'Fine,' we said, 'we're not Army, we're Air Force.'

'The Air Force comes under the Army. As in Army Air Corps.'

We felt offended. 'Not in Britain, it doesn't.'

'So go back there for your rum and coke, bud.'

We looked round. A young sailor was sluicing back the whisky and he looked to be straight out of school.

'What about him?'

'He's Navy. The Navy can drink at eighteen.'

'That's OK, then. Because in Britain, the RAF comes under the Navy.' (May Lord Trenchard forgive me, I thought.)

So why were we wearing Army-style khaki shirts and slacks with funny blue hats on?

'Ah!' said my companion, 'Mac' McIntyre, a notorious leg-puller; 'We started out as the Royal Naval Air Service, then we joined with the Royal Flying Corps to form the RAF. So we're a sort of mixture of the two. In fact, that's what the letters RAF stand for – Rum Allowed Fridays.'

'Today's Thursday', said the bartender.

'Not in Britain, it isn't,' said Mac airily, 'we're a day ahead of you.'

He looked at us in unsmiling disbelief.

'So I'll check it out with the 'Snowdrops' at the next town.' They were the formidable white-helmeted American military police, who were fond of adding the odd exclamation mark to their conversation with a truncheon.

'On second thoughts, make that two Pepsi-colas', we said.

On the fifth day we clambered down from our air-conditioned coach into 112 degrees of heat in the shade. Only in Arizona there was no shade, not in the heart of the Sonora Desert, where our new camp, Falcon Field, was located. Like Hansel and Gretel before us, we felt as if we had been invited to dinner in an oven.

Meanwhile, as we drummed our way across America to the Far West, Dagwood's troopship was seeking a neutral port in the south Atlantic to take on supplies.

We got up early for a first sight of land', he wrote later in his diary:

'The convoy filed into a wide semi-circular bay of golden sand, fringed with dark-green palm trees, with a toy-like locomotive slowly puffing its way round the coast.

Then the town of Bahia came into view. There were tiers of small ochre and white buildings along the shore, and chapels with mission bells on the roof. It was all in a green oasis, set with banana trees and bougainvillea. It looked like an appetising coffee cake, and it just happened to be the identical dazzling scene captured by Walt Disney in the cartoon film, *The Three Caballeros* and the town that inspired the song *Bahia!*

Closer inshore, the magic faded. The small box-like buildings all seemed to need a lick of paint and the morning air stank with the old cabbage smell of rotting vegetation. Litter blew in the wind and piled up round every corner.

Soon loads of fresh citrus fruit were being hauled aboard in large rope baskets, and fresh water pipes were connected up to pump tons of drinking-water into the tanks.

At night, some of the magic returned as the shabbiness melted into the shadows and coloured lights shimmered on the water. After years of blackout at home we had forgotten how bright the lights could be, and the mood was enhanced by the ship's speakers playing the popular song, *Tangerine*.

But that was as close to Brazil as we were going to get. Being a neutral country it could provide emergency supplies but not hospitality to combatants, even though the friendly inhabitants waved to us from the shore.

Next morning, everything had changed. It was announced that Brazil had entered the war – fortunately on our side! A ceremonial parade was quickly organised, and we put on our brand-new overseas uniforms with their gleaming brass buttons, and formed up on the quay in the bright sunshine.

The white-helmeted Royal Marine Band led the way, followed by the Navy and the Wrens in their tropical whites. Then came the Army, and lastly the junior service, the RAF cadets. In perfect step with the drums we marched smartly to the market square, and there listened to an excited address by the mayor in what we could only assume was Portuguese.

Then someone on board made a mistake – we were dismissed for an hour. Without local money we could only wander round the town, and it was hot. So we settled for a snooze in the shade before forming up once more for the return march. It was soon apparent that the lack of money had not prevented the soldiers from obtaining quantities of the local wine, and the march back became a stagger. Even so, thirty or forty of them were still missing, and a hit-squad of NCOs was quickly sent to winkle them out of the bars. They didn't find them all: a dozen or so were left behind to face possible desertion charges, while one man was brought back so aggressively drunk that he was put in irons, chained to a rail on the deck. It wasn't a pretty sight.

The replenished fleet, now well behind schedule, swiftly set sail for the southern tip of Africa, and eventually, after a pleasant and uneventful trip, we caught a distant glimpse of Table Mountain, with its flat white cloud, known as 'the Tablecloth', lying across its top and spilling over its edge.

Nestling below it, safely and peacefully under the sun, was the city and harbour of Cape Town.

Then someone called out, 'Look!' In the water below was drifting wreckage, and inflatable life-rafts with bedraggled seamen clinging to the top and in the water, hanging on to the side-ropes. It looked as if a ship had been sunk by a

U-boat on the very threshold of Cape Town harbour. The shipwrecked mariners waved listless arms of welcome to their rescuers. But to our amazement, the Captain sailed straight past without stopping, as did the other troopship. We set up an indignant clamour to know why.

'Vulnerable targets like troopships don't stop when subs are about', they explained. 'U-boats will hang around wrecked ships, hoping for a second victim. The Navy will see that they're picked up.'

The convoy continued eastwards, steaming straight past the provincial ports of Port Elizabeth and East London, to our destination, Durban. For part of the time we were watched over by a patrolling Lockheed Ventura aircraft of the South African Air Force.

As we finally docked, there was the sound of singing from the quayside. The celebrated Lady in White was greeting us, as she greeted all the wartime ships, with a patriotic rendering of *Land of Hope and Glory*.

I gave a last lingering look of affection at the *Winchester Castle* as we disembarked. Only it wasn't to be my last sight of her. I didn't know it then, but many years later, after the war, I was to once more board the same ship as a civilian passenger on my way to a new teaching job in Southern Rhodesia, or, as it's known nowadays, Zimbabwe.

East London was a bright, clean and sunny town on the Buffalo River in South Africa. The shops were full of everything that had long disappeared from the shelves of a severely rationed Britain, and in the glorious weather we soon lost our pallor and acquired the bronzed, fit look of the locals. Our noticeboard was crowded with offers of lavish hospitality from the townsfolk. They were eager to persuade well-educated English-speaking young men to return after the war to enjoy the beautiful climate and the manifest prosperity. No mention was made of the potentially massive social problems.

Collondale was a military air base just outside East London, close to the wild, unspoilt coastline facing the Indian Ocean. It was operated jointly by the Royal Air Force and the South African Air Force, and it provided intensive training courses in air navigation, which included meteorology and reconnaissance with aerial photography. This last we used to take part in an overlapping survey of bush country north of Durban, where they planned to build a big new air base.

We were number 7 Air Navigation Course, and we had already received basic training with the university air squadrons, followed by the navigation ground school at Eastbourne. We flew in the Avro Anson, nicknamed 'the Annie' – a noisy and slow but very reliable aircraft, which we preferred to fly in at night. In the daytime heat in the stifling, oil-smelling cabins we were tossed about on the thermal air currents, inducing a strong nausea that some cadets could never overcome. They were taken off flying for good.

Two students flew together. One navigated the aircraft along its route, the other measured wind drift, took sextant measurements of the sun or stars, and wound up the heavy undercarriage by hand; a matter of a hundred and twenty-eight turns, and not an easy task in the heat.

The course took three months, followed by exams and assessment of our skills by the instructors, and while they did this we were a given a day off. Most of us headed for the town beach. It was labelled 'safe', meaning safe from the sharks, rather than from the currents. Certainly it wasn't safe from the bush telegraph, which quickly ran round the town, and before we knew it, all the

A Night-fighter Crew

The upper photograph is of Graham White, as a cadet pilot in 1941 at the tender age of eighteen, just before going overseas for training. The white flash on his forage cap denotes that he is a flying cadet, though his rank – until he gains his wings – is the lowly one of Leading Aircraftman.

Inevitably nicknamed 'Chalky' – all Whites are labelled either Chalky or Snowy in the RAF – this made a welcome change from being known at school as 'Aggie' (after his initials, A.G.) and for obvious reasons, 'Fishface'.

The lower photograph is John D. Wooding, his nav/rad or navigator/radio, wearing Sergeant's stripes and flying brevy as awarded on completing training.

In the Royal Flying Corps this badge would have been a winged 'O' for 'Observer' but as this was known somewhat irreverently as 'The Flying Arse-hole' it was changed to an 'N'.

More accurately it should have been 'N/R' but if captured this could have led to some intensive interrogation by an enemy probing for radar secrets.

John was nicknamed 'Dagwood' after the comic strip husband, Dagwood Bumstead, by Jimmy Lowrie for his amiable and laid-back disposition.

local girls from the oddly-named U-no-me Club appeared with picnic baskets crammed with Coca-cola and sandwiches.

But the beach party was short lived. A loudspeaker van was driven on to the sands and blared out a message: 'This is an emergency. All RAF cadets of No. 7 Course must return to Collondale immediately. Service transport is waiting for you on the Beach Road. Do not delay.' The van moved on up the beach to repeat its message.

Grabbing up our uniform and towels we ran across the sands. The waiting transport driver couldn't enlighten us; all he knew was that we were to report to the main lecture hall without delay. The staff pilots were already there, cradling their flying helmets in their laps, and the excitement mounted as the station commander appeared on the platform. 'Cadets of the senior course, you have been recalled because there may be a national emergency, and you could be needed for operational action against the enemy.'

In South Africa? We were the other side of the world! 'A Lockheed aircraft of the South African Air Force on patrol over the Indian Ocean has reported what has been assessed as around a hundred ships approaching the coast. No Allied fleet is in the vicinity, so we must conclude that it is Japanese and possibly an invasion force. Our training aircraft are being armed to attack. You will fly out in formation led by the senior navigation instructor, who will brief you on the flight plan. Good luck to you all!'

Later, as we sat waiting for take-off in the hot, stuffy Ansons, clutching our maps and plans, apprehension gradually began to take over from our original excitement. These lumbering old Ansons wouldn't stand a chance against the formidable Japanese carrier-borne fighters. But there was no time for further speculation. There was a call on the radio and the pilot opened the throttles and we started to move.

We taxied to the edge of the airfield, stopped – and the pilot cut the engines. Then in his clipped Afrikaans accent he said, 'You fellers 'ad better get out, the mission 'as been aborted.' We stumbled out with mixed feelings of relief and disappointment.

Back in the lecture hall the CO was smiling. 'Good news, chaps. A second Lockheed was dispatched to check on the latest position of the invasion fleet. After a careful search he was unable to locate any ships, and assumed that they had made off eastward back to their bases, having realised that they had been detected. Then he noticed something. On the ocean surface he observed dozens of small ship-sized shadows projected from alto-cumulus clouds high above. It was all an illusion!'

We felt very flat after the recent tension, and nobody felt like returning to the beach. But then the public address crackled again. Here is an important announcement for No. 7 course. You have all passed your exams and will qualify as navigators on Friday afternoon.'

That, at least, was one battle that had been won.

CHAPTER FOUR

Land of the Free

In the blissful blue skies and blazing sun of Arizona, far from the grey battlegrounds of Europe, we quickly pushed ahead with our flying training. There were some forty-five cadets on each course (with four courses going through at any one time), and we spent half the day in the classroom and the other half flying over the dry Sonora desert in the blazing heat.

We trained near the small town of Mesa, about halfway between the state capital of Phoenix and Tucson, a town on the Mexican border.

Falcon Field had been built in the desert a few miles from the town, and it had been set up under the name of Southwest Airways by a group of Hollywood actors and producers, as their contribution to the war effort. Indeed, one of our instructors, Hank Potter, was a Hollywood producer, and another, Brian Aherne, was a minor film star. As a result of our nearness to Hollywood – a mere four hundred miles as the covered wagon rolls – we seemed to attract more than our fair share of media interest, no doubt due to the area forming a handy place for film folk to display their patriotism without interfering too much with their careers.

One of my letters home at the time described how our training was interrupted by Movietone News cameramen, who wanted to show us on screen with Brian Aherne, along with the cowboy star Gene Autry, who was an Army sergeant at a nearby base.

Southwest Airways was a private outfit, employing American civilian flyers to teach us to fly, in three stages – Primary, Basic, and Advanced. Or it had been: ours was the first course to cut out Basic and move directly from Primary, using Stearman fabric-covered biplanes similar to the Tiger Moth, to Advanced Flying, with the metal-skinned monoplanes known to the RAF as Harvards. The ground instructors were also American civilians, while administration and discipline remained the responsibility of RAF personnel. These consisted of a senior NCO and three officers, a flight lieutenant, a squadron leader and the commanding officer, a wing commander. These officers acted as invigilators at our exams.

We lived in light, airy huts in the camp, built round a square. There was a canteen, a dining hall, classrooms, repair workshops, and a control tower, and surrounding it all a fence and a gatehouse manned by armed guards. They didn't want anyone sneaking in for free flying lessons. Beyond the end of the runway, distantly shimmering in the desert heat, were the steep cliffs of Superstition Mountain, an area of legend and mystery. It was a holy place to the local Indian tribes, but it also had its own treasure trove, 'the Lost Dutchman's Mine'. Around the turn of the century a prospector (actually German, a mistaking of the word 'Deutsch' for Dutch) had come stumbling out of the hills with his pockets full of nuggets and boasting of the gold mine he had found. Greedy men waylaid and killed him for the gold still on him after he had bought drinks for everyone in the local bar. The mine itself was never found again, although people continue to hunt for it.

Our only way into or out of camp was through the gatehouse, and the guards would religiously record the names of anyone returning late from town, so that they could go on report next day. The trouble was, to the guards we Brits were like the Chinese are to us – we all looked alike. So when, next morning, the Tannoy blared out the names of late cadets who had to report to the office, the list had a familiar ring to it. You'd be amazed how many times George Formby, Stanley Baldwin, and Flanagan and Allen were late back to camp.

You soon learned to keep a sharp eye out for the rich culture of creepy-crawlies which shared both the airfield and the surrounding desert with us. The first thing you did in the morning was reach out of bed and shake your shoes, in case a scorpion had squatted in them overnight. In the cadets' lounge several venomous Black Widow spiders lived permanently under the chair cushions, while outside you kept a wary eye open for poisonous snakes like sidewinders, rattlers and vinegar roans.

One day we found a tortoise wandering among the cacti in the desert sand, and in a spirit of fun we stuck an RAF roundel on its shell with the words 'drill sergeant' under it, then unthinkingly sent it on its way. Unthinking because we later learned that the bright roundel would probably reveal its presence to local predators, such as falcons and eagles. Over the centuries those scavengers of the skies had learned a technique for cracking open the hard shells of their victims. They simply picked them up in their talons, took them to a dizzy height, and dropped them onto the rocks below, like cracking open walnuts.

But our prize find was a Gila Monster, a twelve-inch-long, highly poisonous lizard with pink and brown scales, named after the local dried-up Gila river.

We tethered it by a rope to a tree and gathered round in a circle, as a dare taking it in turns to dash in and pick it up behind the head so that it couldn't bite you, but eventually we tired of the game and let it go.

As for the scorpions that we occasionally came across in the huts, there was a legend that if surrounded by fire they would commit suicide by striking themselves on the neck with their own poisonous tail. Of course we had to try it, and ringed one with a flaming circle of Ronsonol. Sure enough, its sting came curling over its head, and the creature quickly stiffened in rigor mortis. Or so we thought. We put the flames out, and turned away – and the scorpion dashed off into hiding! I swear I heard it chuckling as it did so.

In the desert itself you might come across the odd rattlesnake or the occasional tarantula, but the things that really gave you a headache were the harmless but painful armour-plated insects resembling flying half-inch bolts that blundered around after sunset. How they ever got airborne I will never know, but they certainly didn't seem able to climb more than five feet eight inches high, the perfect level from which to happily zap into your forehead then lie upside down on the ground until they got their breath back.

But the creepy-crawlies weren't all you had to keep a watchful eye out for. Although the camp's sanitary plumbing was far superior to that on board ship, the toilets were still open to public gaze, being a row of porcelain thrones without any vestige of partitioning round them. And no sooner were you ensconced there than a small Mexican lady would promptly appear with a mop and pail, calling 'Leeft your legs!' She would then commence to mop the floor under your raised feet as you sat there. One thing the RAF cured you of was blushing.

Near us in the desert was a forest of giant Saguaros, those long-limbed cacti that resembled policemen on point duty – only these were anything up to forty feet tall. One cadet, illegally low-flying over the desert, staggered back to base with a bent wing and an aircraft covered in green cactus juice.

The camp was protected by armed guards, and they could be a little trigger happy at times. Mike, a member of our hut, had got himself a revolver from somewhere, and one night he seemed reluctant to go to bed. The rest of us told him in no un-certain terms to put the flaming lights out. 'OK, I'll put them out', said Mike affably, and calmly shot out both light bulbs with succeeding bullets. We heard shouts of alarm and running feet, and half a dozen guards with drawn revolvers burst in – only to find six cadets (including Mike) apparently sleeping like innocent babes. They spent the rest of the night patrolling the boundary fence looking for the armed intruders.

We had other disturbed nights as well. Our doctor, Hank, was a US Army Air Corps officer, and a great character. His regulations stated that at an appropriate interval after the cadets had been let out on the town for the weekend they must be given an intimate inspection to check that they hadn't picked up any unmentionable disease from some lady of the night in Phoenix. (This procedure was known as an FFI, or Freedom From Infection, not to be confused with the other FFI, the French Forces of the Interior, or for that matter, the IFF, or Identification Friend or Foe, an electronic method of interrogating an unknown aircraft. Life got very complicated by capital letters at times.)

For some unknown reason, Hank considered that three o'clock early on a Thursday morning was an appropriate interval, under the meaning of the Act, and his favourite method of waking us up was by playing his trombone very loudly in the middle of the hut. That we might not have minded too much, but the trouble was that he played it not only very loudly but remarkably badly, and the only way to shut him up was by giving in, stumbling out of your bed, and baring all before you.

As one sleepy cadet told him, plaintively, 'Doc – I'd sooner have the disease.'

Not that we found all the US Army Air Corps regulations quite so funny as this. Mike – he with the light-bulb notches on his gun – was one of the best pilots on the course and one of the most fearless. In a moment of dare-devilry he did a beat-up of Thunderbird Field, the local American Air Force training base; great fun, though very much frowned upon. But the Army Air Corps operated what was called 'the honour system', whereby any of their flight cadets who caught a fellow cadet breaking regulations was honour-bound to report him. Mike was spotted and his number reported by an American cadet, and he was sent back to England in disgrace immediately. We were appalled. Nothing could have been further from our own concept of honour.

However, we got on extremely well with the ordinary citizens of Arizona, who, we found, possessed a remarkable mixture of curiosity and kindness. Like the lady who, while giving a couple of us a lift into Phoenix one day, discovered that we were British cadets and insisted on going miles out of her way to show us to her cousin, Mary-Lou.

That lady inspected us carefully, as if we were a new breed of exotic pet of unknown temperament, and then delivered her verdict. 'Why, they're just like our boys!' But our driver was determined to prove otherwise, and ordered us, 'You ain't heerd 'em speak yet. Go on – say something!' We duly obliged and she crowed triumphantly, 'There! Ain't that just the cutest accent you ever come across!' Mary-Lou conceded that it was, adding, 'They sure picked up the language quickly.'

* * *

We did our best to inculcate the Arizonians into the mysteries of the British way of life, including our games.

Our demonstrations of cricket and soccer were met with blank stares of incomprehension. This was in no way helped by the uncertain explanations by the non-playing cadets such as myself who had been detailed to mix with the crowds and explain to them the games' subtleties.

But with rugby, it was different. One of our officers (a man not averse to a little self-publicity) harshly criticised American-style football on the local radio. 'We don't consider it very manly', he declared loftily, 'to play games encased in body armour.' This raised a storm of protest from irate local sportsmen, so to placate them it was arranged for us to put on a demonstration rugby game in their High School stadium. The officer quickly realised that his bluff had been called, so he ensured that both teams wore light-coloured shirts, and called for vigorous play. Anyone getting a bloody nose was not allowed to change his shirt ('Keep it on – it looks great!'), so that

The P.T. 17A Stearman Primary Trainer, fitted with a Continental 225 engine

This initial training aircraft had an inertia starter, which involved a groundcrew man literally winding up a heavy flywheel to great speed in the Arizona Desert heat and feeding in fuel as it wound down, hoping that the engine would fire.

Heaven help the cadet if it failed to do this and he was found to have forgotten to switch on before the prop finally ground to a halt. Only the crewman's utter exhaustion in the desert heat saved many a young trainee pilot from being battered to death on the spot with the heavy winding handle.

they soon appeared to be drenched in blood. Anyone limping slightly was carried off on a stretcher to the touchline and told to lie down and not move. Talk about spin! – the stadium began to take on the air of an abattoir on overtime.

Afterwards, the game was described on local radio in lurid and blood-curdling detail, and the officer was asked for his comment on the afternoon's blood-soaked entertainment. ''Fraid it was a bit of a quiet game', he said apologetically.

Pressure on our flying skills began to build steadily as we worked our way through the course and changed from primary biplanes to the more advanced metal mono-planes, and with it mistakes began to be made. During one formation flying exercise a cadet somehow chewed off his leader's tail with his propeller. The plane crashed and a cadet and his instructor were killed. The lad who caused the crash baled out and came down by parachute, with a ten-year hole in his memory from the trauma. He didn't know there was a war on or what he was doing in America – for him it was 1932, not 1942, although later he recovered and, indeed, resumed flying on a later course.

Shortly afterwards Jock Watters, in the next bed to me, suddenly disappeared on a solo flight. Flying was immediately cancelled and the instructors went looking for him. They spotted wreckage on the side of Superstition Mountain, and a jeep raced

The A.T. 6A Advanced Trainer, known in the RAF as the Harvard, fitted with a Pratt & Whitney 650 air-cooled engine

This metal-skinned low-wing monoplane introduced the young pilot to such refinements as wing flaps and retractable wheels. Failure to lower these when closing the throttle in the circuit prior to landing set off a warning horn. A watchful flying control man would also yell a warning over the air. Despite this, one young pilot serenely completed the landing with his wheels up, resulting in a bent propeller and a very red face. When asked why he had not heeded the warning message, he replied, 'I couldn't hear you for that bloody horn!'

across the desert to the site. Jock was still in his seat, one hand on the stick and the other on the half-turned fuel cocks. His engine had cut out and he had desperately tried to crash land, only to realise at the last moment that he had forgotten to change over fuel tanks as one emptied.

He was given a full military funeral. Those of us who had been his room-mates acted as bearers, and we slow-marched the coffin through the town to Mesa Cemetery, for once bare headed in the sun, followed by the rest of the cadets and watched by a large crowd of sympathetic local people. There it was lowered into the grave and his RAF cap, bearing the white flash of an air cadet, was placed on it, according to RAF custom. He joined twenty-five other British cadets who still lie there, together with three of the American cadets who later came to train with us at Falcon Field.

A few years ago an American researcher wrote to me. He was investigating wartime crashes in the area and had come across the remnants of Jock's aircraft, still lying on the side of Superstition Mountain after all these years. Could I help him identify the crash? I sent him the full details, together with a photocopy of our group with our instructor, Mr Mills.

The reason the Yankee cadets came to train at an RAF-controlled camp was as follows: General Hap Arnold, Chief of the United States Army Air Corps, and a great friend of this country, had already been instrumental in arranging for RAF pilots to be taught alongside the American cadets. When the RAF set up their own 'dromes in the States, he retained his interest and came down to Falcon Field on a tour of inspection. There he talked with Al Storrs, our American director of training, an acquaintance of his, who impressed on him the RAF's superior standard of instruction in night-flying training – the Yanks didn't go in much for flying after sunset.

Al told him, 'There's not a lot you can teach the RAF about night flying.' Whereon the general thought it might be a good idea to see how American cadets would fare under the British system. But he didn't intend to lose face over the experiment, and he wisely covered his bets. The Yankee course was handpicked – they didn't want to risk any American cadets being 'washed out' – so they had all been to university, and all had attained a certain level of flying training anyway. We got on very happily with them. They seemed to take well to the freer and more relaxed RAF style of instruction, and many long friendships were begun.

Today, Falcon Field has been swallowed up by the expanding girth of the city of Mesa. Just a small park remains of the once busy air base, and in it, forming a memorial, is the fireplace of what used to be the cadets' lounge. On the brickwork is a brass plaque bearing the names of those killed during training. The locals take great pride in looking after it, and a well-attended remembrance service is held each November.

After the war, many towns in Europe who had good reason to thank the wartime efforts of the RAF – towns like Amiens, where the pin-point bombing by Mosquitoes of the prison walls freed prisoners of the Gestapo – began a like tradition of honouring crashed RAF flyers, tending their graves, and, above all, teaching their children what they all owed to the dead young men. I only wish our own children were taught one quarter as much.

Following Jock's funeral, three of the bearers – myself, Paul and Dougie, went for a quiet meal to try and relax after the stresses of the day. There, we chatted about our careers so far in the service. They had both been at Manchester University and they talked of a friend they had known there, John Wooding. He was in South Africa now, they said, training to be a navigator, and if ever I needed one, they could recommend him. It was just a chance remark, over in a few seconds. Maybe I remembered it because they added, 'He's got a great repertoire of dirty jokes, he'd be good company on those long trips over Germany.'

But he was thousands of miles away and there were thousands of others training to be navigators. The chances of my ever meeting up with him must have been somewhere between 'zilch' and 'non-existent'.

Came the day we had all been working for, and which at times seemed would never come. Wings Parade!

We were marched onto the square, and as it was the graduating course we removed the white cap flashes we had worn so proudly for almost two years. One by one we were called to the front and the longed-for RAF wings were pinned on our chests and sergeant's stripes on our sleeves. There was a low groan of envy as we turned to face the other cadets, then we marched off to join the ladies – members of the DBE – who had been invited to the ceremony and were waiting with poised needle and thread at the back. There, they quickly stitched on our new badges for us on a more permanent basis.

There is an organisation in America, founded in 1890, known as the Daughters of the American Revolution, or DAR, a sort of cross between the WI and the Conservative Women's Coffee Clubs. They are made up of direct descendants of participants in the Revolution of 1776, and they did much to support American institutions and patriotic causes. They saluted the flag and God-Blessed America a lot – that sort of thing. Not to be outdone, a rival organisation grew up of ladies with British antecedents, called the Daughters of the British Empire. (The Arizona branch was 'The Lion and Unicorn Chapter', and it is still in existence.) These days it sounds a very memsahib sort of organisation – you could imagine them shooting tigers before tiffin – but they provided us with a clubhouse in Phoenix that we could use and where we could sleep over at weekends, and they persuaded local families to offer us meals, accommodation, and various outings. They did a splendid job and we owed them a great deal.

Speaking of British people in America, you did occasionally bump into them, and they were all at great pains to assure you of their patriotism and pride in being British, though not quite enough, apparently, to go back and join the fight. Sometimes their assurances became a trifle comical.

Thanks to our Hollywood backers, and in particular to our instructor/producer, Hank Potter, we spent our leave in Hollywood, where we were put up free at the British-America Club, all paid for by these selfsame Hollywood film folk. (Also thanks to them we were invited along to RKO Studios to lunch with Cary Grant and watch his latest film being made under Hank's direction. Cary was very friendly and great fun, and I still see the film at rare intervals on the box.)

While we were walking in the film capital we were hailed by a passing motorist who had noticed our RAF uniforms. 'I say, you cheps, care for a lift anywhere? Hop in!' We dutifully climbed in the vehicle, and its driver, a smooth, plump individual, beamed at us.

'Take you for a jolly old spin round the town, what! Show you the sights.' Which he proceeded to do, pointing out various places of interest on the way in an impeccable upper-class drawl. Out loud we hazarded a guess that he might hail from England.

'Bang on, old boy! You could tell, eh?'

We suggested that perhaps the accent might have given us the teensiest of clues.

'Ah yes, the jolly old lingo!' he chuckled. 'Never lose it, yer know – it's born and bred in a chep.'

At that moment, an elderly pedestrian attempted to cross the road in front of his vehicle, and in purple-faced rage and pure Brooklyn phrasing he suddenly snarled. 'If dat crazy old bat don't watch out she's gonna get an ass full of fender!' He immediately reverted to his previous cut-glass tones without apparently noticing his temporary lapse. You must admit it, when it comes to keeping up appearances the British abroad do it in spades.

This visit to R.K.O. Studios during our leave in Hollywood was arranged by Hank Potter, a film director/part-time flying instructor at Falcon Field. Hank is in the centre of the picture with Cary Grant and Laraine Day, who he was directing in a film. (I am at the front, far right.) After lunching with them, during which Cary was great company and made us most welcome, we watched a scene from the film being made.

Many top radio shows were also transmitted from Hollywood, and with the help of a friendly Canadian sound engineer we were smuggled in to broadcast shows like Red Skelton and Abbott and Costello, as well as visiting the stage-door canteen, where film stars and extras entertained and mingled with servicemen. We were likewise made welcome at several nightclubs. At one of them I caused gales of laughter when the seductive singer who featured in the floorshow did a slow and voluptuous dance of the seven veils round my chair while I slept soundly through her act, oblivious to her charms. NAAFI concerts were never like this.

Our training in the hot south-west corner of America had been a hugely fascinating experience. It was a new continent with so much to see, albeit with a faint sense of *déjà-vu*, in that we had already seen its images on the silver screen in the local Gaumont or Odeon cinemas on a Saturday night.

We had soon adapted to Arizona. The people were friendly and welcoming, the skies blue and unclouded – in the Arizona desert we only had one rain shower in ten months – and the food was wonderful after the rationing back home. We moved quickly through our training and enjoyed our off-duty life.

However, coming from the rather formal conventions of wartime Britain, we were constantly surprised by the wide variation in customs and moral attitudes that we found in the States. These seemed to range from easy-going raunchy Wild West to prim Victorian.

Take the time that my pal, Bill Taylor, and I were hitch-hiking our way to Hollywood for our leave, midway through our flying training. We started to thumb an overnight lift on the Yuma Road out of Phoenix late one evening, and presently a car pulled up in response to our waggling thumbs. There was a young fellow driving, with an older passenger by his side.

'Can you drive?' asked the passenger, and when Bill said he could (I had not yet learned the noble art) the older man turned and said, 'OK, thanks!' to the driver, who got out and walked away. Bill was invited to take the wheel, and as I snuggled down in the back, he then drove the whole way, through the night, some four hundred miles to the edge of Los Angeles, a journey broken only by a brief search of the car boot on the Californian border for illegal citrus fruit. (Apparently, taking a young woman across a State line for immoral purposes, although a Federal offence, came considerably down the list of heinous crimes compared to the possession of one small blood-orange. It was something to do with protecting their beloved oranges from imported disease.)

We discovered that our host was taking the car right across the country, but he couldn't drive the thing! Incredibly, he was going from hitch-hiker to hitch-hiker! So, when, finally, we reached the outskirts of Los Angeles, he told Bill to keep going until we came to another hitcher, when we stopped and asked him the same question, 'Can you drive?' Fortunately he could, so we got out, and our benefactor was then driven off in the early morning light by a total stranger, to continue working his way to some distant and unknown destination.

I've often wondered about this. Had he won the car in a raffle while on holiday? Was he allergic to steering wheels? Or was he, perhaps, a car thief who had failed his driving test?

Then there was that other hitch-hike, this time on my own, when, out of funds, I was thumbing my way from Mesa into Phoenix. A car pulled up, containing three large men, and I was told to 'Hop in, kid!', so I joined the man in the back, behind the driver and front passenger. The first thing I noticed with vague alarm as we sped away was that all three had the sort of faces that would have scared the pants off Humphrey Bogart. They were definitely by Al Capone out of Frank Tyson, but they seemed friendly enough, and when they discovered I was 'a Limey kid' they all started chatting animatedly, including the driver, who scorned such formalities as watching the road, and drove with one hand while looking back at me. It appeared that they were 'Moonshiners' – makers of an evil and illegal colourless liquid, laughingly labelled 'Scotch whisky'. They had been turning out a batch of their product somewhere in the foothills of Superstition Mountain and were now on their way home, and the bottle they were busy passing to and fro was a sample of their work. (They insisted I take a swig: 'It's good stuff – freshly made this morning!'

All I can say is that it was lucky the Germans never got hold of the formula. I swear it would have put a hundred miles on the range of their V2 rocket.) And, as we carefully skirted the small town of Tempe – they had had a bit of a bust-up with the sheriff there – and made for Phoenix, I was regaled with stories of their life. One showed me bullet holes in his arms and legs from shoot-outs with the cops, another gave me advice on how to hide the smoke from a still (use a down-draught), how to escape if chased by police along a dirt road (drag a chain behind your car, it throws up so much dust they can't see where they are going), and other tricks of the trade. Eventually, we reached Phoenix and dropped one man off to a call of 'See you on the night-shift, Buck!', and I was let out in the centre of the city to thankfully watch them zigzag away. What a pity I was too nervous to remember all the advice they gave me, or maybe today I would have been managing director of International Distillers, and Scotland's favourite tipple would be Glen Superstition.

The third incident happened when our whole course did a cross-country flight from Arizona to Texas, supposedly as an exercise to simulate, in distance at least, a trip to Berlin from Britain's embattled shores. We landed at a place called Midland, in the Texas Panhandle, and were put up at what appeared to be a quiet and decent family hotel in the town centre. But we were in the heart of the old Wild West.

I shared a room with two other cadets, Paul and Doug. Maybe we should have been warned when the bell-hop unlocked our door and then politely asked whether we would like a woman for the night – 'Ah kin git yuh any colour yuh want, white, black, brown or yeller?' We resisted the temptation to ask for a green one and declined his offer with thanks, intimating, in our stiff British accents, that it wasn't the sort of behaviour that British gentlemen indulged in when abroad, dam' bad form and all that, and a poor example to the natives. Of course, the fact that we had one dollar twenty cents between the three of us might have had something to do with it. I remember the bell-hop's look of utter surprise at our refusal, as apparently he ran a thriving, and quite acceptable, business there in true frontier fashion. But he didn't pursue the matter at that time.

However, it became clear that he didn't give up so easily, because in the early hours of the morning I was suddenly awoken by the light going on. I struggled from my bed, a sleepy eighteen-year-old clad only in drawers, airman for the use of (the RAF's standard and most unglamorous underwear, being a sort of cross between Bermuda shorts and a badly made shroud), to find a Mexican lady of the night standing in the middle of the room, having apparently walked through a locked door.

Was I interested in some fun and games, she asked.

Now, I couldn't see a dartboard anywhere, and my share of the communal one dollar twenty amounted to some forty-five cents, not even enough to buy the chalk for keeping the score, so I politely declined. Whereon she woke Paul and repeated her offer. He also refused, with the bemused but gallant air of a sleepy Terry-Thomas. In some desperation, no doubt having paid in advance for the loan of our doorkey, she turned to the still sleeping Doug. 'What about heem?'

Knowing Doug's uncertain temper when his sleep was disturbed, we suggested she ask 'heem', and sat down happily to watch the result, but Doug was not an easy man to wake. Despite vigorous shaking he slept serenely on, so she slipped a hand beneath the sheets and gave him what I can only decently describe as a tweak. The result was startling. Doug seemed to rise into the air – I remember thinking that he did a better loop without an aeroplane than with one – and came down with his indignation at boiling point.

All unaware, she repeated her offer of lusty pleasures, only to be cut short by a flow of invective from Doug worthy of a bargee who has just received a water rate demand for his canal. Almost too late, she suddenly got the message that the enraged and beefy young Englishman bearing rapidly down on her with steam coming out of his ears was just not in the right mood, and she turned in terror and ran for her life. We heard her race down the hotel stairs and, through the window, watched her disappear into the night, almost as quickly as our boyhood illusions about the golden-hearted saloon girls of the Far West in a thousand films; and no doubt, as fast as her own illusions about the typical Englishman being some sort of urbane and beautifully mannered cross between Cary Grant and Hugh Grant.

All this was in stark contrast to an incident that happened in more conventional Arizona society. I slept in the next bed-space to Jock Watters (who sadly ended up in Mesa Cemetery when he crashed on Superstition Mountain), and one day he asked if I wanted to go to a party. There would be lots of girls and plenty of food. What the crafty Jock didn't mention was that it was a Sunday School party and there wasn't a girl there over twelve.

Jock had been inveigled into giving the youngsters a talk about how the war affected the life of youngsters in Britain, and was trying to lay off some of the work involved onto others. Once there, he quickly gabbled a few words about air-raid wardens along the Royal Mile and balloon barrages protecting vital haggis factories, and then added, 'But I can only speak of Scotland. Cadet White can tell you far more interesting things about England', and sat down with a smirk on his face.

Totally lumbered, I stumbled through an account of my Home Guard career, with gory tales of bayonet practice and Bangalore Torpedoes – great stuff for Sunday School, you must admit – while the audience listened fairly attentively. Then, to stretch out the time I drew a picture in chalk on a blackboard of a Home Guard stalwart defending Britain against the Nazi hordes. I showed him about to throw a Molotov Cocktail, made out of a beer bottle filled with petrol and with a lighted fuse in the neck. I even decorated the bottle with the triangular Bass Beer label. (Eat your heart out, Rembrandt!)

Resuming my talk, I soon lost my young audience. They were giggling at something behind my back, so I turned and found that a Church Elder had sneaked round on hands and knees and was carefully rubbing out the part of my drawing that he considered would corrupt young American minds. Never mind that my figure was attempting to fry the whole *Waffen SS* to a crisp with a crude form of napalm, it was the beer bottle that he was worried about. He carefully removed all traces of it from their innocent gaze, leaving the Home Guard recruit to defend Britain's shores with nothing but a burning fuse hanging harmlessly in mid-air.

But what, for me, best encapsulated that American ethos of red-blooded manhood combined with a warm generosity was an incident that happened to a fellow Derbean out there. Chris worked at Rolls-Royce, helping build those excellent and much-wanted Merlin engines, but couldn't ignore his growing urge to do a little more to help his country. Surprisingly, in view of his work, he was allowed to join up in the RAF, and was sent off to the States to train alongside the US Army Air Corps as a pilot (this was before the Yanks entered the war).

Halfway through his course, Rolls-Royce, which was trying to get Packard to build its engines, but was having production problems, realised that it had a man on the spot. Chris was taken off flying and sent to sort out the problems at Packard. After the odd spat over 'some Limey' telling the bluff American auto workers how to build aircraft engines, he got on well with both union shop stewards and workers. So much so that they invited him to join them on their regular Saturday night jaunts: 'Just a cuppla beers at a joint we know in town, shoot a little pool, with mebbe a visit upstairs to the little lady in the back room – that sorta thing.'

Chris, rather taken aback at the difference between their idea of a night on the town and his own, tried to cover his embarrassment with the jokey comment that he 'wouldn't fancy going in second wicket down to any of you lot!' They stared at him stony-faced, then retreated down the shop to hold a hurried meeting conducted in fierce undertones. Chris watched in alarm. Had his flippant comment been taken the wrong way, and caused a strike in a vital war factory?

Eventually, the leader marched back and confronted him. 'OK, about what you just said. We took a vote on it and it was unanimous. You get first go.'

But now, newly trained and bewinged, we set off back to Moncton, in Canada, climbing on the train in the 85 degrees of an Arizona winter and getting out into a blinding snowstorm, several degrees below zero. (I had my shoes repaired before leaving Arizona. Ten days in the Canadian snow was enough to wear them out again. When I got back home to Derby I asked our local cobbler to mend them and he told me in a voice of shocked disbelief that they had been repaired with compressed paper!)

Now, home beckoned. And the biggest beckon of all was from the females of the family. We were coming back from a land of plenty, and one particular bit of that plenty interested them. 'Don't forget the Nylons!' was the call across the Atlantic, together with strange coded messages about sizes and deniers and colour shades. Rumours abounded as to what a pair of brand-new nylons would get you by way of a thank-you from luxury-starved, bare-legged English ladies. But first, we had to make space for the contraband in our bulging kitbags.

An edict was issued, that you could take only two kitbags per man on board ship. Lusty Lotharios with great plans for a busy lovelife for years to come were temporarily stalled. Then someone realised that they hadn't stipulated the size of the kitbags! So – you bought two kitbags and stitched them together into one long tube. Do that twice and you still had two kit bags, they just happened to hold twice as much! Long white canvas snakes appeared in the room and were hastily fed to bursting point with all manner of wicked temptation. And as they grew steadily fatter so too did the smiles of their owners.

A few days later we boarded our return ship in New York harbour, under the stony stare of the Statue of Liberty. And what a ship it was! No less than the newly built mighty *Queen Elizabeth* in dull-grey war paint. We wound our way slowly along endless miles of concrete corridors to get aboard, and it was here that we discovered the reason for the two-kitbag-only rule and the snag in the Lotharios' scheme. There were no stevedores and no cranes to hump the luggage aboard, you had to carry all your kit yourself. We were treated to the sight of lads bent double under the weight of those monstrous kitbags, looking for all the world like tiny ants trying to stagger home to the nest with two gargantuan white grubs that threatened to give their carrier a double hernia. The thought made those of us content with a modest few pairs in the back pocket smile happily.

Somehow they shoe-horned five thousand British and US troops aboard the great ship, and then, careless of prowling U-boats, we raced for home without a naval escort.

By building three-tiered angle-iron bedframes they got a dozen of us into each third-class cabin, with our gear dumped in the bath. We slept in three layers, on rough hammocks one above the other, each hammock a flat piece of canvas with eyelets round the edge, through which coarse string was threaded, tying it to the angle-iron frame. It was crude but not uncomfortable – to start with – but of course it became a challenge to the jokers among us. They began sawing at the cord on the bed above, so that it broke in the middle of the night, the top man falling through onto the middle man and both dropping on the unfortunate bottom victim. The amount of string holding your bed in place became less and less until in the end you untied your remaining few pathetic inches each day and carried them round with you until bedtime, when you retied them. We shaved, painfully, in cold seawater, until we decided not to shave at all during the voyage. Nobody cared. We ate twice a day in the magnificent dining hall and had fresh water only from ten in the morning until four in the afternoon. We played poker for matches and stared at the sea, and despite the boredom the days passed quickly and happily. We were going home.

CHAPTER FIVE

Coming Home

Basic training completed, and with bright new flying-badges on their chests, Dagwood and his fellow navigators were shipped home again to Blighty from sunny South Africa.

They joined hundreds of similarly qualified young Aussies, Canadians, New Zealanders, South Africans and Rhodesians, with a sprinkling of BLAVs – British Latin-American Volunteers – the sons of British people who had emigrated to South American countries. People like 'Chile Willy' Williams, a South American gaucho. All had come to help 'the Old Country' in her hour of need. What to do with all these keen young men, who had been trained to fly – just – but not yet to fight?

The Commonwealth airmen were sent down to Bournemouth, where attractive sandy beaches were screened off with coils of barbed wire in case of an attempted invasion. The RAF lads, including Dagwood's contingent, were moved up north, into the echoing empty hotels of Harrogate.

> Arriving there [wrote Dagwood], it was soon apparent that the priority was to build up a huge new air fleet of night-bombers, so most of us expected to finish up in four-engined Lancasters, Halifaxes or Stirlings. We lived in some comfort in the Majestic Hotel facing the Town Gardens, but we knew this easy life would be shortlived, as, daily, there were new arrivals from incoming troopships and departures to the operational training units. So when we were paraded in front of the hotel one morning and the Adjutant appeared with a sheaf of papers, we told ourselves, 'This is it!'
>
> But it wasn't. The officer merely read out a short note. 'Volunteer navigators are needed to train with airborne radar equipment and subsequently fly on twin-engined night-fighters.' He went on to say that radar aptitude tests must be passed and candidates would need above-average night vision. Training would be long and there would be additional flying training before being sent to a night-fighter OTU. We had one day to think about it.
>
> A group of us had become friends in South Africa and we sat together in the Town Gardens during tea break to talk over the pros and cons of such a move. It sounded special and exciting, but there was a saying in the RAF: 'Never volunteer. Trouble will come soon enough.' Some of us thought that our navigational training would be wasted and such a radar course would turn us into mere knob-twiddlers. The prospect of longer training put off a few.
>
> 'We'll settle for heavy bombers', they said. But about eight of us decided that we would volunteer. There were rumours that the Beaufighter was being replaced for night-fighting by the new super-plane, the Mosquito: you never knew your luck.

We were sent for aptitude tests, which involved something like today's control boxes of computer games. Most of us passed easily enough, but we guessed that the night vision programme would be more formidable.

A WAAF officer organised the tests in the night vision centre. 'You are the first batch', she said, 'We hope you will cooperate sensibly. In the middle of the room is a lantern with eight faces. You will each sit opposite a screen exactly four feet away. I shall clip your tunic collar to the back of your seat so you can't lean forward. You have a pencil and pad. When I ring the bell the lights will go out and the small lamp in the lantern will come on. You must try to identify the aircraft silhouettes on the screen. You have five minutes.'

In the darkness that followed we could see only faint grey blobs. Urgent whispers hissed from the darkness. 'Can you see anything?' 'No – she hasn't switched on yet, has she?' Someone said, 'Hang on!' I felt a hand on my neck and the clip was slipped off. I returned the favour, and soon we were straining forward. Then we hastily reclipped each other's collars, just as a second bell rang and the lights flashed on.

'Relax while I check your answers.'

Moments later her voice sounded rather surprised: 'Well, you've all done better than expected. Just a little confusion between the Beaufighter and the Ju 88. The next stage in your night vision training will be in the gym tomorrow morning.' It certainly seemed that we had cooperated sensibly, especially over those collar clips!

Next morning we arrived to find a muscular PTI waiting to greet us behind drawn blinds. 'To see in the dark', he told us, 'you must learn to look slightly to one side, as the most sensitive part of the eye is just off-centre. Everyone put on these tinted goggles to cut out the light, then form a circle round me and we'll start our first game. It's called Ball In The Belly. I have a heavy white medicine ball which I will throw at you in turn. You should see the ball coming faintly so put out your arms to catch it.'

For the first ten minutes we were all knocked flat by the ball, then gradually we saw a faint image, just enough to fend it off. Finally we managed to catch it. We had learned to look off-centre. The next game was even more painful. It was a relay race, zigzagging between two lines of heavy, white-painted wooden skittles. 'Faster, faster!' roared the PTI as we stumbled round the gym. We improved steadily and the instructor handed out sticking plaster for our sore shins.

Later we were given a talk by a medical officer on taking care of our eyes. We must not stare at bright lights, such as car headlamps, as this destroyed our night vision. We must wear our sunglasses each time we went out, even on cloudy days. We had night-time walks in the Town Gardens, and were delighted to spot an owl in a tree that we would never have noticed before. And it was important. Radar would bring us in to a few hundred feet behind an aircraft at night, but our eyes would finally confirm whether it was friend or foe. People's lives would depend on our night vision, as in the final analysis it would all be down to the Mark I Eyeball.

Daily we scanned the notice board for our posting notice. Finally we saw it: 'The following navigators are posted with immediate effect to the Radio Navigation School at Ouston, Newcastle-upon-Tyne.' And the last name on the list? As ever it was Wooding J.D.

CHAPTER SIX

Getting Serious

We landed back in Liverpool on a cold spring day. England seemed much the same after our exile, a little more drab and down at heel, perhaps, a little greyer and rather small after the brilliant weather and wide, open spaces of Arizona. Nothing else appeared to have changed much, except that now there seemed to be more Yanks over in England than we had left behind us in America. And when it came to bringing back goodies for the girls, we had been beaten to the punch! The GIs all seemed to be amply provided with nylons and chewing gum, things that luxury-starved British girls and their kid brothers hadn't seen for years. What's more, they didn't play fair. Red-blooded Englishmen, used to tanking up at the bar with half a dozen pints before they dared venture onto a dance floor with a girl, stood no chance against such over-powering competition. To females who had had to resort to painting their legs with gravy browning and drawing a simulated seam down the back of their calves with eyebrow pencil it was no contest.

In our training, though, things were about to change. In Arizona we had learned basic flying. The roads were so few and ran so straight that not only could we set our compass by them, we could use them as markers for exercises. In World War One, to get into a spin meant losing control of your aircraft and almost certainly crashing to your death. In our training, we had been taught to do deliberate precision spins, coming out of the turn dead in line with the road below. We had even ventured timidly into the night sky and triumphantly landed back again on a brightly lit runway, feeling that we had become masters of the air.

But now, we were getting down to the serious stuff, and we had much to learn. We had to fly in Europe, and it was like going from school to university. Here, the only straight roads were the ones the Romans had driven across the land two thousand years before. From the air any of the highways and paths created since then looked like a madwoman's knitting. We had to learn to fly in rain and cloud and snow, in the blackest of nights, keeping one eye out for enemy intruders, without lights and without seeing the horizon, or even the ground. And above all we had to know where we were in the bewildering green mosaic of ancient fields and farms, trees and towns.

But first we had to learn to control two engines instead of one. So from the reception centre of Harrogate we moved north to Inverness, capital of the Highlands. It was a quiet town, with the inhabitants speaking a clear form of English without any trace of accent, supposedly due to the settling of the area by victorious redcoats after Culloden. In fact Dalcross, the 'drome, was actually on Culloden Moor itself, scene of the last despairing battle and defeat of Bonny Prince Charlie's rag-taggle army.

There we flew Oxfords, the twin-engined light planes we termed Oxboxes, over and around Loch Ness. One of the cadets ended up in the loch; for some unknown reason he simply flipped over onto his back and plunged straight in. They never found him – those are deep, dark waters, and in such a setting it is easy to understand how the legend of a monster was born.

Apart from that, the course was straightforward enough, and the chief thing I recall about my time at Dalcross was being put on a charge for taking two eggs for my tea. That's what I said – for taking two eggs for my tea!

I was hungry. I'd overslept after being on late-night flying and missed both breakfast and lunch, so at tea I went round for a second lot. But it was the day that the rare and much-prized hen-fruit were doled out for our evening meal, and after the plentiful food in the States I had forgotten how precious they were in war-torn Britain. The charge was read out in sombre tones: 'Stealing comrades' rations in time of war', it thundered. It had the sonorous ring of courts martial, followed by blindfoldings, last cigarettes and firing squads at dawn. (Actually, I didn't smoke and I couldn't help wondering whether that would have earned me an extra ten minutes' heavy breathing instead of that last fag before the blindfold.) An indignant WAAF sergeant cook and a pompous warrant officer gave evidence that there was only one egg per man, and I had taken two, which meant someone had gone eggless. What had I to say?

I listed the names of six people who had gone into Inverness without waiting for a meal. If someone went short, where had the other five eggs gone? There was an embarrassed silence, and then the weary and incredulous squadron leader told everyone to get out of his sight before he put us all on a charge for wasting his time.

One of those to disappear eggless and early into town had been Alex, a quiet Aberdonian. It was Friday night and he didn't reappear until late Sunday evening, wearing the dazed smile of a man who has won the jackpot without ever remembering buying a ticket. And the tale he told was the stuff of dreams.

In Inverness he had been stopped by a young Scottish WAAF who asked him where the nearest service hostel was. She had been to see a friend on a nearby 'drome and had missed her train back south. Alex showed her the place, but there were no spare beds. She looked lost and downhearted at the news and on talking to her he found that she was a fellow Aberdonian. But she had an air of deep sadness about her. To cheer her up he took her for a drink and then on to a local dance. There her story gradually came out over the evening. She was engaged to an American flyer and they were due to be married in two days' time. Then she would be leaving her homeland for ever and going across to the States to live, which is why she had come north to say goodbye to her friends. She sounded as happy about the idea as a pork scrattin manufacturer relocating to Israel.

At the end of the dance, there remained the question of her night's accommodation. 'Well, as we've spent the day together', she said calmly, 'we may as well spend the rest of the night together.'

It was a warm June evening and they lay out in the heather outside the town, watching the sun set over the dark green hills and purple water. She looked longingly at the last sight of her homeland and cried gently at the thought that she might never see it again. She told him she wished she could take a little bit of Scotland with her. Alex said he would love to help, but he really hadn't come properly kitted out, as all he had in his field-dressing pocket was his field dressing. But she asked what difference did it make, she'd be married in a couple of days anyway. So he did his best. Technically, it would probably be recorded as off the top end of the Richter scale, and later, by local historians, as Caledonia's most northerly heather crop-circle.

That little bit of Scotland that Alex donated would be in his late fifties by now, and one wonders what direction his life took. Did he end up in the White House or in the nut-house, with psychiatrists trying to work out why he liked to wear his mum's skirts and his dad wondering why he sounded like a set of bagpipes every time he blew his nose? Or did he finish his days as just another tyre mark on skid row? I suppose it all depended which star you were born under. And when you think about it, he was born under all of them.

Twin-engined aircraft, at least in the form of the lightly built Oxboxes, proved to be no great problem; it was mainly a matter of balancing the power of your two engines, one against the other, on take-off. However, learning to fly with one of those engines out of action took some getting used to. You had to lock your leg into an immovable bar to counter the imbalanced thrust of one-sided engine power. But it was a lesson that was to be vital to me on more than one occasion.

From the far north of Scotland we moved down to Grantham, an interminable seventeen-hour journey in a slow darkened train that seemed to take for ever. We didn't know it but the steady transfer of troops to the south ready for the build-up to D-Day had already begun and the railways were overloaded.

In Grantham we learned to fly along radio beams. Turn one way and you heard a short bleep of sound in your earphones, turn the other way and you got a longer note. They overlapped in a narrow central beam and there you heard a continuous tone. Using this as a guide, with radio cross-markers, enabled you to fly in an intricate weaving pattern that put you into position for a blind approach and landing in bad weather. It was vital but soul destroying to listen to, and already becoming outdated. A radio bleeping monotonously in your ears for hours on end while you tried desperately to work out what it all meant and what to do about it was a passport to madness. Yet our flying instructors back in America had spent much of their lives 'riding the beams', as they called it, in their pre-war work of flying mail across the breadth of the United States in all weathers. Some of them would happily sit listening to the sound for hours while they taught us how to fly. It takes all kinds, I suppose, but I was glad when we finished the course.

There was usually something special that you recalled about each camp you went to, and Grantham was no exception. They had a vicious way of waking people up in the morning. Promptly at 7.00 a.m. a service policeman (who else would have such a warped soul?) would hold a cheap and very noisy alarm clock close to the Tannoy and turn up the volume. The ear-shattering bellow that resulted made the Crack of Doom sound like a bishop's burp, and men would leap up in terror before collapsing, trembling, back into their blankets. But worse was to come. You then heard him slowly rewind the thing, ready for a second session. It was torture of a particularly refined and sadistic kind. You knew what was coming, but try as you might, you couldn't steel yourself to withstand it. Suddenly it howled out again and you experienced a second heart-zapping convulsion. Then – the final insult – just in case you might not have heard it, to end it all a voice burbled gently, 'Wakey, wakey!'

We completed the course and prepared to move on to the final step in our training. This would be an OTU – operational training unit – where we would learn to fly the biggest and most advanced aircraft before going on to a squadron and operations over Germany. But where would it be?

The flight commander gathered us round him and broke the news. 'You are all going on to heavies [the big four-engined bombers] and your OTU will be at Forres . . .' We all groaned; it was the next camp to Inverness, and no doubt involved a further seventeen-hour journey back up to Scotland again. '. . . except', added the officer, 'for Sergeant White. He is going as a staff pilot to Ouston, near Newcastle.'

I was incensed. 'Why pick on me?' A stooge job, flying other people around the sky like a taxi-driver! Was I never going to get into this war? 'What have I done wrong?' I demanded, but he just shrugged uninterestedly. Was it the Curse of the Ws again? But I wasn't the last on the list – Doug Wilkinson came after me and he was going off with the others. Then I recalled the form we had filled in when we got our wings. What plane would we like to fly, it asked, in a ridiculous pretence that they were going to take any notice of what you said. Of course, everyone put down 'Spitfire' (though only two or three of the course finally ended up on them).

But not me. There are two types of pilot. There's the Flash Freddy and the Steady Eddy. Now, I was never brilliant at aerobatics like the Flash Freddies, I preferred the earth to stay where it was – down there – not to finish up somewhere round my ears. But I was good at instrument flying, I could fly for hours in cloud or darkness, without ever seeing the horizon, And I liked to cover my bets – two engines were better than one, I thought, it gave you a spare – so I put down 'twin-engined fighter-bomber', which seemed to just about cover everything I could think of. I was probably the only one to do so, and to this day I don't know why I did, but it's very likely why I'm still around today – over a third of our Arizona course were lost in the bomber battles over the Reich. But there was something else – it led directly to my meeting up with Dagwood.

When you've lived as long as I have – and thoroughly enjoyed every minute, let me admit at once – then there comes a time when you need to start making plans. Not plans for this life – it's a bit late for that – but for the next one. But it isn't easy when there is so much that you don't know.

Right from Sunday School days you've understood that you either go to heaven or hell. No messing, it's one or the other. Keep your nose clean, eat up your greens, remember your mother's birthday, never covet your neighbour's wife in church on a Sunday and only ever cheat on your Income Tax, and there's a fair chance that St Peter will smile benignly, tick your name off his list, and wave you on in. On the other hand, if you murder a few people with an AK47 for flogging you heroin that's out of its sell-by date, forget to take your cough mixture before appearing on *Who Wants To Be a Millionaire?*, or ride your bicycle on the pavement, there's no hope for you. Peter will hand you a map with singed edges, a pair of asbestos Y-fronts, and precise directions as to where you can go (using only two fingers), before slamming the Pearly Gates in your face.

But life is never that black and white. No-one is all good or all bad; many a vicar tries pressing the return coin button on a payphone, and many a Scout-mistress fails to Be Prepared. There needs to be a grading system of wickedness so that you end up with some sort of rating. There's an 'O' level and an 'A' level for getting into university, so why isn't there an 'H' level for getting into heaven, and what sort of pass mark do you need to make it? (Or should it be a No-pass mark?) Then again, do they just count the worst thing you've done or is there a topping-up procedure, like in driving offences?

If you knew, you might be able to make amends for one or two of your worst sins to bring you above the pass mark before it's too late. Such as, if you'd committed bigamy, you could hand the oldest and fattest one in to Oxfam in good time, or if you'd robbed a bank you could put your loot into another bank, and they would promptly rob it right back off you again.

So what has brought on all this agony of conscience? Well, there are one or two small sins I'd like to get off my chest here and now, before it's too late. For instance, I've never admitted this before, but when I was posted to Newcastle as a staff pilot, while the rest of the course travelled back up to Scotland to an operational training unit, I took the chance to sneak home on the way. I was totally on my own and I reckoned no one would notice if I travelled from Grantham to Newcastle via Derby. But as luck would have it, after a few hours at home the last train from Derby was late, and it was midnight before I reached the Geordie capital. My destination, Ouston, was a dozen miles further on and I'd missed the last bus. I had no money left for either a taxi or a hotel, and I didn't know the road well enough to hitch a lift at midnight.

It wasn't the first time I'd been stranded. Once, following a pal's wedding in Folkestone, some of us broke into the railway station and spent the night in the compartment of a parked train – first class, of course. But Newcastle was a much busier station and I doubted whether I would get away with it there. Anyway, you don't sleep well in such circumstances, you spend the night worrying whether you'll wake up on the New Brighton Ferry or as part of the latest Commando raid on Dieppe.

My only hope was to try for a bed in a servicemen's hostel. Which I did, but they were all full. I tried the last one, and it was the same. In fact, it had a queue of people waiting in case someone didn't turn up to claim his bed. Like, maybe he'd been lucky at the local dance with some khaki widow. But there were far too many hopefuls hanging round the desk for me to stand any chance.

I tried ringing the police. How about going into the Bed and Breakfast game, I asked, and letting me kip down in an empty police cell for the night? They said, sorry, they were reserved for the local criminal fraternity only, and allocated on a strict first-crime-first-served basis. And when I offered to break a few plate-glass windows in Grainger Street if that would help, they agreed that it might – like, help to get me six months. I quickly put the phone down.

I'd had enough. I was out on my feet and at breaking point, so I walked back into the hostel, past the waiting queue, smiled a good evening to the lady at the desk and casually waved a piece of paper at her as I passed, hoping it looked like a bed receipt. Inside, there was a big sleeping hall with rows of beds but with few of them yet occupied with inert forms. Each bed had a large numbered ticket clipped to its foot. I chose a bed at random in the middle of the room, then went round and removed the number from every bed in the place – even the ones with sleepers in them. I hid them all under my pillow, got in bed and fell fast asleep.

I was roused an hour or so later by dozens of people milling round the room, trying to work out which was their bed. One or two tried to wake me to ask which bed number I was, but I gave out realistic drunken snores and they eventually gave up. In the morning I woke early, tiptoed to the toilets and hid the incriminating tickets on top of a cleaning cupboard. Then I walked out to catch the first bus to camp. The same lady at the desk gave me a sleepy goodbye smile. She looked very tired, as if she'd had a hard night.

Now there might be some fully paid-up member of the Hair-Splitters and Nit-Pickers' Union who would argue that that wasn't much of a sin to forgive, but they miss the point – it might mean a lot to St Peter, you just don't know. You see, it was a Salvation Army hostel, and that makes it sort of family, doesn't it.

That's what I mean, if there was a rating system and I was just above my 'H' level, I might – I'm admitting nothing, mind, but I just might – find one or two other small sins I could confess to tip the balance.

*   *   *

The aircrew staff at Ouston were a hilarious mix of greenhorn pilots and old-sweat instructors. We flew Ansons – the reliable old Annies – and all the pilots were youngsters fresh out of training and still wet behind the ears. All we had to do was chauffeur an instructor and four nav/rad pupils round the sky in an Anson full of radar gear. Two Annies would take it in turn to be the hunter and the hunted, and the pupils would learn how to do radar interception techniques on each other.

The instructors, on the other hand, were veterans of the blitz and cynics to a man. People like the cadaverous Lancastrian, Bernard Cannon, the ebullient but hot-tempered Mike O'Leary, and Nat Addison, the urbane Mancunian who won his first Distinguished Flying Medal as a lowly Airman, First Class; they were hard-bitten warriors of the night skies who had spent fruitless hours chasing their own tails in the darkness over places like Bristol, Coventry and Liverpool, desperately trying (and surprisingly sometimes succeeding) to pick up faint echoes of enemy bombers on their crude and elementary equipment while Britain's cities burned below. (There was an old night-fighter joke that said the Mark I radar consisted of an ear trumpet and a stop-watch. You opened the window and shouted, then timed the echo.)

These instructors were not happy to be flying with such novice pilots, especially when they included people like 'Sally Anne'. He was a young pilot who got his nick-name from being a staunch member of the Salvation Army, and he was very short in height – so short that he needn't have bothered too much about religion, he would have probably managed to squeeze under the Pearly Gates anyway. When flying, he had great difficulty seeing over the long nose of the plane, especially when coming in to land. So he would fly a little, stand up to take a good look round, then sit down and fly a bit more, trying to remember what was where, until he hopefully hit the runway. This prevented him from going any lower, so he would finally bounce his way to a stop. He appeared completely unperturbed by the ripe and anguished comments of his long-suffering passengers.

However, on occasion those veteran instructors would get their revenge. Occasionally we would have to relieve ourselves while flying, and there was a funnel and a long rubber tube down at the back of the plane precisely for this purpose. But the pilot sat at the front of the aircraft, so if he was flying solo he had the option of wetting his pants or doing a mad dash down the plane and an Olympic-standard emptying of the bladder before racing back to wrestle the old Annie back into submission. This was hardly to be recommended, so with just the one pilot aboard, our only alternative (strictly against regulations) was to hand over the controls to our totally unqualified radar instructor.

That gentleman would watch and wait with an evil grin on his face while you walked down to the back, then the moment you started, he would fling the aircraft all over the sky. Generally, the tube stayed quite dry but I can't say the same for the rest of the aircraft.

Or, if the instructor really felt in a mood, he would take the opportunity while you were down at the back end to try his hand at low flying. You ran back but you daren't attempt to take back control while so low down, and all you could do was hang on and pray very hard. On one occasion, an Anson landed and taxied to the far side of the 'drome, where, well away from the prying eyes of the CO, they got out and started pulling wheat out of the engine casings. The instructor had neatly reaped a swath of the farmer's corn with his propellers.

It was at Ouston that I learned one of the basic secrets of the universe – how to deal with delicate electronic machinery when it goes wrong. The answer is simple, you put the boot in hard until it surrenders.

Newcastle had its fair share of bad weather, and our old Annie would often find itself lost in a white world of smog, unable to see the ground beneath us, or indeed anything else. But it was all part of the learning programme. The 'drome transmitted an electronic beacon that the pupils could pick up on the radar set, and they were taught how to home onto it and, with its help, bring the aircraft into a landing approach.

Unfortunately, one day we were in just such a white-out when the radar picture quietly faded from the screen. The instructor didn't turn a hair. He stood one pupil at the side of the set and told him to kick it steadily. At each kick the picture flickered momentarily, just enough for the instructor to home in on the lost beacon, and after a short interval we sailed serenely back home over the hedge and on to the runway.

It is a lesson I took to heart. The more delicate the machine, the more brutal must be the beating. It may not always work, but it lowers the blood pressure and satisfies the soul.

It was also at Ouston that I first came across members of the WAAF, the female side of the Royal Air Force – they just hadn't been around during our training up until then. Between the wars the RAF, along with the other two services, had been a hotbed of male chauvinism. The very idea of having women working on aircraft maintenance was risible, they just didn't do that sort of thing.

But in wartime the unthinkable all too often became the inevitable, and with a growing manpower shortage, to the horror of the old sweats who had spent long, weary, peacetime years striving to attain the coveted three stripes on their sleeve, women began to be gradually introduced into almost every facet of Air Force life.

Of course, unlike today, there weren't any women pilots in the RAF. That's not to say there weren't any women pilots at all. Quite often you would see a small curvaceous figure climb daintily down from a large four-engined bomber she had just delivered single-handed to a squadron, before powdering her nose and mincing off – but they were Air Transport Auxiliaries. They weren't in the RAF but they were damned good pilots.

Apart from this, WAAFs were to be found throughout the service, in the Stores, packing parachutes, driving the small Hillman vans that delivered aircrew out to their aircraft like so many parcels, and particularly in the Signals section, as wireless operators. They were the golden voices of the night, listening out for aircraft in trouble and passing on assistance and information. When you are clinging to life by your finger-nails in a crippled aircraft, trying to make it back, there is no sweeter sound than a woman's voice calling out of the darkness to guide you home.

But, occasionally, there were problems. The pilot and his navigator normally spoke to each other on the intercom. To talk directly to the ground station the pilot would press a switch on his radio, and his navigator could hear this, but he couldn't speak to them. Nor could the ground station hear what the navigator said. This was fine unless the transmission switch jammed on. In that case the pilot unknowingly transmitted his intercom talk over the air. Ground control could hear this, but it couldn't hear the navigator's reply, nor could it contact the pilot to warn him he was talking to the world and to switch off. And on occasion this unguarded conversation could be more than a little fruity.

Take Jock, one of the pilots at a later 'drome, a rough Glasgow diamond. He never minced his words; instead he cracked them wide open and stuffed them full of lurid expletives. He flew with a compatriot as a navigator, a dry and witty observer of the frailties of human nature.

One night, a gleefully spiteful fate ordained both that Jock would be flying the night after he had taken out one of the WAAF radio operators and that his transmission switch jammed in the open position. Almost unbelievably, the same malevolent fate also arranged that the lady in question would be on duty at the same time. There are no prizes for guessing the subject of the intercom conversation.

'Hey, Wully, ye ken I was oot wi' young Jenny last night! Weel, she's always seemed a stuck-up wee coo, but ah'm tellin ye, her pants cam doon like a flag of surrender!'

There was a short silence as the unheard navigator made some lewd and caustic comment in reply. It made Jock hoot with laughter.

'Och, aye – the biggest I've seen!'

The alternating randy comments and short silences, followed by bellows of laughter continued unabated – indeed, increased in imaginative language and physical detail until Jock almost fell out of the sky with laughter.

Meanwhile, the unfortunate subject of the discussion was quietly having hysterics as the choked laughter of her companions grew. But there was no way to stop it – Jock could not be contacted. Finally she fled sobbing from the room, while the hard-bitten RAF sergeant in charge glowered after her.

A fiery-pink WAAF whose duty it was to record all calls in detail, turned hesitatingly to him. 'Do I have to write this down word for word, Sarge?'

'Can you spell it?'

Rather hesitantly, she admitted that she could.

'Then write it!' snarled the sergeant.

At Ouston, too, WAAFs turned up on the flight line as mechanics. Frankly, the senior NCOs didn't know how to handle them. Reducing airmen to tears was a difficult art, honed to perfection over many years, accompanied by selections from an accumulated vocabulary of choice epithets. With women it was all too easy to obtain a flood of tears, so easy that some of the old sweats began to suspect that the reaction was being used as a weapon against them, and they weren't sure how to combat it.

So when one sergeant in charge of maintenance on the old Anson aircraft came across two of his new female recruits doing something rather startling in the line of aircraft inspection and repair he did not immediately fly off the handle.

The Anson was an ancient though sturdy aircraft, and its acknowledgements to the pilot's bodily needs were rudimentary, to say the least. The pilot only had the already-mentioned fearsome funnel and rubber tube arrangement, halfway down the plane, to the right of the entrance door. The tube led to a simple hole in the side panel of the aircraft, whence the liquid proceeded earthwards before, no doubt, convincing some farmer in the fields far below that he should finish his haymaking without delay.

The maintenance sergeant found one WAAF inside the plane, holding up the metal cone to chin level and chatting amiably into it, while the other stood outside, with her ear pressed against the exit hole. 'What the 'ell', exclaimed the startled sergeant, 'do you two think you are doin'?' The outside girl straightened up with a dazzling smile.

'We're checking the intercom, Sarge,' she said.

*   *   *

Inevitably there was considerable physical attraction between the sexes on the more remote airfields, but opportunities for romance were not easily come by. After dark, gimlet-eyed service police patrolled unlit corners of the camp, moving on any amorous idlers.

WAAF quarters were strictly out of bounds to males, and the hallowed precincts tightly guarded with mother-hen efficiency by their female NCOs. The airmen's quarters were plainly impossible areas for any hanky-panky. In those long bare barrack rooms hiding a bird in your bed by disguising her as a large lumpy pillow just couldn't be done.

But the sergeants' accommodation was a different matter. NCO aircrew lived two to a room, and the temporary absence of his room-mate could sometimes tempt a would-be Lothario to try a little covert dalliance.

I once shared a room conveniently next to the stairs with a pilot named Jeff, a likely lad with a lusty appetite. One night I came late to bed, following a long snooker session, but was unable to open the door to the room. Thinking it was jammed I heaved it ajar far enough to snap on the light switch. But the light itself stayed stubbornly unsnapped.

'Bloody bulb's gone!' I said out loud in disgust, but Jeff's voice came out of the darkness.

'No, it hasn't, mate. I've taken it out.'

'What the hell for? And why won't the door open?'

It turned out that Jeff's bed was against it. 'Just go away for half an hour', Jeff told me, and a female voice echoed from the dark interior, 'Yes, go away, Chalky!'

I'm no spoilsport, I went away. But the mess was empty, the NAAFI was shut, and it was starting to drizzle. The only light came from the guardroom and if I wandered anywhere near there, the Snoops would want to know where I was going at that time of night. And they didn't like it if you said 'Barmy'. So I trailed back to the room in a stroppy frame of mind, determined to get my head down regardless of whatever floor-show was going on around me.

As I forced the door open, Jeff's bed sounded like a rusty trampoline changing gear while going up a steep hill.

'Look, I'm going to bed. Just pretend I'm not here!' I told the wall of darkness loudly, then felt my way to my bed and flopped on to it. As I did so, my hand came down onto warm, naked, hairy flesh and I leaped to my feet again before someone started counting the number of hands around the place and coming up with an odd number, one of which was remarkably cold. But there was no expected shriek of offended womanhood.

'Jeff! Whose bed are you on?'

'Mine.' Not surprisingly, he was a little short on the conversational side.

'Well, what about the – er – whoever's with you?'

'She's here as well,' he said, rather breathlessly, 'that's the usual arrangement, mate.'

I began to wonder if he was using my bed as a subs bench, with a spare, stripped ready for action, for when they changed ends.

'Then who's over here on my pit?'

'Oh – that's the CO's dog.' He seemed disinclined to elaborate further, leaving my mind in a whirl of speculation.

The CO! Which bed was he on then – and what sort of orgy was going on in here? I tried to recall whether you had to salute an officer in the dark when you were in pyjamas and he, presumably, wasn't showing his rings. I decided I'd best take to my bed and feign sleep. Somehow I managed to worm my way under an unoccupied bit of blanket and snuggled down.

But before the trampoline lullaby could send me drifting off to dreamland it stopped abruptly. There was much tugging of clothing and snapping of elastic as the lady got ready to depart. Then, from out of the darkness I suddenly received a smacking kiss. It felt as if I'd been given a quick topcoat of lipstick by an over-amorous paint roller.

'Goodnight, Chalky!' she trilled softly, and disappeared.

My first thought was to try and remember whether the Decontamination Centre stayed open twenty-four hours a day, but I fell asleep trying to recall where it was, anyway, and the next thing I knew, it was morning.

'That was a funny dream I had last night', I told Jeff as I yawned my way to my feet. 'I dreamed I had a dog on my bed.'

'We both did,' said Jeff, rather ungallantly, 'only yours had four legs and it's still there.'

I followed his pointing finger and found a black Labrador curled up comfortably on the floor under the bed. It normally never left the CO's side. I shooed it out and it wandered unresentfully away down the corridor.

'How did that thing get in here?' Jeff shrugged: 'I dunno. It followed us in last night and sort of settled down.'

It never came to our room again, or even gave so much as a knowing wag of the tail when it passed us down at the flights. Jeff thought that maybe the service police had tried hot-wiring the dog to spy on him, but I remembered that doleful Labrador gaze and thought it was more likely the reincarnated spirit of some long-dead airman, wistfully trying to recall memories of lusty pleasures in a previous existence with a spot of doggy voyeurism.

Then again, maybe we were both barking mad.

One day I climbed out of the aircraft, followed by the instructor, Mike O'Leary, and his four pupils. It was cold and wet and it hadn't been a good trip. Someone made a comment about the filthy weather, and I agreed. 'It's not what I'm used to. Give me good old Arizona sunshine any day.'

At that, one of the pupils, a tall lad, looked round.

'My pals trained as pilots in Arizona', he volunteered: 'Paul Welch and Doug Wilkinson . . .'

I looked at the name tab that all pupils wore on their left chest. 'Ah yes, John Wooding! They mentioned your name . . .'

We exchanged a few words, but I didn't see him again, as a few days later he moved on to the next stage in his training at a 'drome up in the Scottish Borders, and for the moment I forgot all about him. The place was called Charterhall.

Meanwhile, my pal Jamie and I continued to explore the delights of Newcastle. It was a place full of surprises. One night, we wandered down Grainger Street and into the Haymarket, where we found a small pub, the Half Moon. It was full of happy Geordie chatter but empty of uniforms. We were the only servicemen in the place, which made a pleasant change, and the beer was good. Halfway through a pint of ale we noticed a man stroll into the bar and calmly turn straight into the ladies' loo. No one batted an eyelid but us.

'Did you see that, Jamie!'

But a couple of minutes later a young copper entered. He, too, turned at once into the ladies'. Before we could say anything, the law returned, pushing the original miscreant in front of him. 'I've told you before, keep out of there', he said mildly, and went out again.

The man stood by the bar and watched him go.

'You having a drink or what?' asked the barman.

'Later', the man said, calmly, 'I'll try a bit of what, first.' He grinned and immediately went back into the ladies' loo. He never came out again before we left and no one took a blind bit of notice.

We tried to warn a couple of girls we were chatting to, as they made for the Ladies'. They just smiled and went in anyway.

'They didn't seem very bothered', I said. 'They're probably too innocent to understand what we were talking about – the one I spoke to said they were just out of a convent – something like the Church of the Reformation.'

'They've got a funny accent round here', said Jamie, 'the way mine pronounced it, it came out as "Reform School".' We decided maybe we wouldn't wait for the girls to return, it might be a better idea to catch the bus.

Back at camp we suddenly spotted the name 'Half Moon' on a notice-board outside the Guard Room. 'The following premises are strictly out of bounds to all personnel and all ranks at all times!' it declared. 'THE HALF MOON in the Haymarket, Newcastle.'

It made you wonder what went on in the Gents.

Interesting place, Newcastle, in wartime.

Three weeks later the flight commander called Jamie and me into his office. We were moving on. We had done our stint at staff piloting, lugging a radar instructor and his pupils round the Geordie skies in our faithful old Annies. Now we were to rejoin the conveyor belt that fed a constant stream of fresh young pilots into the black cauldron of night warfare.

Before coming here, I had been cocooned in a wodge of flying cadets, moving inexorably from place to place, all learning the same new knowledge and skills like a class in school, all of us straining every nerve to attain that almost mythical goal, an operational squadron.

Now, by stepping aside for a while and becoming part of the mechanism that drove that conveyor belt, I had got a rather different idea of what RAF life was all about. I had chatted to the wise old sweats spending their 'rest' period from operations by instructing newcomers to their trade, and I had listened to their marvellous, cynical tales of action in the night skies, and I think at Ouston I had grown up a little.

Only now things had changed. Now we were leaving, but not to a bomber operational training unit. I had been indignant at having been side-tracked to this place, yet by moving here Jamie and I had all unknowingly entered the small and select club that was the night-fighter world.

The old-sweat instructors said goodbye and asked where we were going.

'Charterhall', we told them.

'Ohmigord – Slaughter Hall!' they said, their eyes widening. It was the first time we had heard the nickname. They said goodbye again. Only this time it sounded as if they really meant it.

CHAPTER SEVEN

Pigs Might Fly!

The call to continue our training had come as a surprise, but our stint as staff pilots at Ouston had got us into one of the most exclusive clubs in the RAF, that of night-fighting. The trouble was that the operational training unit we were bound for was in the Borders, that desolate area between England and Scotland that had been fought over by the two countries for centuries. Personally, I never did work out why either one of them would want it.

It was autumn, hardening into winter, and there are few bleaker places on God's Earth at that time of year. Charterhall was about thirty miles inland from the coastal town of Berwick-on-Tweed, which was another way of saying thirty miles beyond the end of the earth. Dagwood and his companion navigators from Ouston were already there on the previous course to ours. He describes his arrival at the notoriously nicknamed 'Slaughter Hall.'

When we left Ouston the staff had given us a heartfelt 'And the best of British luck, chaps!' They had an idea of what we were in for.

We lived in draughty old Nissen huts and they supplied no fuel for the big round stove in the centre of the room. Instead, they gave us a large axe, indicated the abundant trees outside, and invited us to help ourselves. We spent much of our time foraging for fuel, be it tree trunk or broken furniture – and I'm not saying how the furniture got broken.

On our rare time off we would brave a cold walk or cycle ride into the nearby small towns of Greenlaw or Kelso, where there was an occasional dance in the Corn Exchange or an ancient film at the cinema. Otherwise we sat on our beds and thought back nostalgically to the not-so-long-ago warmth of the South African sunshine.

It was at Charterhall that we met up with the pilots who were to make up the other half of our crew. The first two weeks were less stressful for the navigators than the new drivers because we were taken up in the Mark II Beaufighters by experienced training staff and shown how to use the radar interception equipment. The young pilots had the daunting task of learning to fly those ferocious aircraft, so different to the light, well-mannered planes they were trained on.

They were set a rigorous regime of dual and solo flying, culminating in 'circuits and bumps' (take-offs and landings) carried out entirely on their own, starting in daylight and continuing into dusk and finally into darkness with the landing-lights switched on.

During this initial period everybody was busy trying to sort out a good pilot to crew up with. You came together as two groups of complete strangers, eyeing each other warily, and you were given a week in which to get to know each other and make your choice. To help us the CO gave us a little chat on arrival. Look for someone you felt you could get on with for long periods at a stretch, he said. (That was a laugh for a start, the one thing we couldn't do in the aircraft we ended up in, the Mosquito, was stretch!) Make sure your intended crewmate had no little mannerisms that were likely to irritate you. (Like, perhaps, a pilot saying, 'Look, no hands!' when coming in to land?) Even better if you felt that you could become firm friends and spend some of your leave together. Look for someone, he said, with a similar outlook on life, and try and find common interests or intellectual pursuits that you shared. ('I hope tha drinks a decent drop of ale, lad. That camel's puke they brew down south will likely mek thi go blind, and there's no room for a dog and a white stick in these aircraft, tha knows.') Then once you were crewed up (he went on), get to know and understand each other, so you developed almost a sixth sense between you. Back your partner all the way, your lives could depend on the trust and understanding you have built up.

I must have been slow off the mark, because each time I approached a likely prospect he would say, 'Sorry, mate, I'm already fixed up.'

I began to feel a slight sense of panic. Perhaps there weren't enough pilots to go round. Maybe I would have to learn to fly my own plane as well as do the navigating and operating the radar?

Eventually I came across a quiet chap called Jerry. He seemed shy and nervous, and when I suggested we might make a good team he said doubt-fully, 'I suppose so. You're the only one who's asked me.'

I thought to myself, 'I've picked a right one here!'

Most of the others seemed happy with their pairings. My pal, Jimmy, found a namesake in Jimmy Chipperfield, scion of the Chipperfield Circus family. They flew together for two years and Jimmy married his pilot's sister, Mary. After the war he joined the family circus as transport manager and spent his working life organising the movement of lions and elephants and other wild beasts.

In the days following crewing-up, the navigators cycled round the edge of the 'drome to watch their prospective partners trying their hand at landing the Beaufighter. It was not an occupation for people of a nervous disposition. 'Here comes old Jerry now!' they shouted to me gleefully, as a plane dropped the last ten feet onto the runway and went bouncing off like a table-tennis ball. 'We hope you've got good life insurance.' I shuddered nervously and gave a weak smile. Later I sought out Jerry and, diplomatically avoiding mention of the dreadful landing, asked how he was getting on.

'Oh, fine – I think. But it takes a bit of getting used to.'

Next day, I watched him approach for a landing far too fast, bounce wildly and claw his way back into the sky again. As I cycled back, I decided that in future it might be better for my nerves not to look, even from the crew room window.

After two more days a disconsolate Jerry sought me out to say that he had been suspended from the course and was being sent back to the sorting centre at Harrogate. I felt a mixture of relief and anxiety. Now there was a definite shortage of pilots.

'Don't worry,' said the training officer, 'he's not the only one who couldn't cope with Beaufighters. I've asked for replacements and you'll move on to the next course. They're sending a couple of staff pilots from Ouston to make up the numbers.' I wondered who it could be. Not, I hoped fervently, our tiny tambourine basher, Sally Anne.

Jamie and I travelled by train up to Berwick-on-Tweed and then on by RAF lorry to Coldstream and Charterhall. Our first introduction to the new 'drome did little to raise our spirits. Charterhall was a camp that was carelessly scattered across a large chunk of countryside. It was a couple of miles from your billet to the sergeants' mess for your breakfast, and a further two to the 'drome. It was almost as far again round the 'drome itself to the flight lines on the far side. True, every aircrew member was issued with an old boneshaker of a bicycle, but discipline was strictly enforced. Getting a puncture and turning up late got you the illogical punishment of having your bicycle taken off you, making you later still. Should your mate take pity on you and give you a lift on the back of his machine then he too was dispossessed of his bike. But such handicaps paled into insignificance compared with what we were supposed to skid around the sky in.

At Charterhall we had to learn to fly the savage and dangerous Beaufighter Mark II. There was a saying on the 'drome – 'You haven't lived until you've flown a Beaufighter Two – and you won't live long when you do.' But that was all to come. First, it was partner-picking time. So take your partners for a gentlemen's excuse-me war.

In the Army, you did as you were told, if you knew what was good for you. When they said 'Jump!' all you said was, 'How high?' It was the same in the RAF except that when they said 'Jump!' you asked 'From which aircraft?' All decisions were made for you except one. And that one the RAF always insisted was yours alone to make, even under the pressures of wartime training. You were completely free to choose your own flying partners. Matching up of crews took place when pilots and navigators met for the first time, and were given seven days to pair up before starting final training on operational-type aircraft, prior to posting to a front-line squadron.

Seven days to sort out someone on whom your life might depend was not long. Yet, somehow, the system seemed to work. On big bombers, like your Lancaster or Halifax, the navigator was just one of a group of seven or eight people. He stayed tucked quietly away in his corner, scribbling lines on maps and staring at stars, pretending it all meant something. (He'd probably work out your horoscope for you if you asked nicely.) And when the pilot called on the intercom to enquire where they were, our navigator laddy would come out with observations like, 'That's probably Europe we're passing on the starboard side right now, Skipper!' Or, 'Take your hats off, lads, we're in the choir stalls of Canterbury Cathedral.'

Of course, day-fighter types never used navigators at all, which was just as well. There wasn't room in their cockpit for anyone else, not with those huge handlebar moustaches and those enormous egos. They just charged round the sky following their leader, in a mad rugger scrum, shouting 'Tally-Ho!' and picking fights with people. But then, they didn't go all that far from home anyway, especially in bad weather. Between the wars it was not unknown, when lost, for them to land on the vicar's lawn and ask the way back over a cup of Earl Grey, but by World War Two aircraft were getting a bit too big for that, so they would just call on the radio for a course to steer.

Actually, we night fighters didn't use navigators either, we used a navigator/radio (known as a nav/rad), which is a slightly different species. Not that their name was much of a guide as to what they did. For a start they didn't really navigate – they could but they didn't need to, they were guided to within two thousand feet of the target by a ground controller and then left to get on with it, afterwards being told the way home again. Come to that, they didn't use the radio either, the pilot did. Instead, the chap in the other seat was a skilled radar operator, trained to translate a few moving blobs of green light into a picture of what was happening out there. He was our eyes in the darkness.

Later, when we moved on to long-range night-fighting over Germany, we didn't have the luxury of a ground controller to guide us, we had to do everything ourselves. The nav/rad had to work out where we were by using a little electronic box, known as Gee (as in 'Gee, how the hell did we end up here?'). Of course the Germans lost no time in jamming the signals, but then, they tended to be like that, very unsporting. In any case they could only jam it up to ten miles from their coast. And should the worst come to the worst, you could always line your starboard wing up on the Pole Star and aim for England. It wasn't an easy island to miss.

But more than anything the nav/rad was an equal half of a team. He and the pilot were completely dependent on each other, which is why it was so important that you got your choice of flying companion right in the first place.

I surveyed the new intake of navigators and wondered how you picked one out of that lot – maybe they would let you have one on sale or return? I wished I'd taken more notice of how well the pupils had done back at Ouston; this lot had only just come through there, but I couldn't remember a single face. In the end I opted for a cheerful, buck-toothed lad from Chesterfield, on the grounds that it was almost as good as coming from Derby.

That was on the Monday. I had sorted everything out on the first day, and sat smugly back, watching others scrabble around frantically as the days, and the available choices, diminished rapidly.

On Friday, the final day (after that a navigator would be chosen for you), young Buck-teeth calmly informed me that he had changed his mind, and decided to crew up with a pilot who also came from Chesterfield. Did I mind?

I minded bitterly, and stalked off, fuming. Yet I remembered the CO's advice – choose someone you could trust. He had soon shown how much I could trust him.

Had I but known it, I'd had a lucky escape. Young Buck-teeth turned out to be a nagging fishwife of a navigator, who drove his pilot mad with his suspicious questioning of every move the other made. 'Are you sure you've got the wheels down, Ray? You're coming in a bit fast, aren't you . . . ? Look out for that ambulance, Ray . . .' I'd have probably needed another nav/rad anyway: that one I'd have swiftly throttled with his own parachute harness.

But now I was left high and dry, and there seemed to be no one left to crew up with. In a black mood I went and sat in the sergeants' mess grumpily to await lunch.

Someone flopped into the seat beside me, interrupting my reverie. I vaguely recalled the face from somewhere. 'Hi! Remember me?' asked Dagwood. 'Tell me, is there anyone on your course who needs a navigator? My pilot's been thrown off, so I've got to move back a course and recrew.'

'There's me', I said.

'Great!' he said. And that was that. Dagwood was equally relieved.

The rapport between us was immediate and reassuring. I watched him bring a Beaufighter smoothly down onto the runway and my cares seemed to disappear. We were to fly together until the war's end, and stayed friends for over fifty more years.

We were a right pair.

Sometimes during your service life, you flew aircraft that were, to put it politely, mildly eccentric in some way.

Pilots learned to tolerate things like the starboard impulse magneto on the Tiger Moth needing a massage with a hammer before the engine would start in cold weather, or the Griffon-engined Spitfire trying to stand on its nose if you put both brakes on at the same time as you taxied round the airfield. You took such things in your stride. But just occasionally you came across an aircraft that seemed to be down-right evil, and seemed to breathe an air of sheer malevolence from the moment you climbed in them.

The Beaufighter Mark II was one of those. Black sheep of a fine family, and given every start in life, it was a real pig of a plane. And pigs might fly, but they don't do it very well or without giving a whole heap of trouble.

The first (Mark I) Beaufighters had been produced in a desperate rush in 1938, as war-clouds gathered ominously, to answer an urgent need for a twin-engined fighter-bomber to replace the ageing and under-powered Beaufort. To save time they reused the wings and tail-plane of the older machine. The Taurus engines were replaced by the more powerful Hercules, the nose was shortened drastically to give the pilot a superb view and the crew was reduced from four to just two, pilot and navigator.

It all looked fairly promising, if a mite over-heavy (snap the wings off and it would make a passable stand-in for a Sherman tank). That was until you got down to the small details, like how you actually got in and out of the thing. My own guess is that the design for this was sub-contracted to a team of eccentric Chinese acrobats from Blackpool Tower Circus. The pilot entered under the belly of the plane via a metal hatch bearing a short ladder, which gave access to a well behind the pilot's seat. However, there was no room to pass round the seat to enable him to sit in it, so he had to operate a side lever that collapsed the back and arms, so allowing him to clamber over into position, complete with chute and dinghy. Then he relocked the seat and prepared to fly. The hatch was closed from the outside and formed part of the floor behind him. At the other end of the plane, hidden from sight behind armour-plated doors, the navigator struggled through a similar hatch opening of his own.

That was the easy bit.

Getting out again in anything like a hurry was a much more athletic feat. First, the pilot opened the hinged outside escape hatch by remote control, leaving a gaping hole in the floor behind his seat, then he released his safety straps and collapsed his seat once more by its unlocking lever. Meanwhile, set in the cabin roof over his head were two long steel tubes, which is where the Chinese acrobat bit came in.

Pilot Officer Tarzan now had to reach as far back as he could above his head, grasp the tubes, and haul himself, parachute pack, and dinghy, backwards until he dangled over the dark hole in the floor below. He then dropped down through the still airspace created by the open flap into fresh air. Always assuming, of course, that down was still down and hadn't suddenly changed to being up, a not unknown event in flying.

On his way out, Pilot Officer Tarzan had to dodge the navigator's open hatch at the rear, (hoping he had been sporting enough to mention that he was thinking of

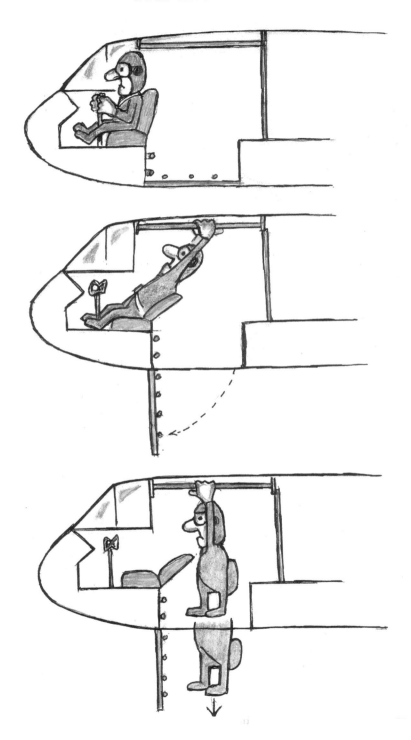

returning to earth by the scenic route.) The navigator always beat you into fresh air: he had only to open his hatch and step on the square yard of nothing that appeared in the floor – no hanging about on metal poles for him. And if you managed to miss the open back hatch there was always the tail-wheel to clobber you.

(I often wonder what became of old Jimmy Becket, a navigator with an odd sense of humour, whose idea of fun was to sneak up behind his pilot, Butch Baker, while he was coming in to land and collapse his seat under him.)

Despite such eccentricities, the Beaufighter Mark I was a rugged aircraft that charged round the night sky at a fair but unexciting rate of knots, proving, in its role of night-fighter, to be a reliable, if rather underpowered, platform for the freshly developed airborne radar.

But while Bristol was churning out Mark Is at top speed (they also built the engines), the enemy was busy bombing Britain's aircraft factories flat, a habit viewed with some alarm by the British Government. It left it with a lot of eggs in one basket, and the basket was within easy egg-breaking reach of German bombers. So someone had the bright idea of fitting a batch of Beaufighters with different engines as an insurance policy. And what better to use than that reliable thoroughbred, the Merlin, produced in the far safety of Derby, under its protective blanket of East Midland mist at the end of Bronchitis Valley. Thus the Mark II made its debut – and it proved an utter disaster.

Altogether 337 Mark IIs were built with the Rolls-Royce engines, and no fewer than 102 of them – thirty per cent – crashed from one cause or another. These included just two shot down by enemy action and – as if they didn't have enough to contend with – one destroyed by a USA Spitfire. The Merlin engines gave the aircraft such a built-in swing to port that it tried to take off in ever decreasing circles. You had to open up the port engine slowly and carefully halfway before attempting to advance the starboard throttle, yet the heavy aircraft was underpowered, and if you didn't accelerate reasonably quickly you risked not getting off at all. And if you messed up the landing, going round for another try became a desperate juggle with Jesus.

At this point, with the impeccable logic of the Mahogany Bomber pilots in Air Ministry, it was decided to take the Beaufighter IIs off the front-line squadrons, and put them onto training stations. Presumably they reasoned that any trainee pilot managing to stay alive on such aircraft for more than five minutes would find operations over Germany a doddle.

Eighty-four Mark II aircraft were sent to Charterhall. Thirty-nine of them (that is forty-six per cent) crashed, eighteen of them during take-off, landing, or over-shooting. Four force-landed, six plunged into the sea, five into the ground, and four caught fire in the air. Two of them simply disappeared off the face of the earth, and it was one of these that came close to finishing up as a coffin for Dagwood and me.

One night I was taken off flying because of a badly infected and swollen eye – the only time in my life that I ever had a stye – and a friend, Don Pinney, and his navigator took our place and our aircraft. It was a foul night, thick with cumulo-nimbus cloud along the coast. The plane simply disappeared from the ground controller's screen in the middle of the exercise, presumably into the sea.

'Dangerous icing' was the general opinion. 'There's no such thing,' scoffed the Bligh-like chief flying instructor, 'only dangerous pilots!' (He was a terrifying figure to young green-horn pilots, yet a short time later, when a non-flying squadron leader barged in ahead of me as I collected my supper after a hard night's flying, this same chief flying instructor took the meal out of the man's hands and handed it to me, saying, 'You've earned it – he hasn't!' A hard man, but fair.)

To be fair, Slaughter Hall already had its fearsome reputation even before the Beaufighter IIs arrived. Richard Hilary, acclaimed author of *The Last Enemy*, had lost his life there some ten months before we arrived. He was trying to get back into the air after suffering horrific burns in a day-fighter in the Battle of Britain, and he was flying the predecessor to the Beaufighter, the Blenheim Mark V, at night.

The Blenheim, wonderplane when first produced before the war, was by then outdated and slow, and the addition of a long, peculiar nose to the Mark V to accommodate a bomb-aimer cut down the pilot's view savagely. In my opinion Hilary should never have been sent up in such a plane, certainly at night, after his appalling experiences. If nothing else it was grossly unfair on his navigator, Sergeant Wilfrid Fison.

Not surprisingly, there was no dual instruction on the Beaufighters – pupils were expendable, instructors weren't – and those gentlemen had no intention of flying in the aircraft if they were not at the controls. Instead, you had two sessions on a Beaufort, an old bomber that flew like a brick shit-house (you climbed in the Beaufort by stepping down from the wing to the cockpit floor via the top of the Elsan. So an important item in your checklist was 'Check Elsan lid closed!'). After that even a Beaufighter II felt reasonable. You did a couple of trips as passenger in one, standing behind the instructor-pilot, peering over his shoulder trying to see how he flew the thing. Actually you could see the square root of sod-all, but you were standing on the escape hatch, which bore a remarkable resemblance to a hangman's trap-door. So not surprisingly you spent the trip remembering that he operated the lever that opened it, and trying very hard not to annoy him.

After that you read up the technical notes on the plane, then took off and flew it on your own – the first time that you had handled the controls – while the rest of the aircrew watched at the end of the runway, making ribald comments about your incompetence to your new and nervous navigator. If you survived two solo flights without even slightly killing yourself they risked sending your navigator up with you.

Afterwards, it was back to endless hours of training in the old Beaufort, learning instrument flying the hard way. The cockpit became the nearest equivalent to a medieval torture chamber yet devised. You spent the entire flying time sweating under sodium goggles. These things stopped you seeing anything outside the cockpit; all your eyes could make out were the clock faces on the instrument panel as you pulled the heavy aircraft into accurate steep turns, climbs and dives. You even did a blind-landing approach – flying without seeing the ground, turning and losing height to your instructor's orders until he took over at the last moment. There was a bump as your wheels touched, and you lifted your goggles to find you were running along the ground. It was fearsome stuff, but tremendous training for what was to come in the dark skies over Germany.

Night solo flying training started with 'Duskers'. You took off still in daylight and kept going round and round, doing take-offs and landings as the shadows grew longer and the light faded, until you suddenly found yourself flying the thing in pitch darkness. The worst time was twilight, when the fading light played tricks with your eyes, clouding your judgement.

There followed endless nights of take-offs in the dark, making mock attacks on each other, under the control of a ground station, and returning blearily before dawn, hoping you wouldn't make a pig's ear of the landing and have to stagger round again. Your chances weren't too high.

I recall one time I could get no reply from my navigator, Dagwood, hidden behind his armour-plated doors. His escape hatch was loose and kept banging painfully open against his shins. He tried leaping on the slowly rising hatch to close it, mistimed his jump, and found himself desperately clinging to the edge of a large hole without a parachute pack on, his voice frozen in terror at the sight of the countryside far below.

A little later a Beaufighter crashed in flames coming in to land, killing the young crew. My navigator and a fellow Londoner volunteered for funeral duty, taking the coffin down to the capital to attend a service for a mate who had smeared himself thinly along the runway. Anything, they thought, for a weekend away from this grim place and the bonus of a night off in the Smoke with their girlfriends. They reported to the morgue in best uniforms, where a small, unconcerned WAAF told them, 'He's over there – pop him in the box!' 'He' turned out to be a canvas bag, roughly sewn to human shape, with any recognisable body bits inserted in the appropriate place. The bag wasn't very full, and they couldn't face handling it. 'You great sissies!' jeered the little WAAF scornfully, and unceremoniously dumped it in herself. A prissy WAAF officer announced, in all seriousness, 'I doubt if they'll let you take the coffin on the Tube – you'd better get a taxi from King's Cross.' They didn't need to, because the coffin didn't get that far. Somehow they lost it on York Station while changing trains, and didn't see it again until it turned up at the church on a railway lorry halfway through the service. Later, Dagwood was the first to admit that he'd had better weekends.

Eventually, we moved to a satellite 'drome a few miles away. As we did so, a new batch of aircrew came in, one of them, Arthur, a pre-war friend of Dagwood. He avidly sought reassurance from us that the 'drome's nickname of Slaughter Hall was an over-the-top joke. 'Well, we're still here', we said comfortingly, but sadly within two weeks Arthur was dead.

Totally different from Charterhall, I remember the new 'drome, Winfield, with great affection. There were only twelve sergeants in the mess, with one WAAF cook, a wee Scots lass who knocked off at five each night, leaving us with a haggis for our supper. It was my first taste of the delicacy, and it was superb with the local ale. We took it in turn to be barman, and one of the lads could pound a reasonable tune out of the ancient piano. There was absolutely nowhere else to go, so we spent the evenings in great RAF singsongs and games. It was our Happy Hour.

My only other memory of the place was not so good. One night I retired early to bed in the Nissen hut, leaving the others drinking and playing darts with an elderly team from a distant village. I slept in the middle of the hut, and the only light switch was at the far end, not an ideal arrangement. In the darkness it was not unknown for idle people with full bladders to stand on their beds and open the windows. It was also not unknown to be woken in the small hours by a howl of anguish as a gust of wind slammed the window smartly shut.

On this particular night, unknown to me, while I slept the visitors were given beds for the night, as it was too late for them to get home. In the small hours I woke to feel someone leaning against one side of my bed. The next thing I knew was that a jet of urine was shooting over me very close to my chin. I could hear it splashing into my best shoes on the far side, making a glug-glug sound as they rapidly filled. I daren't utter a sound in case the perpetrator should swing round in automatic response to any noise, when I would have copped the lot. But as soon as the flow stopped I dashed out of bed and snapped on the light. It was an old boy who had drunk too much and couldn't find his way to the door.

I was incandescent with rage, not least because I'd just carefully cleaned the shoes. Despite pleas from the others that it was snowing I threw him out. What happened to him I never discovered, but if you ever take a lonely side-road near that remote camp – or where it used to be – and in the wee small hours you come across an ancient figure trudging forlornly along in the snow I'd like to ask a favour. It'll be a ghost, of course, but just stop and tell him I'm sorry.

At Winfield, we went on to the newer Beaufighter Mark VI, a vastly different machine with more powerful engines. True, on one flight the port engine packed up, covering the windscreen with oil, but unlike the Merlins, on the remaining engine we sailed confidently back home with little trouble.

It carried a newer type of radar, the Mark VIII, which only had a single circular screen instead of two rectangular ones. You were the dot in the centre of the circle and other aircraft appeared as a curved arc of light. The distance from the centre to the arc gave the range of the other plane. The completeness of the arc and the position of the gap in the circle indicated whether it was above or below, and to the left or to the right of you. It was rather like looking at a streetlight through the end of an empty beer bottle, which, I suppose, could be why we got on with it so well.

In fact the Beaufighter Mark VI was very much a pilot's aircraft, robust and powerful (at least low down, it wasn't too good at height), with a panoramic view from the cockpit, giving the pilot the impression that he was flying a cinema organ. Not so good for the poor navigator, though, particularly when trying to navigate, operate the radar, and load the ammunition all at the same time, in the draughty tunnel of a fuselage. However, there were occasions when he got his revenge.

When night-flying was cancelled we usually celebrated at the mess bar, and next day, while climbing to height in the increasingly rarefied air, our queasy stomachs were loud in their protest – freely emitting what we called bum-barks. We didn't so much break wind as shatter it into small pieces. Should this originate from the long-suffering navigator in the back, some quirk of the Beaufighter's air-conditioning system ensured that the evil cloud promptly charged forward down the fuselage and gathered in an all-pervading miasma of highly charged flatulence in the pilot's cockpit. Who says those Chinese acrobat-cum-aircraft designers had no sense of humour?

Today, the unlamented Slaughter Hall is no more. A sad and desolate place, it has vanished almost without trace off the face of the earth. Almost, but not quite. Bill McCash, chairman of the Falcon Field Association (to whom I am indebted for the information), was travelling up to Edinburgh in March 2003, and happened to take the A697 road via Greenlaw and Coldstream. Just before arriving at these ancient places, he came across a small sign pointing down a side road. It said, 'To the RAF Richard Hilary Memorial'.

It was a mile and a half to the quiet, leafy spot and the monument was set on a corner of two minor roads. Of polished dark grey marble, it stands about four feet high behind a semicircular drystone wall. The gold lettering below states:

Near here, and very early on the 8th January, 1943
Flight Lieutenant Richard Hope Hilary, RAFVR
and Sergeant Kenneth Wifrid Young Fison, RAFVR
were killed when their Blenheim V crashed at Crunklaw.

This memorial is dedicated to their memory
and to that of the many other officers,
NCOs and airmen who lost their lives
while serving at RAF, Charterhall
May 1942 – May 1945

'The last enemy that shall be destroyed is death.'
1 Corinthians XV 26

And on the back of the memorial:

Richard Hilary fought in the Battle of Britain
with 603 (City of Edinburgh Squadron) RAF.
Shot down and severely burned in 1940,
he recorded his experiences in his book
'The Last Enemy' before returning to
flying duties in November 1942.
Before the war he had stroked the Trinity College VIII
to the head of the river at Oxford.
Wifrid Fison, his radio observer, had been
awarded a Hockey Blue at Clare College, Cambridge
in 1927. He joined the RAFVR in December 1941.
The two men had flown together
for less than two weeks.

Beneath a plaque on the semicircular wall giving details of the people responsible for
the erection of the memorial is a lamp set in a small square concrete block. It is the
last surviving runway directional light from RAF Charterhall.

CHAPTER EIGHT

Little Snoring

I was home on leave following the end of our operational training, and I was awaiting news of where we were to report for our first squadron, when the telegram arrived.

'To Sergeant White, 564,' it said, 'Report to RAF, Little Snoring by 23.59 hours 1st April 1944.'

Little Snoring! – it sounded like something from a Will Hay film. I was convinced it was an April Fools' Day joke, it was the sort of name the lads would think up for a leg-pull. It was signed by someone in 100 Group. Well, I thought, that proved it! There weren't a hundred Groups in the RAF, surely! I knew there were no more than half a dozen or so in Bomber Command and about the same in Fighter Command, where we expected to go. Unless course, it was an overseas group . . .

But I dismissed that idea at once, because just as we were departing the blood-stained runways of Slaughter Hall a call had come through for ten newly trained Beaufighter crews to go overseas. Our hearts sank. Overseas usually meant a posting to North Africa or the Far East, and neither option was an inviting prospect. Funny things could happen overseas.

Take my pal, Don, out in the North African desert. One day the Messerschmitts roared over, ground-strafing the British lines, and they all dived for the nearest slit trench, the only cover in the flat desert landscape. But Don and his pal made a slight mistake. The trench into which they hurriedly dived wasn't a slit trench at all, but a latrine trench that had come to the end of its useful life and was awaiting its covering of sand. When the two re-emerged no one would come near them and there was no spare water around for them to wash themselves. So their officer ordered them (no doubt by loud hailer) to take the unit's truck, drive to the coast and not come back until the blue Mediterranean water had turned a deep brown for at least a mile out to sea. Now that was the sort of thing that tended to happen to me, and I wasn't eager to tempt providence.

And things like that weren't the only hazards to be faced in desert life. All that desert sand tended to collect in all kinds of bodily nooks and crannies. Which was why people who lived in those parts, and were historically experienced in such matters, kept their nooks and crannies to a minimum. In fact, when it came to odds and ends they went to great lengths to trim the ends off their odds. Whereas any extra bits and pieces I was born with I preferred to keep inviolate. (Not to mention keeping them in gentian violet, the purple wash that RAF medics tended to daub over your crotch at the slightest excuse.)

(Though given the choice, I'd rather have half Blackpool beach silting up my sewage system than end up in the Far East. There, it was said, if you were taken prisoner, a Jap officer was quite happy to do the trimming for you with his Samurai sword, free of charge and without asking, simply for failing to bow low whenever the Emperor's name was mentioned.)

Not that desert sand was the only hazard to be faced – if faced is the right word – in a North African posting.

Access through the Mediterranean had long been barred, first by Mussolini's navy and later by German aircraft. So Britain had been forced to send replacement planes via Takoradi, flying across Central Africa to Egypt. It was a hazardous journey, crossing – on metaphorical tiptoe – reputed cannibal country before turning north across endless miles of empty desert. The aircraft were mostly single-seat fighters, so they travelled in a loose gaggle, mother-henned by a twin-engined Beaufighter, whose navigator acted as pathfinder. And in case he had to make a forced landing, it was said that every pilot carried the notorious 'goolie-chit'.

Legend had it that the women in nomadic desert tribes were in the habit of removing the family jewels from any unbeliever found wandering in the wild, with the aid of a sharp knife, so the quaintly named goolie-chit was a polite note to whom it might concern (and I can't imagine anyone being more concerned than the unbeliever himself), offering a reward for the return of any crash-landed airman, providing he was complete down to the last detail. In fact, especially to the last detail. Otherwise. you might just as well have left them with the cannibals on the way.

Butch Baker (he with the eccentric navigator at Charterhall) ended up doing this job, playing sheepdog across Africa until bored out of his skull. Having taken his charges into a desert strip for the night, he relieved the tedium by beating up the tiny 'drome. Unfortunately he hit the radio mast, their only contact with civilisation, then crash-landed on the sand, to find, when he tried to stand, that he had broken both legs. Neither Butch nor the Beaufighter could move, nor could they radio for help. He wasn't the Middle East's most popular pilot.

But if the desert end of the trip held its dark terrors, Takoradi, at the start of the journey, was little better. Though somewhat improved from the worst days of equatorial fever, memories of the era still hung about the place. My mate Harold, an engine fitter, was posted there, on the coast of Guinea. It was a steaming swamp of a place, so full of germs that they had to make an appointment to infect you. At one time, unsurprisingly, it was labelled 'the white man's grave'.

While working on an aircraft out there, Harold needed a replacement manifold for the Bristol radial engines but he couldn't find one in the Stores. So he asked his sergeant.

'Try over in Half-dead,' said the NCO, 'I think there's a spare one in there.'

'Half-dead?' Harold was mystified by the name. The sergeant pointed out an old hut on the edge of camp. Years before, when the place was busy earning its grim label, fever was so rife that this particular hut lost half its occupants to the disease. Although later used for storage it was ever after known by its sombre nickname of 'Half-dead'.

So, all things considered, I'd rather not move anywhere south of the English Channel, thank you very much.

Fortunately, my customary luck at winning the toss had already ensured that Dagwood and I would not have to be carried screaming aboard a troopship. And anyway, a place bearing so improbable a name as Little Snoring could only be in England. So despite the imminence of All Fools' Day, I thought it best to check. I found the place as a very small dot on a very large map of Norfolk, not surprisingly bang next to Great Snoring.

But finding it on a map and actually getting there were two very different things. During the war it was always quicker when going anywhere by train to travel via London (I didn't say it was quick, I said it was quicker). Aberdeen to Carlisle? Go via St Pancras! Cornwall to Cardiff? Change at Paddington – which is why I rang Dagwood and arranged to meet him down in the 'Smoke' and we'd travel up to Norfolk together.

But my devious journey had another, sadder purpose. A letter had followed me home from the blood-stained runways of Charterhall, bearing the awful news that Bert, my companion through Stratford-upon-Avon and across the big pond to America, had been killed in a flying accident.

Despite his seeding in the Promotion Stakes, prompted by his education at Dulwich College and his occasional turnout for the Wasps at rugby, Bert had not got a commission on gaining his wings. He was a rebel at heart and they weren't keen on awkward customers in the hallowed halls of the officers' mess.

We had been reunited on our way back from training at Moncton in Canada, then travelled back across the Atlantic together as sergeants. At Harrogate, we split up once more when he moved on to day-fighter training – his ambition had always been to fly Spitfires, and unlike me he was a natural fighter pilot – so we were parted once more. Our friendship was unusual, that of a public schoolboy from south London and a grammar school lad from the industrial East Midlands, yet it had endured. There was a strong bond between us dating back to Stratford-upon-Avon days, when we had happily shared our last pennies, pints and punishments together.

But he never could hold his tongue in the face of stupidity. So he was turfed off his course by a pompous and bloody-minded squadron leader and condemned to a target-towing job off the coast of Northumberland. Day after day he trawled the long canvas sleeve out to sea off the Farne Islands, and while other pilots tried their best to fill his drogue full of bullet holes Bert ground his teeth in impotent fury.

We met up in Newcastle when I was at Ouston and spent a great weekend together, splurging out on front-row seats at the local music hall, chiyiking the long-legged chorus girls on the stage and laughing gleefully at the foul-mouthed comic.

Before we parted he told me he was getting married and asked if I would be his best man. Of course I would! But Captain Bligh refused me time off from Slaughter Hall and a mutual friend took my place. Now, only weeks after the ceremony, Bert was dead. His engine had cut out over the sea and he couldn't reach the shore. They never found his body, nor that of his observer.

In my last letter to him I had moaned about the horrors of Slaughter Hall, and his reply called me an ungrateful bugger for not appreciating the chance I was being given. Years on, I mused on how I had survived thirty-three ops over Germany while Bert, longing for action and the prospect of dogfights on his beloved day-fighters, died doing a boringly 'safe' job that he hated. Fate is funny, sometimes – utterly and cruelly funny.

By the time the letter reached me it was far too late to attend his funeral, but we had promised each other, should anything happen to either of us, that we'd check that each other's family were okay. His parents made me welcome, containing their grief in their quiet and courteous manner, as did his darkly pretty wife. I was offered a bed for the night – they lived in a big old house backing onto the Dulwich College grounds, where Bert had spent his schooldays.

That evening there seemed to be some sort of ruckus going on over the fence, that broke in on our stilted conversation in the garden. A team from the American Army Air Corps, baseball fanatics to a man, had challenged the ultra-British college to a game of cricket. At any other time I would have found the event hilarious, with its baseball-style shoulder-high batting stance, together with the most uncricketlike Texas-rebel yells of encouragement by the raucous spectators on the hallowed college turf. But it did help relieve a little of the tension.

I called on Bert's folks several times after that, and they always welcomed me. One time, as we went to bed, Bert's dad, in the quiet tones of a receptionist querying an early call, asked, 'If the buzz-bombs come over, would you like us to give you a call? We usually go down into the basement.' What, me? Hide from a toy aeroplane propelled by little more than a parson's fart? I should say not. We were made of sterner stuff in the RAF.

A little after midnight I heard it in the distance, like the devil's motorbike scudding across the sky. It got louder, and I burrowed deeper into the pillows. Then, seeming almost overhead, the sound stopped as the tiny terror weapon plunged silently to earth. It was the most terrifying few seconds of silence that I've ever endured. There was a tremendous blast of a nearby explosion, and by the time the windows had stopped rattling I had joined them in the basement. It was my closest experience of being on the receiving end of bombing, and it showed me what Londoners had been quietly enduring for so long.

Next day, as arranged, I met Dagwood in a pub just off the Charing Cross Road and we had a drink before catching the train up to King's Lynn. The place was crowded with servicemen, including an amiable young American – he couldn't have been more than nineteen – who began chatting to us. He wanted our advice. There was a dame down the bar who was offering him a ten-minute quickie round the back for a quid and did we think this was a fair price?

Why he thought we would be conversant with the going rate in such an occupation was not clear, but we suspected that he only had a hazy idea as to what a quid was. Still, we obligingly inspected his proposed inamorata. From that distance she appeared so far removed from the first flush of youth that she had probably learned her trade while keeping a sharp eye out for the Bow Street Runners, so we gave as our considered opinion that a quid would be about right, providing he negotiated a discount of around nineteen and six.

He seemed even more confused about the lesser values of the Imperial coinage. Nineteen and six? That sounded like two discounts. Could he add them together and, say, demand a cut of twenty-five bobs, or whatever those things were called? It was a delicious thought, demanding a twenty-five shilling discount off her standard one-pound fee, so we suggested he go for it! Then we went for it – hurriedly leaving for Liverpool Street Station. The lady was beginning to give us dirty looks, and many of her kind had minders nearby. And they minded very much if anyone tried to interfere in their client's commercial transactions. What sort of deal, if any, he eventually achieved we don't know, but let's hope it was big enough to pay for a nice bit of raw steak to put on his black eye.

Dagwood and I reached Fakenham railway station, deep in the dark heart of Norfolk, late at night after a brain-numbing journey from London. As the doors banged shut behind us and the train slipped sleepily out of the station once more, the minimal lights flickered out and the staff slid off home before we could seek answers to our questions. Like, how far away was the camp and how did we get there?

Another crew from Charterhall, Ginger and Big Brian, had arrived on the same train, and the four of us stood in the darkened station yard, our piled kitbags in a forlorn heap, listening to a lone owl hooting. It was beginning to weep with rain. Nothing else stirred in the blackness.

We found a decrepit phone box and crowded into it, using a cigarette lighter to find the number and our last tuppence to ring the 'drome for a lift, though for that money we doubted we'd have time to say much more than 'Help'.

A callous duty sergeant told us the transport section had better things to do. He suggested we dump our kit in the left-luggage office and walk. We explained that the staff had left the left-luggage office for the night but not the key. He didn't sound surprised. He didn't sound bothered either, and said in that case we'd have to hump our kit all the way, wouldn't we. Ginger said he'd pass the message on to the squadron leader, and say it was from the duty sergeant. Whereon the duty sergeant suddenly remembered a Bedford truck that was coming down that way in about ten minutes' time.

When it arrived, the driver asked where was this squadron leader then? We said he'd left his kit with us and decided to start walking and we'd probably pass him on the way back, but we didn't. He must have got a lift, somehow.

They put us in damp beds in a large empty Nissen hut at the end of a turnip field – a Nissen hut was like an enormous dustbin half buried on its side in the earth, with a big iron stove in the middle. There was no fuel for the stove and no sheets for the beds, so we folded our towels over the edge of the rough blankets to protect our razor-raw necks from barber's rash. The wash-house was another Nissen hut in the next field. It was a wash too far so we didn't bother – anyway, not washing was warmer. Supper was a packet of rubber crisps from an empty and echoing sergeants' mess. Yet despite our weariness we found it hard to sleep in the chilly hut. There was no comforting lullaby of droning aircraft engines filling the night, such as we were used to at Charterhall, and everywhere was as quiet as the grave. Which was just about what we had come to.

Next morning, we signed in at headquarters, collected our allotted ancient bicycles and cycled round the perimeter track to our new squadron office on the far side of the 'drome. When we got there we almost fell off our saddles in horror. Standing in front of the huts were two of the squadron's aircraft. We all groaned and said, 'Oh no! Please – not Beaufighter Mark IIs!' But they were.

It was not a happy squadron we had come to. True, it was early days yet, and although not newly formed, it had been doing entirely different work. So what had we expected? Well, speaking for myself – maybe I still carried too many romantic ideas, inspired by the *Boys' Own* Magazine, of the Dawn Patrol, despite the harsh realities of service life so far – but I had expected a warm 'Welcome to the squadron, chaps' from a quiet, firm-jaw-clamped-on-a-pipe CO and a hearty handshake from the others. Instead, the unit seemed little different from the harsh training regime we had just completed.

It started right at the top, and showed itself, as it usually did, in the relationship between the officers and the sergeants. If it was a happy squadron, the crews mucked in together and nicknames were the order of the day. If it wasn't then they split into two separate groups with little contact between the two.

The commanding officer I found to be a cold, supercilious man, reputed to have served much of his service in the Far East. He seemed to have little time for his NCOs, whom he appeared to rate somewhere around the dhobi wallah, or washing orderly, level. Certainly he had much to do to pull the squadron into shape, but the crews, although new, were keen and willing. I just didn't believe it was the right way to go about it.

We knew we were in 100 (Special Duties) Group, yet we had no idea what the group did, and we didn't even know what our future role in it was to be.

In the next couple of weeks we did a little local flying in the battered old Beaus, looking round the area, and we fired a few rounds of 20 mm cannon at the sea. But I don't think we could have hit it because we weren't allowed to claim it as a 'probable', let alone a 'destroyed'. But mostly we had lectures, followed by school-like tests in everything from aircraft engines to meteorology. I happened to come top in one test – on the Merlin engine – but instead of a word of praise the CO kept the officers behind and berated them for letting a sergeant beat them. Which just about said everything.

One thing troubled us. Half the squadron navigators were just that – navigators, not navigator/radios. What's more, the new crews coming in – and they came in steadily – were the same. This meant they had not done any radar training and it seemed that our own hard-won skills in night interception techniques would not be needed. What was going on?

I knew my flight commander from when I served under him at Ouston. He was a kindly and approachable squadron leader, and I offered to take Ginger and Big Brian along with Dagwood and myself for a quiet off-the-record chat with him.

It was typical of my luck that he was out, but that the CO wasn't. What, demanded that worthy (almost genially for him!) did we want with the squadron leader? Suddenly I found myself heading a very short, narrow queue as the other three seemed to shrink into a line behind me. I took a deep breath.

'We'd like to move to another squadron', I said.

He went pale with suppressed fury. He couldn't believe that a bunch of mere sergeants weren't thanking their lucky stars at the chance of serving under him. I tried to explain that we were trained radar teams and we didn't want to waste that training.

'What makes you think we won't get radar?' he demanded.

'Because none of the new crews have been trained on it.'

He had no answer, so he gave a contemptuous sneer, rather like a streetwalker offered payment in out-of-date Green Shield stamps. 'So you're the defensive type, not the offensive type!'

Offensive? Defensive? I didn't know what the hell he was talking about. 'We just want to do what we were trained for.'

'Well, I don't want your type on my squadron!' he raged.

He called everyone together, ourselves included, and told them of the contemptible behaviour of 'certain people on this squadron'. (He made it sound as if we'd planned to take the squadron aircraft and defect to Germany with them. I wouldn't have trusted the planes to get that far for one thing, and I certainly couldn't see the Germans accepting them if we had.) He went on to say that we would be posted away at once, and that went for anyone else with similar despicable ideas.

Afterwards, the other sergeants crowded round and demanded to know how we had managed it. Just go and tell him you want out, I advised them; only, of course, they couldn't screw up the courage. Their hesitation must have cost quite a few of them their lives. Before we left, my old squadron leader gave me a sadly reproachful smile of sympathy. 'You'll be sorry, Chalky, this is going to be a tremendous new operation – you don't know what you're missing.'

He was right, I didn't. But neither did anyone else at that time because 100 Group was just being formed and was kept secret from the rest of the RAF. (Its operations were to remain so, under the 'thirty-year rule' until quietly slipped out in 1975, by which time not many people were still interested.)

In fact there was little to show of what was to come. At one time the squadron's aircraft had been officially reported as 'having been standing in the open for two years with the state of serviceability grave, while the training of the aircrew was described as woefully inadequate'.

But the new group had a lot going for it. It was being given the highest priority in machines and equipment by 'Bomber' Harris, head of Bomber Command. And it was decided that Beaufighters were no longer suitable for the work and the group would re-equip to the newer Mosquito night-fighters.

However, this squadron was destined for a low-level intruder role. However, flying so low over the continent at night meant that the then radar was useless so initially they would fly without any. They would be all but blind, flying low in the darkness. It was a daunting prospect, and one that explained the lack of radar training of the new navigators.

But we knew none of this, because we weren't told. Would we have wanted to stay had we known? I don't know. It takes a special type of blind, near-suicidal courage to fly so low at night over unknown and unlit country. Working almost blind, with no margin for error, you keep going because you fear the scorn of your friends and you convince yourself that nothing would happen to you. I don't think I'm that good a liar.

Yet in the end the squadron did a tremendous job, albeit without our help. They suffered horrific losses, but they flew deep into a darkened Europe without radar, finding their way in the blackest of nights to the German night-fighter bases and circling on watchful sentry duty, attacking anything trying to take off, until relieved by the next crew.

As to how low they actually went, one pilot told me of a night when he was flying right down on the deck only a few feet above the Baltic. You could usually tell when the German radar was tracking you because it made a ZHRRR sound in your head-phones. But this time there were a succession of such sounds, as if the whole German radar was onto them. Then tiny lights began flashing past them and he realised that they were the hooded lights on the mast-tops of ships. And they were all but level with them! Just in time they realised that they were heading straight into Kiel Harbour, and hastily turned away.

Their success can be judged by the fact that *Luftwaffe* pilots coined a new word, '*Moskitopanik!*' to describe the fear those low-level intruder attacks evoked among the German crews. They had to resort to desperately low levels, what they termed '*Ritterkreuzhoch*' ('Knight's Cross Height') to avoid detection. Or as we might have called it, Victoria Cross level.

And the intruders' accuracy can be demonstrated by the following tale. While being interrogated about his life at Melsbroek, the main airfield to Brussels, a captured *Luftwaffe* corporal told how he had lost his way back to the base in the blackout after a night out in the Belgian capital. 'So I just walked toward the sound of the enemy intruder plane!' he said.

Not surprisingly, such work exacted a fearsome toll, with scarcely one crew in three surviving. In the Nissen hut where they slept one bed in particular seemed to be jinxed. A newly promoted pilot officer was first to go, on his first operation. From then on, to the end of 1944, no one who slept in that bed survived beyond their third operation. Eventually, they took the bed out because no one would sleep in it. Such is the power of superstition among men under stress. The bed was No. 13.

Not all those missing were killed, some cheating death in spectacular ways. On one daylight raid a crew had to ditch in Wilhelmshaven harbour, but their aircraft sank only a few feet. They had landed on a sandbank, and could only sit there, waiting patiently for the next bus to the nearest POW camp.

CHAPTER NINE

'What Goes Around Comes Around'

While we waited for our posting away from Little Snoring we were totally ignored, so much a small bunch of outcasts that we felt like walking around preceded by the ringing of a leper bell and a cry of 'Unclean!' We half expected to be returned to an operational training unit to learn how to fly while wearing leg-irons, perhaps ultimately to man a bank of oars along each side of a Stirling bomber. But, to our surprise, despite being sent to Coventry, Dagwood and I ended up in Kent.

We had been moved over to Fighter Command, and we landed up in Battle-of-Britain country. It was all lush green meadows, cherry orchards and oast houses. Only a few years previously workers in these fields had stopped to watch as needle-nosed fighters laced the white clouds together across the deep blue skies with white condensation trails as the fateful battle raged over their heads in that golden 1940 summer.

No. 85 squadron, the unit we were bound for, had flown Hurricanes in that battle. It was a splendidly élite squadron, its pages garlanded with famous names and rich in history. It had since converted to night-fighters.

Our new base lay in the rich heart of Kent, on the crown of a low green hill above the village after which it was named. It was a comfortable peacetime 'drome, so different from the tin-hut-in-a-turnip-field accommodation at Little Snoring. Yet it had no concrete runways to fly off, it was simply a large green field, all that had been needed for fighter aircraft when it had been originally built. In a belated attempt to improve the bad-weather capability for heavier aircraft in time for the coming battle, it had been hurriedly fitted with two makeshift runways of inter-locking mesh strips, known as Somerfeldt tracking, that gave a grip to aircraft tyres in the mud.

Dagwood and I walked up through the village from the station and on up the hill to the camp. Halfway to the main gate we passed The Startled Saint, a pub made famous during the battle when it acted as a second home to the aircrew and was known to them as The Strangled Virgin. Its sign showed a medieval monk with modern aircraft buzzing around his head. The saint in question was St Leonard, who helped bring Christianity to pagan England. Legend has it that he rested on the mound on which the pub stood on his journey north, and the sign was an artist's impression of what the saint's reaction would be to the modern-day 'drome, were he to pass this way today.

Just beyond that, opposite Smokey Joe's, a small simple café that catered mainly to the needs of airmen, we met up with Jamie and his navigator Tom, mates from

Ouston and Slaughter Hall. They were going down to the village, and they were welcoming friendly faces to our new home.

But the most welcoming prospect of all was the sight of the menacing aircraft squatting on the flight lines outside the squadron office. They were Mosquitoes. Not the original sleek, shark-like plywood planes, but their latest bulge-nosed successors. The ungainly bulge, giving them a vague resemblance to an airborne Schnozzle Durante, hid the electronic gadgetry of the latest radar. This was equipment that would never be allowed over enemy territory, in case an aircraft was shot down. Instead it was reserved strictly for ADGB squadrons. (The initials stood for Air Defence of Great Britain, the new silly name for Fighter Command – even in those days they couldn't resist replacing a simple blood-stirring title for a meaningless jumble of initials.)

So we had got our wish and ended up on one of the top night-fighter aircraft fitted with the latest radar in one of the prime squadrons defending the country's night skies. There was just one small snag, there was no one to defend it from.

But first, I had to solo on the new aircraft, and this was done on a Mosquito Mark III, the dual-control version.

Normally, the Mossie cabin was so small that the navigator was set a few inches further back than the pilot's seat so that they didn't bang elbows. But two pilots in there together required side-by-side seating, meaning you just about needed a shoe horn to get in. And as an extra control column was set in the floor for the second pilot, the only way you could get out again in a hurry was by that second column being quickly removable. I always thought that this removable column would serve as a handy weapon when you were both fighting to get out of the same tiny door at the same time, but I was careful to keep such thoughts to myself.

Fortunately, a mere thirty minutes' tuition – little more than a few circuits and bumps – was all that was required before I was sent happily off on my own. But, as always, there was a small complication. It was a hot day and continuous take-offs and landings meant that the engine temperatures were starting to rise dangerously. If I didn't get airborne quickly, so that the rush of air cooled down the radiators, the engine coolant was likely to boil over, a cardinal sin. Having to cut your engines at the end of the runway before take-off and be towed ignominiously back to the flights would have earned you a reputation that would have been hard to live down. So I wasted no time in racing to the end of the runway and rushing through my pre-flight checks.

When I looked up, ready to go, there was a Spitfire curling in to land. Just time to take off in front of him, I thought, so I swung onto the runway and slammed open the throttles.

Reaching fifty feet I throttled back to climbing speed, looked round the cockpit and relaxed. Everything seemed fine – until I glanced sideways and found the Spitfire desperately staggering along hanging onto the air almost on my wingtip.

As I explained, it was a grass runway with a metal grid reinforcement. The hot weather had fried the soil to a fine tilth and I had unwittingly blown a cloud of dust into the Spitfire pilot's face as he came in to land. Oops! Ah well, I thought, I'll apologise to whoever it was over a pint, later. But there was suddenly a blast of invective in my earphones.

'Hello, Control! Who the hell was that idiot who just took off in front of me?'

The voice of the traffic controller nervously admitted that it was Driver Two Three. He added an obseqious 'Sir!' to the end of his sentence.

'Well, get him out of the sky and into my office, now!'

I went cold. Only one man dared talk to the controller like that, and he was the station commander. He didn't fly very much, and as a result was a little rusty. He liked a gentle flip round the sky now and again, but didn't welcome anything or anyone getting in his way. Besides a cloud of dust, it seemed that I had raised some very important blood pressure.

Control called me up. I was supposed to be doing circuits and bumps, but I had suddenly decided it might be wise to be somewhere – anywhere! – else for a while. People as well as engines needed time to cool down. I was listening out on Channel A on my radio – we carried two push-button boxes of five radio channels each – and as soon as the call came I hurriedly changed over to Channel B. When he changed to Channel B, I promptly pressed the C button. He chased me through every channel until he cornered me on the last one – I had to be listening out on one of them!

I calculated that the station commander had still only cooled down enough to allow me to remuster to ship's figurehead on a submarine, so I resorted to a trick I had learned at Ouston. You plugged your helmet into the radio by means of a long bayonet-type plug. If you took this out, placed it in your mouth and wet it thoroughly before reconnecting it, it produced a satisfying howl on the radio, so loud that nobody could hear a thing you said. Then, when you landed, you reported your radio wasn't working – which they could clearly hear for themselves – but by the time they checked it over, the plug had dried out and they couldn't find a thing wrong.

I finally came in to land after half an hour, to be greeted by the impatiently waiting air traffic controller. The station commander had tired of hanging around and had handed him the job of dishing out a severe dressing-down.

'I believe this was your first solo on a Mossie?' he began, and I admitted as much.

'Silly bugger!' he said. And I don't think he meant me.

'By the way, don't pull that radio trick too often, will you!' He grinned and turned away, and that was that. The RAF now had one more newly qualified Mosquito crew, ready and willing to hack any raider out of Britain's night skies. There was only one small snag. The *Luftwaffe* was refusing to come over any longer and be hacked. Once more, we had nothing to do. Every time we got near this war it seemed to move some-where else; I was beginning to think it was deliberately avoiding us.

Still, life was very pleasant there. We investigated the local hostelries, and learned the correct order in which to drink in them. You always started at the lowest pub in the village, a grotty place where the beer was great but the music was grating. This was supplied by a local with long matted hair seemingly plastered down with Bostik rather than Brylcreem. He played a violin very badly, and it wailed further and further off key as the evening wore on and its owner got more legless.

When you could hold no more of the liquor or stand any more of the music you went on up to Fat Phoebe's, a nice place with insipid beer, and hung on to a half pint all night, hoping no-one would buy you any more.

Phoebe herself, a great hogshead of a woman, was fond of entertaining officers from the camp for the night. It was said that one squadron newcomer, waking to find himself in a double bed next to a deep indentation in the mattress, lavishly tipped the barman who brought his morning tea not to tell Phoebe's husband. The barman duly gave his word, but not his name. After all, had he revealed that he was the spouse in question, the man might have asked for his tip back.

But our idyll was shortlived. Within a couple of weeks of our arrival there, and after no more than four hours' desultory local flying, we learned that the squadron was on the move. Together with another ADGB squadron we were going back to Norfolk to join the mysterious 100 Group once more!

So what was with this new group – were they going to use radar or weren't they? We had talked our way out of it because we wanted to use our newly learned night-fighting and radar skills, and they were taking on ordinary navigators to do low-level work where radar was useless.

Yet now they were calling on two top interception squadrons fitted with the latest airborne radar, equipment that had been banned from going over the Continent because it mustn't fall into enemy hands! To understand it we must go back to the development of air warfare since the Second World War began.

The bomber would always get through. That was the accepted theory at the outbreak of war, a theory postulated by a certain General Douhet of the Italian Air Force. And it was generally true, but the said bomber wouldn't always get back home again. The fast single-seat fighter, carrying no more than one man and a clutch of guns, would always outrun the bigger bomber with its large crew and heavy bomb load, and severely damage the bomber formations – providing it could find them.

Thanks to newly discovered radar this wasn't too difficult in daylight, as the *Luftwaffe* found out to its cost in the Battle of Britain, and as the RAF had already discovered when its old, lightly armed bombers were hacked from the sky during the German *Blitzkrieg* attack on France and the Low Countries. Sensibly, the RAF turned to operating its bombers at night.

This worked for a while, even though they didn't actually hit anything except the odd cow. At night, the defending fighter couldn't see you, but neither could you see the target. Which didn't matter too much, as they were only dropping pamphlets at first, and anyway the paper came in handy for cleaning up after the cows became understandably nervous. New navigational devices improved matters. Bombers began travelling in a tight stream to overwhelm the defence (and as a result a thousand of them all but destroyed Cologne). But radar light enough to be carried in an aircraft made them easier to find by enemy night-fighters, so the RAF tried fouling up the German radar by dropping clouds of 'window' – strips of aluminium foil – and as a result flattened Hamburg. In turn the Germans developed new interception techniques, and in a raid on Nuremberg everything went square-pear-shaped. Ninety-eight RAF bombers were destroyed in a single horrifying night.

Meantime the American bomber force ('the Mighty Eighth', as they were wont to term it, in their modest way) arrived, and scorned night-flying for day-flying. They reckoned their massive, multi-gunned bomber formations could smash their way through to any target, covering each other with protective gunfire. With their gyroscopic bombsight (they claimed they could 'drop a bomb in a barrel') they could ensure very precise destruction of military targets in daylight, and everyone could sleep in their own beds at night. The only snag was that their planes were so full of fuel and ammunition that there wasn't much room left for bombs, which was the whole point of going in the first place. And you can't drop a bomb, even a small one in a big barrel, when you can't see the barrel. Clouds cloaked the targets and the mass formations were torn apart by flak and Focke-Wulfs on their long flights. The Yanks suffered the sort of horrendous losses that even they could ill afford.

The solution to both problems, day and night, were long-range fighters that could escort and protect the bombers all the way. It wasn't easy. You needed aircraft big enough to carry the fuel for such a long trip, yet small enough and fast enough to take on the home fighters when they got there.

In the end they fitted the British Merlin engine into their Mustang fighters and added disposable drop-tanks under each wing, and that did the trick. The RAF answer was to use twin-engined night-fighters – they also had to carry a load of radar equipment and an operator to work it – so, with a rather more complex problem, they set up a new group. And they gave it the Mosquito, the plywood-bodied, twin-engined 'Wooden Wonder' that, as a fighter, seemed able to outrun, outgun and outfly anything in the night sky. What's more, it needed a crew of just two. But there was still a problem, no-one had ever tried long-range night-fighting over enemy territory before.

The sky is a vast place. Even in daylight a fighter pilot turning away in a dogfight can suddenly find himself alone and lost. Without the hastily developed radar chain RAF fighters could never have found the German bombers in time, if at all. Radar ground controllers could take a fighter in to two thousand feet, but after that the blips of light representing each plane merged together on the radar screen. From there on it was up to the fighter pilot, using the Mark I Eyeball.

At night, as they discovered at the start of the blitz, two thousand feet wasn't close enough, and the bomber could seldom be found. Not until the first crude radar sets light enough to be carried in a plane were developed was that final gap closed, and even then, the Mark IV set was severely limited. You could never get a greater range than your own height: the radar waves bounced back from the ground and swamped your set, and the maximum range anyway was sixteen thousand feet. That was just enough over Britain, providing you were at a fair height and the ground controller took you in as close as he could, then, most importantly, told you the way back to base.

But now they were asking crews to operate over Germany in support of the bombers, tackling the *Luftwaffe* fighters on their home ground, with very-short-range radar and no ground controller to guide them to the targets, to say nothing of helping them get several hundred miles back home again.

In the end, the answer was simple – use the Germans as ground controllers! After all, who better to know where the targets were than the targets themselves?

Radar works by transmitting a radio beam and then picking up the reflections that bounce back off other aircraft. The German night-fighters transmitted radio beams to pick up RAF bombers, so if we were to tune in to the same wavelength we could use those beams to home in onto the night-fighters transmitting them. The result was a device called Serrate.

There was just one snag. Serrate could pick up an aircraft from far off, it just couldn't tell how far off. You get the range by checking the time between transmitting your beam and getting the echo back. But the Serrate set couldn't know when the beam was transmitted. You knew, say, that there was an aircraft five degrees to the left and ten degrees above you, but it could be anywhere from four miles behind to fifty miles ahead. So it could all end in a long and fruitless chase, but it was better than nothing.

And all this equipment had to be stuffed into the tiny Mosquito cockpit, about the size of a Morris Minor. A very full Morris Minor. We can just imagine the design conference when they built the thing. 'Let's see, we'll need the normal Mark IV radar set, together with this Serrate thingy . . . and better fit a Mark XV backward-looking set in there as well, so they can check if any blighter's sniffing at their tail-end. They'll need a Gee navigation set to find out where they are – there's a small gap behind the pilot's head if the navigator kneels on his seat to reach it.They'll still need to take all the normal navigation equipment, though, to find their way home because the Germans can jam the Gee transmissions. They'll need to go about eighteen hundred miles, so better fit an extra tank or two in the belly besides the hundred-gallon drop-tanks on each wing. Now then, anyone any ideas where we could slot in a pilot and a nav/rad wearing full flying kit, three pairs of gloves apiece, a Mae West and sitting on a parachute and dinghy?'

100 (Special Duties) Group was set up on 23 November 1943, when the bomber losses had begun to mount sharply to unsustainable levels. It was given the task of protecting the RAF bombers over Germany, firstly by attacking enemy night-fighters, both in the air and on the ground, and secondly, to jam enemy radar systems and radio messages.

To do this, the group was given five fighter squadrons plus a mixed bag of Flying Fortresses and Halifax bombers to transmit a wall of electronic noise across the middle of the North Sea, called the Mandrel Screen, to shield the approaching bombers until the last moment. The fighters were used either low level, patrolling enemy airfields and shooting at anything that tried to take off or land, or high level as bomber escorts, guarding the flanks of the bomber stream or circling enemy assembly beacons.

And the reason for the change of heart about using the latest radar over enemy territory was that the Serrate system was working, but not too well. Contacts were being lost when changing over from it to the basic radar set at close range, and anyway the Germans were starting to use new radar wavelengths. Later we were to try out a new gadget, called Perfectos. This homed onto the identification signals that the *Luftwaffe* aircraft put out to tell their own side that they were friendly (similar to our own IFF, or Identification Friend or Foe, transmissions). However, the system didn't last long because the Germans thought up a cunning plan to counter it – they switched their sets off. On the other hand, the radar on the new squadrons didn't need Serrate, or Perfectos, come to that – it had enough range of its own, around twenty miles on a good night, and at any height. The group wanted to harry the German night-fighters at every level, from the moment they took off until the moment they landed. All of which is why our new squadron found itself at a bleak and cheerless 'drome out in the Norfolk bundoo, just north of Norwich.

And to ensure the new radar's secret equipment stayed just that – secret – they were fitting a standard RAF demolition charge in each aircraft, with a large red firing-button in the cabin. The vital part of the new equipment was a thing called a magnetron valve. It was hinted that anyone crashing in Germany and failing to destroy that bit of his radar before dying would be in deep trouble. (They probably planned to use a medium to inform you that you'd be given Seven Days Confined to Coffin with Loss of Gravestone.) It was, perhaps, a pity that no-one thought to test the detonator at the time against the vital valve. When they did try pressing those big red buttons at the end of the war, the explosion barely scratched it.

But there's a saying up North – 'I won't take me coat off, I'm not stopping!' The new squadrons, too, didn't have time to take their coats off, they were suddenly needed elsewhere, and in one hell of a hurry. They had the only planes capable of catching the newly launched doodlebugs at night. The tiny terror weapons were starting to be launched on London in droves, and the two ADGB squadrons were quickly recalled south. Even they had trouble catching the pilotless flying bombs – they had to use an injection of laughing gas in their engines before they could over-take and destroy them.

But four of us, Jamie and I and our two navigators, could have used a whiff of that laughing gas ourselves to cheer us up. Because before returning to Kent our CO had been asked if he had any experienced crews to spare. One of Group's Serrate squadrons was short handed.

Yes, of course, the squadron could spare a couple of crews. Not exactly operational, mind, but they had definitely soloed on Mosquitoes. We'll send them straight over.

We felt like a litter of unwanted Labrador pups callously dumped at the roadside while their owner hightailed it home.

CHAPTER TEN

'Johnno'

The airfield we finally ended up at – our third in as many months – was no more than a dozen miles from Little Snoring, yet in every respect it was a world away.

West Raynham had been the last 'drome to be built before the war started, and it was the culminating example of the RAF's peacetime planning. It was isolated but with well-constructed buildings and hangars, set on a low hill, and with only two concrete runways instead of the more usual three, but with the main one being a useful two thousand yards long. It was set so close to the neighbouring 'drome of Great Massingham that the two airfields were encircled by a single ring of circuit lights. The place was occupied by the two Serrate fighter squadrons of 100 Group, 239 and 141, charged with the task of bomber escort and special duties. We reported to the 239 Squadron office.

There we were welcomed by the adjutant, an urbane, friendly ex-solicitor, and one of the first people to stick his head round the door as we settled in, to ask if we were coming down to the village for a jar or two, was Mike O'Leary. The much-bemedalled, happy-go-lucky but trigger-tempered Irishman was one of the old-sweat radar instructors from Ouston days. His driver, Neville Reeves – Golden-Balls – the finest pilot I ever knew, and a lowly flying officer when he taught me at Slaughter Hall, was my new flight commander. He was now a squadron leader, charging up the promotion ladder and deservedly so. I began to feel a sense of the select club attitude that pervaded the night-fighter world, a feeling initiated and fostered by my days at Ouston.

There was a tremendous spirit in our new squadron, much of it engendered by the CO. He was a straight-talking man who cared for his crews. If you took a step out of line you were reminded of what was expected of squadron members in no uncertain manner, and then it was at once forgotten. A man after my own heart.

True, we had gone a step backwards with our return to the Mark IV radar. Its severe limitations were fast making it obsolescent, and our Mark II Mosquito aircraft were somewhat over the hill. Their engines were starting to show their age, being rather grudgingly donated by their previous owners in Bomber Command – well, you don't give away your best machines, do you! – but at least there were no odd-engined Beaufighters, no ageing Beauforts, no senile Defiants. Well, almost none.

We were sent next door, to Massingham, to learn the finer points of the Serrate operating system, and wouldn't you know it – the sets were fitted in Beaufighter VIs! They were to have a final goodbye go at me.

Massingham 'drome has a slight bulge in the centre so that as you open up for take-off you can't see the other end of the runway until you get to the middle. I reached that fleeting viewpoint, Hercules engines pounding breathlessly, to find an Irish airfield worker pedalling his way slowly towards me on a decrepit old bike! But he was a reasonable man, bejasus, and got off the bike (though not the runway!) to watch me admiringly as I swerved past him. He even removed his hat in case one of those big fan things on the front blew it off. I felt a murderous urge to knock it off with the head still inside.

But that was just for openers. As I heaved the big Beau into the air, the port engine chose that moment to stop working. It spewed oil all over the left-hand side of my windscreen so that I couldn't see through. A few seconds earlier it would have been an Irish cocktail of blood, oil and second-hand Guinness.

I had barely reached safety speed, but I struggled up to five hundred feet and then scudded round the circuit at a dangerously steep angle on my one remaining engine, trying to see the 'drome through the clean perspex roof of the cockpit. On that particular runway you came in over the top of the railway station – I was so low that it was lucky the train signals were set at GO. Somehow I got the plane down again, to find that every con-rod in the front bank of cylinders had broken and punched its way through the crankcase, wagging freely in the fresh air.

After that, operations held few terrors for us, and soon we were warily dipping our toe in the war by setting out on our first night operational flight into northern France. Our detail was to patrol the eastern side of the new D-day landings against enemy intruder aircraft, but the *Luftwaffe* night-fighters decided to sit this one out and we saw nothing. Still, it was a funny feeling, sitting up there, knowing that only a few thousand feet below us in the darkness spies were spying, resistance men dying, and Gestapo men were gestapoing like mad all over the place, while we could just fly home to our egg and bacon supper.

And nights when we weren't flying we spent wandering round the Norfolk countryside relaxing as hard as we could.

Life changed dramatically in many small villages in the flat farmlands of Lincolnshire and East Anglia in the Second World War as the RAF moved in and built the new airfields needed for the big bomber armadas. The locals had their crops covered in concrete and their footpaths cut off with barbed wire, while in their ancient pubs, blue-uniformed strangers took over their dart boards and their daughters. So it was not surprising that a state of armed truce often existed between locals and newcomers. For our part, we servicemen – townies to a man – found little to do in the quiet countryside after flying was done for the day.

Most camps had a cinema, and a small theatre for ENSA concerts, but the films were often old, featuring the likes of a voluptuous Betty Grable or a grossly top-heavy Jane Russell – and only served to emphasise how low the meat ration had been reduced to. Or it was Errol Flynn, nonchalantly recapturing Burma single handed, without breaking into a mucksweat. We didn't mind that so much – he was welcome to our share of old Moulmein pagodas looking lazy at the sea – it was the way he always ended up being awarded a double helping of Rita Hayworth or whoever, by a pathetically grateful general. It was all so far fetched. In real life anybody managing to winkle the Japs out of the jungle single-handed was more likely to be fobbed off with a Victoria Cross than a Victoria Beckham, while anyone freeing Paris would be lucky to earn a kiss on his Place de la Concorde from General De Gaulle.

The ENSA concerts were no better. The quality of the shows seemed to vary in inverse proportion to your distance from London. Down there the big theatre stars ventured timidly out to places like Biggin Hill, barely outside the capital, drank all the gin in the officers' mess and then staggered thankfully back to their West End shows, feeling very noble. To us, the nearest thing to a great metropolis was

Fakenham – sin city of the sugar-beet belt – so you can guess the standard of beer-soaked comics who were dispatched through darkest Norfolk to entertain us. As for the somewhat elderly ladies of the chorus, I'm afraid we rather ungallantly referred to them as 'the Dogs of War'.

Our only other places of entertainment in the surrounding countryside were two ancient pubs, and it didn't take us long to get thrown out of both of them. In the first, the RAF were banned as 'trouble-makers' after one of our number complained of a tadpole in his beer. The locals hinted darkly that we must have put it there ourselves for our own nefarious purposes, like trying to claim a free replacement pint. We strongly denied that we would ever do such a thing to one of God's creatures – not in that beer, anyway – but it did no good.

I must admit the second landlord deserved a little more sympathy. One night we did keep pushing the hands back on the big grandfather clock in the bar until long past closing time, so that he kept ladling out his precious beer ration well into the small hours. It didn't do the clock a lot of good, either. But as we told him as he slung us out, if you can't take a joke, don't take a pub.

Which left us very much at a loose end. We were allowed one trip a week into Norwich on the RAF bus, but the place was full of Army types and Yankee airmen from the big American air bases, which could be an explosive mixture at times. Like the night at the big dance hall there – the oddly named 'Samson and Hercules' – when an amiably fuddled Yank asked a fiery little kilted Gordon Highlander for the Last Waltz. It almost was his last waltz, too. So on the whole we preferred the peace and quiet of the mess and our own company, where we usually ended up playing penny poker. Depending on how near it was to payday, the pennies became salted peanuts or even broken matches.

Then a new crew, Sergeant Pilot Arthur Johnston (Johnno) and his navigator, Bill Cheetham, walked in. Bill was a large, placid Lancastrian who didn't say much and didn't play much, but Johnno's eyes lit up when he spotted our cards. Could anyone join in our game of whist, he asked, and when told it was a poker school, he said, not to worry – he'd pick it up as he went along. Just tell him whether it was played with five cards or three.

Our mouths watered – you don't get too many people in a poker school who don't know the difference between three-card brag and dealer's choice, and they don't often have real money to play with. Not for long, anyway. We looked forward to a profitable night. We were quickly disillusioned. Once in the game, to our alarm he calmly produced a green eyeshade and a box of plastic poker chips, and looking for all the world like a Mississippi river-boat gambler, fanned out the cards in a smooth, slick shuffle as if they were tied together. It was our first introduction to Johnno's sense of humour.

He seemed to know outrageous variants of the game. 'In this round,' he would announce, casually flicking out the pasteboards faster than the eye could follow, 'fours, whores, (meaning Queens) one-eyed Jacks, and the King with the f——ing axe are all wild.' Eleven wild cards! We took longer to work out who'd won than we spent playing the game – but somehow Johnno's five aces always seemed to beat everybody else's five aces. He quickly cleared us out of our last salted peanut – the currency at the time – and then ate the ante before we could win them back, so we couldn't play any more. Instead he took us on and thrashed us at snooker, with skills honed in his father's pub, magnanimously accepting our IOUs for the debt.

He quickly became notorious on the squadron. Where there was Johnno, there was trouble – trouble such as slipping a Very cartridge (a coloured signalling flare) down

the crew room chimney, and then getting the squadron clerk to light the stove because it was chilly. We staggered out of a thick green pea-soup pyrotechnic cloud, with bulging eyes in purple faces as we gasped for air. Johnno also initiated the Six Feet Six High Club inside a parked Mosquito long before the notorious Mile High Club of decadent post-war commercial aviation. 'Come up and see my cockpit' became a standing invitation to the ladies.

I made the mistake of enlisting his help to transform my best blue uniform into a suitable candidate for exchange. The sole arbiter of whether your uniform was worn enough to merit you being issued with a replacement, was the Stores flight sergeant, a crabby-tempered old sweat rejoicing in the name of 'Fussy' Bridges. You would think he paid for the garments himself, the way he microscopically inspected each stitch before disdainfully turning down the request.

'What you want to do', Johnno advised me, 'is use your razor to shave the pile off the cloth under the arms and on the elbows of your jacket. It will put ten years' wear on your uniform. While you're doing that, Dagwood and I will work on the trousers so you can claim the stitching's going and you'll soon be indecent.'

I was happily giving the unoffending tunic a short back and sides with my razor when suddenly I heard a great tearing sound behind me, and looked round in horror to find my two companions standing holding a leg each, and trying hard not to laugh. 'I said that stitching was going', said Johnno amiably. 'Now they'll have to change the slacks before you freeze to death.' And with that, they both walked off, grinning.

In great trepidation, I slid unobtrusively into the Stores and arranged my doctored tunic in a strategic pile on the counter to hide the dismembered slacks, hoping to get the friendly WAAF corporal to see to me. No such luck. 'Fussy' liked to deal person-ally with aircrew. In his eyes, since they did no real work they had no need to change anything, and he loved telling them so, adding his favourite little joke for the benefit of all and sundry: 'The only thing you lot are ever likely to wear out, lad, I don't carry any spares for!'

But today, he seemed almost in a mellow mood, barely giving the freshly shaven tunic a glance before tossing it to one side and saying, 'Oh, orl right, then', and reaching for the slacks. I lunged for them at the same moment, hoping – desperately – to beat him to it and toss the slacks nonchalantly after the jacket, but somehow we got there at the same time. And – somehow – we ended up with one leg apiece.

For a moment we stood facing each other – it was the only time I ever saw Fussy lost for words. He stood looking at the long single tube of blue cloth in sheer disbelief. I offered him my own cloth leg. 'May as well change that one at the same time', I suggested, trying hard to sound casual. 'There's no point in splitting a pair.'

Just then, one of the Stores WAAFs sniggered, and that brought Fussy out of his trance. He slowly raised the single uniform leg in the air, and in a strangled voice, demanded, 'And what am I supposed to do with this?' On reflection, I don't think that he really wanted an answer, because when I started making suggestions – like, a windsock at a helicopter station, or a spare suit for Douglas Bader – Fussy went berserk.

'I could put you on a flaming charge for damaging Government property', he shrieked, 'An' I will if you don't get those slacks repaired right away.' Unhappily, the camp tailor refused to stitch up a garment that was going to end up as an oil-rag anyway, or at least until I added a hefty tip over and above his usual fee. Johnno was becoming an expensive person to know.

But his greatest joy was low flying. Players and spectators at one of our rugby matches flung themselves to the ground as he roared across the pitch at zero feet. His excuse of having accidentally swerved on take-off was greeted with scornful disbelief, especially by the station commander, who happened to be in the team at the time. The Old Man told him that there was a difference between playing fly-half and half playing at flying, and he had better learn it, and quickly.

But Johnno was never down for long, and on the next pay-day – when we were all flush with a fortnight's pay (fourteen pounds each, including flying pay) – he proposed we celebrate by patronising the Saturday night hop in the nearby small town. It was held in the local Corn Exchange, a building we referred to as Cowpat Cottage.

The trouble was, how to get there. There were only two buses a day, and as we used to say, one of those didn't run till tomorrow and the other was cancelled yesterday. But fortunately, the RAF issued everyone with old-fashioned sit-up-and-beg bicycles. What they didn't seem to do, for some odd reason, was issue quite enough chains for the bikes, with the result that there was an outbreak of bicycle chain burglary at closing time. The last man out of the pub, or the cinema, leaped happily on his parked cycle, only to be painfully reminded that the Bicycle Chain Bandit had struck once again, leaving him with a long, slightly bow-legged, and rather painful walk back through the dark country lanes to camp.

On this occasion, we entered Cowpat Cottage after an invigorating bike ride from the mess and looked round in happy anticipation. At first glance, it didn't look too promising. The band consisted of a drummer, a pianist and a saxophone player who doubled on the accordion, and they seemed to take it in turns to play the right note. No alcohol was allowed, but a refreshment bar served teas and – would you believe? – pease pudding sandwiches! It didn't look too promising at second glance, either. We were checking the Gents to see whether we could smuggle in a few jars of the local painkiller through the back window, when Johnno made a suggestion. 'There's not a lot of talent in, tonight,' he observed, 'what say we liven things up a bit with an Ugly Dance?'

We were baffled but intrigued, and he explained the rules. Everyone put a half-crown into the kitty. The winner at the end of the evening would be the one who asked the ugliest woman in the room to dance and spent the entire evening in her company. Not only that, but he must chat pleasantly to her between dances and listen enthralled to her conversation, supply her with drinks and refreshment, finally wishing her goodnight and expressing his appreciation of her company and dancing prowess. The one thing he must not do was show the least hint of a grin at any time, either at his own or anyone else's companion. The slightest twitch of the lips would bring instant disqualification and a forfeit.

It was quite an evening. Large-toothed ladies with small moustaches who hadn't been asked for a dance since Mafeking Night were eagerly sought out to blush and blossom on the dance floor, bewildered by the attention they attracted. They had never known an evening like it, and they loved it.

After a while, though, things started to get a little out of hand. The local youths, at first hostile, thinking that the sudden influx of blue uniforms would mean fierce competition for the sparse local talent, were successively relieved, then puzzled as to what exactly was going on. Somehow – either they put two and two together or someone let drop a hint – they suddenly cottoned on to what was afoot, thought it a great wheeze, and decided to join in. They seemed to get the idea that they could win the prize – although we refused their contributions – and they left their normal partners to either dance with each other all night or sulk in a scowling group in wall-flower corner. The dance organiser realised that something was amiss but couldn't work out what or what to do about it, at least not without hitting his pease-pudding sandwich sales. He tried Paul Jones and Ladies' Excuse Me dances, but they didn't seem to work – those long-in-the-tooth ladies suddenly turned into sabre-toothed tigers and pursued their prey with amazing speed. They'd waited a long time for this and they weren't giving up easily.

It was then that a warrant officer from headquarters walked into the dance with his girlfriend, a small hard blonde WAAF sergeant who sank pints and all ideas of lust with equal speed. Johnno went over to them.

I doubt if the WO and his partner ever discovered why they were suddenly handed one pound five shillings in half-crowns by some young flight-sergeant pilot and congratulated on their win when they had only just come in. Possibly they thought it was some sort of spot prize, and we certainly weren't going to disabuse them. For one thing, the man had the sense of humour of a warthog with piles and for another he didn't like aircrew. Had he discovered the truth he was liable to call in the Snoops, or service police. So we decided it was time to be somewhere else and got out fast. Later, in the nearby pub, we protested at Johnno's choice of winner, but he pointed out that we had all burst out laughing when he awarded the prize and so had disqualified ourselves. Though he did offer to buy a round of drinks if we paid our forfeits.

I was the last to leave the pub and return warily to Cowpat Cottage for my bike – I had visions of a wizened version of Lilly Marlene waiting underneath the lamplight for me – but all was clear. However, the moment I sprang into the saddle I realised with dismay that the dreaded Bicycle Chain Bandit had struck again. In disgust, I dumped the bike in the hedge bottom and set out on the long, lonely walk back to camp along the dark lanes. Just over halfway back, I heard someone whirr past me in the dark – his bike had no lights, of course – then it stopped, and I heard Johnno's navigator, Bill Cheetham, call, 'Is that you, Chalky?'

I should have known better by then to answer to anything that had the slightest connection with Johnno, but I was tired, so I explained the reason for my enforced walk (Bill had been drinking elsewhere.) 'No problem!' he said, 'I'll give you a lift.' I did point out that he was riding a WAAF's bike, and the lack of a crossbar might make it a bit awkward, and he seemed vaguely surprised at the news. Bill tended to help himself to the nearest machine, and few cared to argue with him. But he always left it where the owner could easily find it again. Like hanging from the top of the flagpole on the parade ground.

'OK, you can sit on the handlebars, then', decided Bill amiably.

Don't ask me how I got up there in the dark, except that an overhanging tree came into it somewhere, but soon I was ensconced on the front of the machine, my feet on the flimsy front mudguard and clinging to the handlebars behind me for dear life. As we charged along the dark lanes at high speed, I felt like the figurehead on the *Marie Celeste.*

The last bit of the journey was down a very steep hill, round a sharper than ninety degree corner, then up another hill and into camp. Bill was pedalling very hard down the first hill, in fact he only paused in his pedalling in order to pass on some technical information to me. 'I don't have any brakes!' he said, 'But don't worry!' I assured him I wasn't. I was too terrified to be worried.

'I've done this lots of times before', added Bill. 'Now, at the bottom of the hill, when I yell 'Lean!' I want you to lean over about thirty-five degrees to the right, OK?' He resumed his pedalling. All too quickly we reached the bottom, and to Bill's prompting yell of 'Lean!' I leaned as far over to the right as I dared. The trouble was, he didn't have any brakes – as he'd said – but he did have metal brake rods, and, in my panic, I gripped handlebars and rods together, very tightly. Bill's fingers just happened to be between them, and he yelled in agony and fell off the back.

It was at this point in time that I decided a quick recap of my life so far might prove helpful. Here I was, perched on the handlebars of a bike, halfway round a steep bend at the dead of night, at an impossible angle and going like the clappers. But there was no-one on the back. I quickly concluded that providing I survived the rest of the bend, my post-war career was decided for me. Without doubt, an apprenticeship as a clown in a circus beckoned. The next second, the bike had slid from under me. I went flying through the air and made the finest three-point landing I have ever made in my flying career, the trouble being that the three points were made up of both knees and the palm of my right hand.

Squadron commanders were always being badgered to send aircrew on courses. Never mind how the war's going, there's a course on a Blind Approach Training Flight, get someone over there right away. With my skinned palm and bashed knees I was favourite for the job, and off I went to Wittering, on the Great North Road. It was a small 'drome, made into a very much bigger Emergency Landing Strip by joining it to the next 'drome along, Collyweston. The trouble was – the join showed: there was a dip halfway along the runway.

Not that that would have mattered had they not sent Johnno to collect me at the end of the course, in an Oxford. It was too much of a temptation – he did a low-level beat-up of the place, flying so low that he all but disappeared into the runway dip, setting the blood-wagon (ambulance to you) and the fire engine racing out in alarm.

This was serious stuff. The Old Man was a decent type and turned a blind eye where he could to our behaviour on our own base, but a complaint from another unit made it official. There were ominous threats of a court martial.

Johnno kept his nose clean for a little while. He was not yet cleared for operational flying, and he fretted to join us as we did trips over Orleans, Kiel, Heligoland and Darmstadt. Then, on 28 August 1944, he was detailed to carry out his final exercises prior to full operational status. This was a 'Haystack' (as in 'finding a needle in'), the code for two aircraft doing night interceptions on each other up at twenty-five thousand feet, followed by a low-level flight over the North Sea and in at Scarborough, a simulation of a night-intruder trip where you hugged the sea below the German radar defences before climbing a few hundred feet and tearing over the coast at high speed to dodge the heavy flak.

I still recall Johnno's big grin as he climbed in the cockpit. 'Oh boy!' were his last words to me, 'Beating up Scarborough at night – and all legal!'

Afterwards, we heard they did the Haystack exercise with the other new crew – and then they simply disappeared off the face of the earth, as if they had never been. Nemesis had finally called in her debts.

Next day, the CO told us to take the Oxford after our night-flying tests, and go look for him, so we scoured the wave-tops out to sea and up to Scarborough for a couple or three hours, without success. We didn't expect any. Although we did our ditching drill religiously, the Mossie almost always broke in half at the back hatch when it landed in the water, and went straight down. Nothing has ever been found of them to this day.

My own guess? There are three small hands on the altimeter clock of a Mosquito, to show hundreds, thousands, and tens of thousands of feet high. Diving from a great height to sea level at night – as they did after the first exercise – it's easy to be mesmerised by the spinning hands and think you're still at ten thousand feet when you're actually at sea level. I think they went straight in.

Johnno's mother never accepted his death, but kept his room as he'd left it until her dying day. They ran a pub, and she expected him to come walking back into the bar one day, as large as life. I wouldn't have put it past him. What we didn't know, because he never told us, was that he was married, but his wife had run off with an American airman, taking their little girl with her to the States. He never saw them again.

Afterwards, though, I did recall a conversation I'd had with him one night in the mess bar. He was in both his cups and a bit of a dark mood, and he told me of the time he was travelling home and was chatting on the train with a Yank going to the same place. Johnno asked if the man knew the Red Lion, his parents' pub. The man did. And the blonde barmaid? asked Johnno, meaning his wife, who worked there. The Yank's face broke into a big grin. Didn't he just! he chortled joyfully – only the second best screw in town!

I was aghast. 'What did you do?'

'I didn't do anything,' said Johnno, staring thoughtfully into his glass, 'I knew it wasn't true.'

'Of course it wasn't,' I agreed loyally, 'you know how Yanks like to shoot off their mouths.'

'Yes, totally untrue', repeated Johnno, 'I wouldn't rate her better than fourth or fifth.'

That's what I mean about Johnno: you could never tell when he was joking and when he wasn't.

All these memories were brought back, recently, when I visited friends in Nottinghamshire and diverted on the way back to walk in a quiet green wood near Newark. It was here that Mosquito DZ256 crashed back in November 1944.

In June of that year Taffy Bellis and his pilot, Dennis Welfare, flew in this plane to shoot down a Messerschmitt 110 that blew up in a ball of flame. The Mossie passed through the debris, and much of its tail fabric was burnt away, so that they had to struggle back three hundred miles, steering by the differential power of the two engines.

In July, duly repaired, Dagwood and I flew it on patrol over Belgium, without incident. Three months later a new pilot, John Roberts (who had flown the other aircraft on Johnno's last Haystack exercise), flew this same DZ256 to a Lancaster 'drome to carry out interception exercises with one of the big bombers. The Mosquito was to carry out mock stern attacks, coming up under the tail while the bomber attempted a violent corkscrew evasion in classic escape style.

The inexperienced pilot brought the Mossie in too fast, and as the bomber climbed, he pulled the nose up and hit the massive slipstream from the four Merlin engines at a dangerously low speed. The sleek night-fighter flipped over into a stall at seven thousand feet over the woods, and then spun from the sky. You must move fast in such a situation, but the new man didn't. It didn't come out of its spin until fifteen hundred feet, and then he didn't get it quite right. Too low, it flipped into a spin the opposite way and slammed into the edge of the wood. He didn't stand a chance. Nor did the Lancaster flight engineer who had persuaded the pilot to take him along for the ride in place of the normal navigator. He broke the unspoken rule of airmen – never volunteer.

It was a lovely quiet evening as I walked through the woods, with the tall trees arching over my head like the fan tracery of a great green cathedral. I thought of the four crews, and how it was the two new boys who were long gone – Roberts and Johnno – after all the long years of training and before they had even got to the war.

Still – if you had to go, better in a place like this in the heart of England than some unknown cold and clammy grave in the waters of the North Sea, like poor old Johnno.

And yet . . .

They say immortality lies in the memories of others. Today, I could tell you nothing of the worthy John Roberts, but Johnno I'll never forget. Funny how we always remember the rogues.

CHAPTER ELEVEN

Twenty-four Hours

It's three minutes to eight – there might just be time to catch breakfast in the sergeants' mess if we hurry.

I lean across to the other bed and shake Dagwood, my navigator. The two of us share the small room with a pile of flying kit, a few personal belongings and a powerful reminder of second-hand beer – and together we quickly pull battledress over pyjamas and a scarf round our necks to hide our lack of a tie from a gimlet-eyed station warrant officer. Then we do an emergency take-off down the corridor, banging on Paddy's door as we go. He has no chance of making the meal on time, but we enjoy watching him sell his soul for a plate of baked beans.

In the sergeants' mess dining room, aircrew usually sit together at the same long mess table, in a monastic silence. Most of them have either been flying the previous night or roistering into the small hours because they weren't flying, so we have an unofficial no-talking rule at breakfast. You are allowed to grunt a surly 'morning!' to the mute company, but bright chatter on any other subject, from Ju 88s getting lead enemas up the exhaust to local barmaids getting led astray up the Rose and Crown, leads us to silently up porridge plates and decamp *en masse* to the next table, leaving the chatterer in splendid isolation. It's a great conversation stopper. Paddy turns up late and tries his luck at the serving counter with Crocodile Skin, the cookhouse corporal WAAF. He returns in triumph with a plate of baked beans and fried bread, in exchange for the promise of a night to remember at the next NAAFI dance. To our ribald advice about not looking at the mantelpiece when you poke the fire he cheerfully observes that with a bit of luck he'll be posted missing before then.

I decide to treat myself, and hand in one of my precious egg ration to the cook, with detailed instructions on how to serve it. This provokes catcalls of derision from the ground staff members of the mess. Eggs during wartime – fresh eggs at least – are non-existent luxuries except to two highly privileged classes – operational aircrew and pregnant women. The rest of humanity, including disgruntled ground staff sergeants, have to make do with the bright yellow powdered version that looks as if the hen was force-fed on Chinese pollyfilla, and they are not pleased. Our kind offer to make them all pregnant on the spot is rudely refused. We desist from taunting them about the half pint of fresh milk a day that we and nursing mothers also get. There's only so much a man can stand.

It's 9.00 a.m., and, fully dressed, we wander down to the squadron flights, calling in the main hangar as we go on the pretext of 'testing our oxygen equipment'. Gulps of pure oxygen are a great cure for last night's hangover.

In the crew-room, a large untidy den at the end of the hangar, full of easy chairs and wire-fronted lockers for our flying gear, our eyes go at once to the chalked list of names on the Operations Board. One column gives the tally of operations flown by each crew; our last one was Number 12. Not that we're suspicious, of course, but we'll be glad when Trip 12A is over and we're on to Number 14.

Thirty is the magic total for a full tour of ops, at least for the time being, but the Air Ministry is not above raising it while you aren't looking. We don't complain too much. Finishing a tour means a spell at an operational training unit, teaching new pilots to fly, and that could be really dangerous.

Dagwood and I are just back from leave, and as someone seems to be flying almost every night, we aren't surprised to see our names at the top of the board. As the first all-weather fighters, the rule seems to be, if the bombers fly, then we fly. If the bombers don't fly, we still fly – usually on spoof raids, pretending to be little wooden Lancasters so that the *Luftwaffe* wastes precious fuel trying to intercept us and shoot us down. If the weather is so bad over Germany that they lock the gates and have an early night, we fly over England instead, where the weather's probably worse, doing exercises with the bomber training units. And if nobody at all will come up and play with us we indulge in a game of hide and seek with each other in the darkness, an exercise known as a 'Haystack'. Depending on your companion, a real haystack on a black night can be a lot more fun.

Chiefy, the flight sergeant in charge of aircraft maintenance, wanders in to report to the CO. One of the pilots made a heavy landing last night and C Charlie will need an undercarriage check. Chiefy dreams of an Air Force entirely without pilots, so that nobody bends his beloved planes, or even gets them dirty. When that day comes he'll weld the hangar door shut and retire a happy man.

No-one knows the target yet – they're still casting the chickens' entrails up at Bomber Command – but those on the duty list take off on a night-flying test. Each crew checks out the plane they will fly that night, the pilot that the engines, controls, and some ninety-odd gauges, switches, buttons and indicator lights are all working, and the navigator that the radar sets, navigation aids and other highly secret electronic equipment work smoothly and well.

Spare crews go off to do things like instrument flying practice on the Link Trainer – a sort of Wendy House with bellows – or aircraft recognition tests. These consist of identifying tiny models in almost total blackness, so that half the time we're not sure we're even watching the right wall. (Supposedly to prevent cheating, our collars are clipped to the chair back, but this is believed to be more a protection for the WAAF officer who is giving the test in the darkness.)

After half an hour in the air, testing each and every control and switch, you land again, faults are put right, and you test it all again in the afternoon. If it's still wrong you get a funny look and the CO tries the plane himself. Invariably he finds nothing amiss, due to Chiefy's cunning ploy in always giving him the worst plane on the squadron for his own. After flying that, he pronounces every other aircraft superb, and tells you to get on with it.

Then, just before the NAAFI arrives with our morning fix of rock cakes and tea, there is a phone call from Group HQ – tonight is to be a 'Maximum Effort'. This means that anything that can be thrown at the sky and manages to stay there while Chiefy counts three goes. They even commandeer the plane that's flying down to London to pick up the CO's wife's handbag for the officers' mess dance, so we know it's something important.

Back in the mess for lunch, we find the phantom crossword fiend has struck again. Someone with a warped soul gets to the *Daily Telegraph* first, and fills the puzzle with wrong answers, driving aficionados crazy with baffled fury. We strongly suspect the station warrant officer – who we are convinced is in the pay of the Gestapo – until we notice that several of the answers begin with an H, a letter he seldom uses except in the wrong place, effectively ruling him out.

After lunch we call on the girls in the parachute section to pick up our repacked chutes. We complain of a hole cut in the parachute silk the size and shape of a pair of knickers, and demand the right to check all suspects. Our humour is not appreciated by the two bored redheads on duty; they have heard it all a thousand times before. In the crew room those of us not on repeat night-flying tests settle down to an afternoon's technical talk on engines, followed by a test ('Give the firing sequence of the four-stroke engine.' 'Bang, bang, bang, bang', says Paddy), but this soon deteriorates into a discussion on the performance and aerodynamic characteristics of several local ladies. Later, we hurriedly spill out of a heavy poker session to watch the flight commander vainly try to save his beloved sports car, which is on fire. He has washed it down with 150 octane aircraft fuel, then jumped in and pressed the starter a little too soon. We vote him a lot funnier than last night's ENSA show.

Then, just before tea, comes the Tannoy call for briefing. 'There will be a meeting of aircrew and all interested personnel at seventeen hundred hours in the lecture room at Station Headquarters.' Presumably it is phrased in this way to deceive

A group of NCO aircrew from both squadrons gather round a map table following briefing to discuss the operation and things to watch out for en route. The author is on the left.

enemy agents camped out at the end of the runway, or, more likely, local girls checking up on any Squadron Lothario doing a runner.

Five o'clock and all the crews on duty gather in the headquarters block upstairs lecture room. There is some friendly banter between the two squadrons, then we are called to attention as the the station commander enters, followed by the two squadron commanders. The big curtain across the end wall is drawn back to reveal a large map of Europe, festooned with multi-coloured ribbons, the colour of the chalk listing your name matching the colour of the ribbon marking your route. Tonight's raid is on Bremen, with a diversion towards the Ruhr. We are on bomber escort duty, long-range night-fighters patrolling under, above, and alongside the unseen bomber stream at fifteen-minute intervals, like sheepdogs circling a flock to keep the wolf pack at bay. The other squadron is doing low-level intruder patrols over German airfields and *Luftwaffe* assembly beacons.

Now the Met. officer slides onto the platform to give us details of the weather. A large depression is centred over the North Sea and our course is plotted in a great circle round it to give us a wind at our backs all the way. He is a smooth character with Brylcreemed teeth, and you half-expect him to try and sell you a second-hand Bentley before take-off. His nickname is Two-way Thomson, and he has no intention of risking a cosy job by doing anything foolish like committing himself to a straight answer. 'Things could go two ways tonight', he announces. 'Either there will be solid ten-tenths cumulo-nimbus cloud from about seven feet six all the way up to thirty thousand feet, with lots of icing – or it will clear and we'll get bright moonlight all the way.' As he sits down we give him a sardonic cheer and he beams happily.

The intelligence officer now takes centre stage to tell us how the war's getting on generally, starting with the latest position of the front line. He could have saved his breath, as we claim we can always tell when we cross it – the anti-aircraft fire gets more accurate. Next we are given the signal colours of the day, both German and British, and what places to avoid. He sounds like an anxious mother: 'Don't go near any Yanks or sailors.' They tend to shoot first and check their Aircraft Recognition books afterwards to see what they've hit.

A small, scruffy civilian with a large forehead and baggy eyes has been skulking nearby, and he is introduced as a boffin from the Radar Research Centre at Malvern. 'Tonight you'll find a small black box between the elevator trim indicator and the radio', he tells us. 'When you switch it on it sends out signals like a Flying Fortress.' (No, he doesn't mean it orders up hamburger and coke.) 'We've discovered the Germans can home onto American radio transmissions, so what you do', says the little man, 'is cruise slowly along, pretending you're a Flying Fortress, and wait until a *Luftwaffe* night-fighter comes up under your tail. Then you do a 360-degree turn and shoot it down.' We vote him even funnier than the flight commander, but stop laughing when we realise he means it, he isn't an ENSA comedian come in by the wrong door.

At this point the navigators drift away to group round the navigation leader, who gives them routes, wind speeds and other secret formulae for the practice of the Black Art, while the pilots scribble courses and times on small simple charts, known as Captain of Aircraft maps. Consisting of little more than the bare outlines of the coast and a few main towns and rivers, we use the crude maps to beat the German night skies for game and, hopefully, find our way back again.

Each of us collects a wad of currency for the countries we overfly, and Paddy speculates out loud whether it's enough to bale out and hole up in a bordello until Montgomery arrives. Various escape aids are on offer should we have to walk back from Germany: plastic combs with small files in the spine, silk handkerchiefs printed with escape maps, tiny compasses set in brass buttons, and Continental-type photographs of ourselves to fit into Resistance-made identity papers. After all that effort, it seems a bit ungrateful to simply fly back. Finally, we are handed the flimsies – secret radio information printed on lemon-flavoured rice paper, the easier to swallow in case of capture. Flying makes me hungry and I seldom return without the edges nibbled to shreds.

And now, there's nothing to do but wait. Aircraft are to take off at fifteen-minute intervals, starting at eleven. We ourselves are due off at midnight, and we fill the time with aimless snooker, letter writing to loved ones (and if there's time, one to the wife) or listening to ITMA on the radio.

We get the occasional passing invitation. 'Not trying the local hop, then?' 'Can't, we're on tonight. Tell Big Brenda I'll see her tomorrow.'

'Coming down to the Crown for a jar, later?' 'Nah, we're on. Leave a few bottles behind a chair in the mess, for when we get back.'

One of the older navigators, Ted, sits quietly on his own, staring at nothing in particular. He seems unusually subdued, answering in monosyllables. When a passing WAAF waitress asks whether he's flying, he nods and drops his voice so the rest of us can't hear, then says he wishes he wasn't, not tonight. He is a solidly dependable Geordie on his second tour, and it is so unlike him that she moves away, troubled.

At nine, the operation is put off for several hours. They have issued Sulphur Benzedrine tablets – 'Wakey, wakey' pills – and those who have indulged start worrying that the effect will wear off too soon. Most prefer to keep them for more important occasions, like mess parties. The phone rings and a female voice asks for Sergeant Woodstock. That'll be Woody's nurse from the local hospital. We tell her, sorry Darling, you'll have to sleep on your own tonight, old Woody's gone home on leave to the missis. The voice icily claims to be Mrs Woodstock, and we put the phone down hurriedly, wondering whether to apologise to Woody, deny everything, or just bale out over Bremen.

The hours tick slowly by. Gradually, the mess empties and falls silent as people wander off to bed, and we finally clamber into our flying kit. Battledress over long white pullover, sea-boot stockings, escape-type flying-boots, and woollen gloves inside leather gauntlets. It's cold up there. The thin silk inner gloves we keep as filters for removing the red stain from official petrol so that we can use it in our cars. Few take along their issue revolvers since Spud Murphy was shot down and tried to John Wayne his way back home, with tragic results.

Down at the crew room, the adjutant acts as dispatcher as the aircrews drift slowly in at intervals. We sign the Form 700 in Chiefy's office, which says if the aircraft drops to bits now it's our fault, and walk out to B Baker with a start-up crew. Time now for a last pre-flight check before we climb in – a matter of kick 'em and count 'em, and don't take off with less than two of anything – and finally we indulge in the ritual of the Last Leak. This despite a recent Air Ministry Order saying, 'Air crew will not urinate on their aircraft undercarriage before take-off.' Apparently it corrodes the landing gear, which says a lot about wartime beer, but we still do it. They should try flying in a cramped cockpit for four or five hours and see how they like using the Fearsome Funnel.

One of the airmen plugs in the starter trolley to give temporary power, cutting off the lights – it's possible to start on the batteries in an emergency, but it's too much of a strain from cold. With some difficulty, we clamber in and strap up in the darkness.

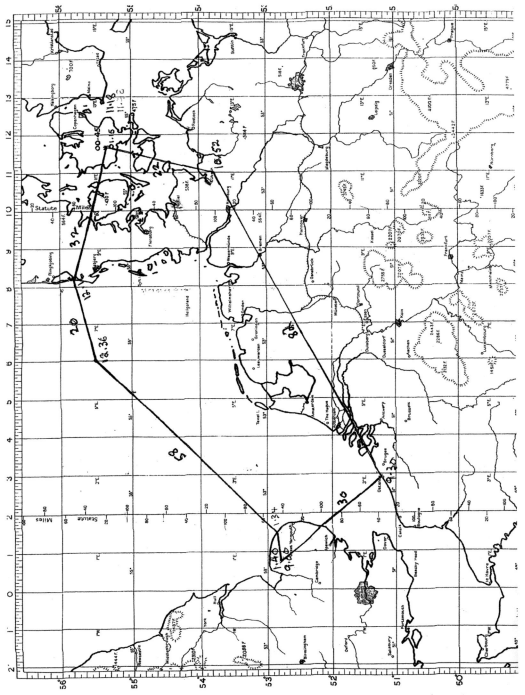

Facsimile of Captain-of-Aircraft map. Newcastle–Prague version. Times at each turning point. (True size 45cms x 30cms.) Flying time in minutes shown for each leg. Total 4hrs 10min.

The inside of the tiny cabin seems to be full of Mae Wests, dinghies, navigation bags, arms, legs and flying-boots – one of the penalties of having a navigator who is six feet plus when fully unrolled.

Check the brakes on, fuel on outer tanks, throttles set half an inch open. Then, signal with a flick of navigation lights, and the unseen airman, holding twin torches, rotates first one and then the other. I press the starter to set the big port engine turning, while the second crewman primes it with the Kl-Gas pump as it jolts round, at first stubbornly, then bursting into a smooth-throated roar. The starboard engine follows and they pull away the chocks.

'Driver Two Three, taxiing out.' You waste no words, and Control replies, laconically, 'Roger, Two Three. Clear to taxi.' Then we lurch out to the end of the runway, zig-zagging between rows of red and green lights, in an ungainly waddle that belies the sleek and deadly lines of the Mosquito.

At the end of the runway I run up each engine in turn and flick the switches to see if the magnetos lose their nerve, but there is no hiccup.

Control affirms, 'Clear to scramble, Two Three.'

In the darkness I quickly go through the familiar take-off procedure.

Throttle one inch open, tighten throttle nut.

Trim tabs. Set elevator one notch nose-heavy, rudder one mark right, aileron central. Mixture on automatic. Fine pitch.

'Fuel on outers?' The tanks are the navigator's job, but you feel behind you and check it anyway, by touch.

Flaps up – hang on, it's the short runway and we're carrying a couple of fifty-gallon drop-tanks; better make that ten degrees down – supercharger on automatic, radiator flaps open.

Compass – set red on red. Adjust the gyro.

Camera switch, guns, oil pressures, check temperatures, oxygen on – it blows softly in your face like a teasing woman – brake pressure up.

I turn down the ultra-violet light on the instrument panel to a faint glimmer, and the green light of an Aldis lamp flashes on us from the chequered caravan at the end of the runway.

It's time to go.

A squealing turn onto the runway and line up, then throttles open, fast as you can but keep it smooth, bang up to the stop at twelve pounds boost. Get the tail up quickly for rudder control. Hold it steady, don't let her swing. The twin rows of lights flow by, gathering speed. We should unstick at 125 mph, but it seems slower coming up than usual, and the end of the runway draws unnervingly near. A quick glance down shows that the power is dropping, and I suddenly realise the throttle nut isn't tight enough, the port throttle is drifting back from the vibration of the Merlins. I slam both throttles forward through the gate, breaking through the safety wire into emergency boost.

The last lights hurtle past, and we stare into darkness. I finally manage to heave it into the air and get the wheels up fast as we start to climb. That boundary hedge won't need trimming for a while.

Then we reach safety speed, 170, and I throttle back, pretending everything is normal. There is a sarcastic silence from the other seat, then Dagwood says, 'We may have to go back for more maps, I didn't know we were going by road.'

I pretend not to hear and call Control. 'Two Three airborne, climbing on course.'

'Roger, Two Three. Over to Channel C. Out.'

We climb steadily into the night. From here on we sever our umbilical cord of radio and are totally cut off. There is no comforting voice to call on for guidance or help. For four hours we will be on our own, ranging over a hostile continent in complete darkness, two men in a long plywood box, stalking and being stalked by an unseen enemy. It will be like playing tag with a tiger in a midnight wood – while riding a bicycle with no brakes.

After twenty minutes in solid cloud, flying only on instruments, with the sudden surge of the supercharger changing gear the only thing to break the monotony, we come out into clear air at thirteen thousand feet. Dagwood stares at his radar screen. The flickering Christmas-tree-shaped base lines are flooded with green blips of light, as a great unseen armada of heavy aircraft crosses the sky just above us. We are in the heart of the bomber stream, over us an army of men move up to battle in the darkness, in a thousand tiny groups of seven to a crew. One in twenty of the big machines, perhaps more, are on a one-way trip, and in a few hours their crews will be sleeping in turf pyjamas or booking-in to the Stalag YM. It is no time to say hello to nervous trigger fingers, so we slide past carefully, and in a few minutes the ghostly fleet fades into the night behind us.

Into Belgium, at Ostend, and we level off at twenty thousand feet, our operating height, turning onto our new course. Somewhere down there in the blackness we cross the front line, but we see nothing.

Twenty-five minutes later we are over the northern edge of the Ruhr, near Münster, and without provocation the sky suddenly erupts in orange splashes of anti-aircraft fire. We hear only the nearest shells, bursting with a soft crump sound. Instinct screams out to duck and weave, to try to dodge the bursts, but they are too evenly spread, it is a box barrage. Like players in a giant game of Battleships, the enemy don't take aim, they blindly fill an aerial space with as many shells as they can in the shortest time. The longer you hang around the more chance there is that they'll hit the jackpot, so you fly straight and level at top speed, and soon leave it behind.

An hour after Ostend we suddenly get a contact. Dagwood is brooding quietly over his electronic box and I am mentally calculating the fuel consumption, when he gives a shout.

'Contact! Twelve thousand feet, ten degrees at three o'clock.'

I turn slightly starboard so that the blip of light slides to the centre of the radar tube.

'Steady! Dead ahead, coming down fast . . . looks like a head-on, prepare to turn thirty degrees starboard.'

It's the Whiting manoeuvre, the only thing to do in a head-on, when you have a maximum range of no more than sixteen thousand feet and a combined closing speed of around six hundred miles an hour. The little blob of green light charges down the screen like a Formula One glow-worm.

'Four thousand feet! Turn starboard now.' And as we complete it, 'Turn hard port two hundred and ten degrees . . .'

The green hands on the blind-flying panel clocks lurch to one side and we are pushed deep into our seats. There is no up, no down, no horizon; we rotate slowly in a world of black velvet, the only things in the universe. There is nothing out there any more – the radar echoes are blanked out by the turn – only the slowly spinning gyro compass seems to be moving. One ninety, two hundred, and we start to come out of the turn. We should be right behind him.

Dagwood sings out in triumph. 'Got him! Two thousand feet and closing. Climb five hundred, turn ten degrees port.'

I see nothing, but, totally trusting, I follow the directions blindly. We creep slowly in to twelve hundred feet. Where the hell is he?

'He's diving – turn port – hard port.'

Damn! He must have picked us up on his Naxos rear warning device, and he's running for the electronic shelter of the ground returns. The little green numbers whirl again as I ram the stick forward and a great unseen hand tries to prise us from our seats.

'He's pulling away – increase speed – keep turning hard port.'

Increase! What speed are we doing, anyway? The altimeter seems to be racing round faster than the propellers. Then suddenly it's over.

'We've lost him.' He disappears into the expanding glare of electronic interference that floods the radar tube as we plunge towards earth. There is nothing more we can do with our limited equipment – if only we had the new Mark X, but they won't release it yet for use over the Continent. We slowly climb back to height.

Ten minutes later we are over Bremen and the fireworks have already begun. Fires burn in a great swath across the city, peppered with the coloured Pathfinder flares, and probing searchlights wave wildly like a man trying to beat off angry wasps. Far off to the north a tiny candle flares suddenly in the night sky, then slowly tumbles to earth, still burning. A second follows and then, shortly, a third. We've been told they are 'Scarecrows', a German pyrotechnic device fired to simulate a burning bomber and unnerve the bomber crews. Not true. These are real bombers, men and machines being torn from the sky by cannon fire. It is too late to help them.

One searchlight suddenly moves across and skewers us against the black sky, flooding the cockpit with a blinding glare. Other lights swing in to grip us in a cone. We know what Max Miller must feel like stepping out on stage at the Victoria Palace. Or maybe the Glasgow Empire might be more accurate – we must get out before the flak starts.

Wrench the stick back into your guts and turn hard port, then nose down and hard starboard. You seem to turn and twist so slowly yet the second corkscrew is enough to lose the light and you thankfully curl away into the dark. They pick you up a second time, but less confidently, and you repeat your escape. But no flak – there must be German night-fighters around. Dagwood switches over to the backward set and searches under our tail like a dog for fleas, while I turn onto the first leg of our patrol line, towards Kiel.

We reach our turning point again and start the last leg, near the end of the patrol. Away to the north-west we have seen firing over Kiel, but nothing round here for a while – there's more life on Mars on a wet Sunday. But somehow, turning in the dark, we have drifted east, over Lübeck, only this time there are no searchlights, no flares, no warning of any kind.

On the ground they had probably tracked us patiently on their screens, waiting for the right moment; now they fire six shots from somewhere down in the darkened city. Normally, Dagwood will slightly detune the set at intervals to pick up any probing radar beams from the guns, but we are caught momentarily off guard. The first thing we know is a blinding flash directly under the nose, hurling us upwards in the air, followed by the soft 'crump' of the explosion and the rattle of shrapnel against the belly. A second explosion follows, under one wing but further away, the rattle thinner, then four more shots. But by then we are peeling off, and for long seconds I throw the plane around like a drunken duck, risking any potential damage against the need to get clear.

But there is no more firing: they must have known they would only have the one chance. We check what we can, then Dagwood gives a course for home. However, there's no knowing precisely where we are, so I use the golden rule. When in doubt, stick your starboard wing on the Pole Star and aim for England. It's near enough until you clear the jamming and pick up the Gee navigation signals.

Now it's downhill all the way, losing height for over an hour as we let down steadily over the North Sea. We're on main tanks and I keep checking the fuel gauges in case a tank has been holed, fighting to stay awake as the oxygen mask leaks puffs of gas into my eyes. Once, my eyes glaze over for a fraction of a second and I suddenly find the Pole Star has shifted to a funny angle. I straighten up and hope Dagwood hasn't noticed. He sits with his face against the rubber visor of the radar, and I half-expect a snore on the intercom, but it never comes. At twelve thousand feet we hit cloud and Saint Elmo's fire dances along the wings. Scary but safe, it means there is no dangerous icing.

Ten minutes to go to the coast. Dagwood has checked our position on the Gee navigation system, then rechecked in startled disbelief as we find we are dead on track. It doesn't happen too often. We begin to pick up calls from other aircraft, and decide that it's time to put our Early Down Scheme into operation.

Normally you call to join the circuit when you're at a thousand feet over base, but as the number of returning aircraft builds up the controller stacks them at five-hundred-foot intervals over the runway. Last man out of twenty has to climb to a weary ten thousand feet again and slowly let down, five hundred feet at a time, as each aircraft peels off and lands. With the possibility of damage a little gentle cheating is in order – we calculate how many aircraft are waiting, and decide to call up to join the circuit while still fifteen minutes away.

'Two Three over base. Permission to join circuit.' We draw a reasonable four-thousand-feet slot while we flog those last few miles home. A suspicious voice out of the night growls, 'You bloody liar!', but fortunately the controller doesn't hear. One of these days everyone will catch on to the fiddle and he'll have twenty aircraft theoretically stacked above his head in dead silence. At intervals, Control moves everyone down one place.

'Clear to land, Two Nine, all aircraft down five hundred. Acknowledge', and the waiting planes reel off their call signs and new height. We spend our last fuel in a mad dash for base.

And then it's 'Clear to land, Two Three', as, just in time, the perimeter lights appear in the near distance. I ignore the circuit and curl straight into the final approach.

Throttle back, wheels down and locked, ten degrees of flap – as I go through the landing drill the approach angle indicator light flicks from green to red. Too low. A burst of engines and we're back in the green. Full flaps now, nose up, power off, and we sail over the unseen boundary hedge at a speed of a hundred and fifteen, then draw back gently from the rising line of lights like a reluctant virgin. Hold it – hold it – we're high, but a second burst of power checks the falling speed as we sink. Now a kick on the rudder to counter a slight cross-wind – forget three-point landings, you wheel it in: better rudder control.

The tyres kiss the concrete ribbon with a sigh of relief, and then you are fighting to keep the aircraft straight as the runway lights slow to a stop under your wings. We squeal off round the perimeter track and into line by the hangar, and I cut the engines. And suddenly there is a deep, aching stillness everywhere. A sleepy airman opens the tiny door and puts the small metal ladder in place.

He asks, 'What did you get?' and we tell him 'Back!' We feel like adding, 'And don't think it was easy.'

Outside, it is cold, with the bright pink of dawn starting to flood over the fields. The big engines are silent at last, but for the steady creak of cooling metal, and the hot strong smell of petrol and rubber everywhere. Somewhere in the clear bright air the birds start to sing morning prayers. We push our gear into a wire-fronted locker and walk down to debriefing through a dribble of blue uniforms making their way to work, fresh faced for the new day. With our ears still deafened from the bellowing Merlins, and the angry red brand of the oxygen mask etched deep into our cheeks, they seem not to see us, we are yesterday's ghosts.

At debriefing we clutch mugs of hot, sweet tea while an Intelligence Officer plies us with more questions than a jealous wife. Had we seen any lights? What were they doing? He doesn't seem to think 'Shining' a very helpful answer. Beacons, then? Ack-ack fire? Yes, we had a bit of that. What contacts did we get? Where? We wait for him to give up and try not to yawn.

Back in the mess, eyes like bicycle rear lights, we are halfway through our bacon and egg night-flying supper when the Chiefy comes in. He is not happy, B Baker has twenty-eight pieces of flak in it. We are impressed, we didn't know he could count that high. He cheers himself up by speculating what vital part of my anatomy the largest piece might have ruined had it not struck the cannon under my seat, and goes off whistling.

Tired crews drift in and flop before tired food. The word goes round, two crews aren't back yet. Ted and his pilot and Paddy and his navigator are still out there some-where. No-one has heard anything: in the control tower they sit waiting, patiently

listening to the silent sky – someone tries to calculate how much longer they can stay up if they have a Ronson lighter with them.

Then a cold bed, with black-out curtains, stiff with dust, failing to keep out the intruding daylight. We lie waiting for the noise of the Merlins to fade from our brain and drifting sleep to soften the red-rimmed eyelids. But in vain.

'You asleep?'

'Nah! Fancy a game?'

We sling on our gear and tramp over to the snooker room. It smells like a four-ale bar the morning after Mafeking Night, and we wipe sticky cues on grubby curtains and begin. Joe Davis's crown is in no danger, after ten minutes the pockets remain virginal and there seem to be more balls on the table than when we started. We decide to try the pit again, and this time we crash out before our heads touch the pillow.

Half an hour later we are wakened by Jimmy. Ted and his pilot are still missing, but did we know Paddy had diverted to Brussels with burnt-out flame-traps? Trust old Paddy! Brussels, newly liberated and full of Free French, free drinks and grateful ladies, why didn't we think of that? Better warn anyone going to the NAAFI dance that Crocodile Skin will be alone and on the prowl.

'By the way,' says Jimmy, 'you're on tonight.'

Not again! But apparently we needn't come down until later, the flight commander will do our night-flying test. We have a better idea, he could do the rest of the trip as well. 'You know him', says Jimmy. 'He's given himself a 48-hour pass to try and get his car repaired.'

I yawn and check my watch. With a bit of luck we might make breakfast.

CHAPTER TWELVE

'Behind the Wire'

The step sideways that both Dagwood and I took into the night-fighter world (albeit involuntarily on my part) was so sudden and complete that neither of us had much idea what happened to the rest of the people on our courses. We knew they had moved on along the inexorable conveyor belt that fed the Bomber Command training machine. Yet we never came across any of these people again in the service. We must have been pretty close to them at times, but we were never in a position to say, 'Oh, hello, mate – fancy seeing you!'

We seldom saw many of the big bombers, anyway – the giant Stirlings, or the Lancasters or the Halifaxes – even though on operations our job was to protect them. I remember being surprised while enjoying a pint on leave with an old school friend, to find that he'd been the pilot of a Halifax that I'd homed in on to check our radar during a night-flying test, but that was rather different. Ken's squadron was on a neighbouring 'drome anyway, and, like us, part of 100 Group – they used to patrol out over the North Sea all night long, transmitting a wall of electronic noise, known as the Mandrel Screen, that the bombers could secretly assemble behind.

Occasionally, though, if there was nothing much on, we might be sent over to a bomber station somewhere (it was usually some place in Lincolnshire) for a spot of so-called 'bomber co-operation'.

I remember flying across one night to a big bomber station – it was the first time we had landed at a bomber base. It was vast, and we tagged along behind a gaggle of aircrew to find the briefing room. With seven or eight men to a crew we had never seen so many aircrew swishing around the place, some of them with fairly high rank. In the group we were trailing along behind were a couple of squadron leaders with pilots' wings on their chests, rings on their arms and spaghetti in their skulls. 'I say, Rod, see that night-fighter Mossie that just flew in?' asked one. 'Yeh,' said Rod, 'wizard little job . . . never tried one – might take the Queen Bee for a quick buzz round in it.'

'I think not, mate!' I thought. The Queen Bee was the top WAAF officer, and he spoke as if it was a new sports car. 'Not with all the equipment we've got on board – you stick to driving your buses.' But if he'd pulled rank I could have had a tough argument on my hands.

Their briefing was very different from our own cosy little get-togethers, where there could be fewer than fifty. Here, there were hordes of aircrew in a theatre-like assembly, and on the platform the night's exercise was discussed between the squadron commanders and the group captain with great seriousness. Then a thought struck them.

'Is the Mosquito pilot here?' they asked the hall, and I stood up. There was a murmur of surprise that a couple of mere flight sergeants would be on such work.

In Bomber Command circles, such aircraft performed Master of Ceremonies roles, and their pilots' sleeves often had more rings on them than a hoopla-stall attendant. 'Oh!' they said, and that was that – they weren't going to waste their time seeking my opinion on anything.

Had they done so I would have said something like, 'Be gentle with us, lads, we are not like that other lot – the home night-fighters. We have no ground controller homing us in on you, and our Serrate equipment only works against German night-fighter radar. Which leaves us with an old Mark IV radar set – the only one they'll let us take over there. And it's primitive, maximum range of three miles, which is not a lot at night. Try anything violent and we won't end up in the same sky.' But as I say, they didn't ask.

We intercepted the first aircraft, sliding up under its belly like a randy Yorkshire terrier on to a Great Dane bitch, flicking our lights to show a sort of 'Bang – you're dead!' signal. But with a convulsive twitch the big plane reared up in the darkness in an approved corkscrew, and almost fell on top of us. Not surprisingly, by the time I had finished getting out of the charging monster's way it had disappeared off the face of the earth – or at least off our radar screen – the same thing, so far as we were concerned. Maybe Rod was a frustrated Spitfire pilot. We spent some time looking round for him, but apparently he had dived, which reduced our range still further. So we gave up and went home.

The air traffic controller was very surprised to see us back. 'What are you two doing here?'

I explained. 'Why didn't they practise with the ADGB boys with their Mark X radars? It would have given them a lot more experience.'

He said, 'I mean that bomber's reported you doing interceptions on him all the way to Skegness – he claims you've carried out six attacks on him so far – he's been using more corkscrews than a barman in a brothel!'

'Whatever turns him on!' I said, 'Let's just hope he's not playing tag with a Ju 88 intruder!'

But even on such occasions we never seemed to run into anyone we knew from Arizona or South Africa, come to that we seldom met up with any bomber aircraft at all. Or not in the flesh (or should it be the aluminium), so to speak. Most of the time, the bomber stream was little more than a rash of green blips of light across Dagwood's radar screen. Though now and then, in the far distance, we might catch a glimpse of a Lancaster twisting desperately in a cone of angry searchlights, like a trapped moth, or a Stirling torching down to earth on the edge of a burning town. And I would wonder if maybe – just maybe – that was Dusty, or Bill Taylor, or Henry Morgan, or any of the Arizona gang, in the process of saying goodbye to this world. But air warfare is very impersonal, and perhaps it's as well that you couldn't put a man's name to a machine. In fact, it was more than fifty years later, when I turned up rather unexpectedly to a reunion, that I found out what had happened to some of them.

Doug Wilkinson was an old friend from Arizona days in 1942, where we learned our basic pilot training. Perhaps more than anyone, he had been responsible for my crewing up with Dagwood.

When we returned to the UK in 1943, sporting shiny new 'wings', the remainder of the course, including Doug, went on up to Scotland to fly the big, four-engined Halifaxes, and during the reunion I asked how many operations he had flown on them. He cheerfully admitted to 'A half!'

He was shot down on his first raid over Germany, ending up in a *Stalag Luft* POW camp, in East Prussia, a bleak and bitter place with each day a cold rehash of the previous one. Gradually, over a pint, he told me what life had been like there for a 'Kriegie', or prisoner of war.

There were few things in the day-to-day life of such a camp (said Doug) that relieved the mind-grinding boredom of its inmates or, even better, managed to raise a morale-boosting laugh simply by the sheer absurdity of its construction.

However, there was one ingenious device that unfailingly managed to do so, and it was used by the camp guards (known as 'Goons') to empty the latrines when needed. The machine was known as 'the honey-wagon' by the US Air Force POWs, but the RAF Kriegies knew it by a more direct Anglo-Saxon term. Still, the ironic Yankee name will do for now.

The honey-wagon was a tank mounted on a horse-drawn carriage, and on the body of the tank were three main features. At the lower rear was a hand-operated valve to which a flexible hose could be attached. On top of the tank was a cone-shaped outlet, held closed by a spring-loaded metal disc, while on one side was a priming pump and a small rotary trapdoor.

The operation of the mechanism was simplicity itself. A hose from the latrine was connected to the rear inlet valve, and paraffin was injected into the tank. Then a lighted match would be put into the rotary trap-door and trans-ferred to the tank itself. The result was rather spectacular as the ignition set off the following chain of events. It began with a loud mechanical belch as the disc lifted against its spring. This was quickly followed by a sheet of flame, an enor-mous bang, and a cloud of finely divided corruption. Almost as an afterthought, the vacuum resulting from the explosion slurped up the contents of the latrine and deposited them into the tank. Bedspring – as they might say in the car adverts – *durch technik*!

Most experienced Kriegies knew enough to stay well clear, and upwind, of the machine when it was operating, but new arrivals tended to dive instinc-

tively under the nearest cover, where they were likely to meet those more senior – and incurably flak-happy – guests of the Third Reich. Strangely, the rather stringy horse that drew the contraption appeared to be the one creature least affected by all the fuss, and it took little notice.

This gem of German technology was operated by an emaciated Russian prisoner of war, a man dressed, quite literally, in rags, and he was equipped by the guards with a box of the local German matches in order to carry out his task. These matches became an important scource of barter in trade negotiations between the main Allied compound and the smaller attached one holding Russian POWs. Somehow, the bedraggled tsar of the honey-wagon managed to persuade his escort that the German matches they had supplied were of such poor quality that it was totally impossible for him to obtain more than one bang per box. Inevitably, a brisk trade in food-for-matches sprang up, with visible improvements in the dress and health of the Russian entrepreneur.

Russia was not a signatory to the Geneva Convention, and as a result, their prisoners were treated as virtual slave labour by their captors. So in 1944, at Christmas time, the RAF Kriegies had a whip-round and sent food in to them from their own precious store. Legend has it that a grubby but grateful thank-you note was smuggled back, which read, 'Gallant comrades, Lords of the Air, please send more biscuits!

As the Russian armies began to draw dangerously near to the camp, it was hurriedly decided to march the prisoners away to the west to safety. This involved a trudge across the frozen wastes of Poland and north Germany in the depths of winter. In a letter, Doug sent me an account of an event on that epic march, when a surprise visitor dropped in on them one night.

It happened [said Doug] during a six-hundred-mile plod across north Germany to safety in the first bitter months of 1945. Life was hard and rough, and bitterly cold, but the elderly Commandant, bless his stiff Prussian upbringing, still had honourable if old-fashioned ideas about his responsibilities towards the men under his command. He usually managed to sort out some kind of shelter for us for the night. During the day's march we would pick up bits of wood or anything that would burn so that, with luck, at the end of the day we could have a scalding hot brew to go with whatever food Providence had sent our way during the daylight hours. It was a monotonous and mind-numbing existence.

Except once! One evening at dusk we were marched into a walled estate in which was a large handsome house and two brick-built barns with thatched roofs. The place was immaculate, obviously belonging to some Nazi Party bigwig. The blades of grass were standing to attention and even the bricks looked scrubbed and polished. The Goons, or camp guards, took over one of the barns and we were put into the other, with plenty of straw. But then the stern edict went forth – fires were strictly *verboten*! So we had to bed down without our precious hot brew. Still, it wasn't too bad, really – the straw made life tolerable, and after twenty minutes or so icy feet slowly thawed out and wet clothing began to steam nicely. It was really rather snug, and sleep came gently that night.

That is, until about two o'clock in the morning! Something must have attracted the attention of a low-level intruder Mosquito because he suddenly appeared out of the night and dropped a bomb on the Goons' barn. He following this up by setting fire to both barns with incendiaries, and happily rounded off the entertainment by shooting up the place. It was quite exciting for a while. The man next to me got a bullet through his thigh, but with great presence of mind managed to scrabble among the straw until he recovered the offending missile as a souvenir. We were quickly herded out behind the stout stone boundary wall and spent the rest of the night watching the Brock's Benefit from this relatively safe vantage point, enjoying the radiated warmth.

With the dawn, we were finally allowed back in to pick up the daily routine of toilet, breakfast and *Fertigmachen*. We were good lads. We remembered the order not to light fires, so we didn't. We didn't need to. Our kitchen fire was fifty feet wide and a hundred feet long! The best bits were the massive ten-inch-square beams that ran the length of the barns like great Yule logs, which by now were charred on the outside and radiated intense heat, enough to singe the eyebrows on our sweating foreheads. Courtesy abounded. There were politely murmured enquiries in beautifully modulated English tones. 'Would you care to use the back burner, old scout, or do you prefer the grill?' It was wonderful. Boiling shaving water! Red hot tea! Out came bits of food hoarded for an occasion such as this. A fragment of bacon from a Red Cross parcel, the egg acquired at the risk of a bullet from an adjacent farm, a Canadian cracker – all fried in Prima margarine and washed down with piping-hot char.

By eight thirty we were clean, dry, beautifully close shaven and warm inside for the first time in days. And we were smiling happily, but not too widely, because the Goons had fixed bayonets and were looking more than a little peeved. But inside we laughed. And laughed. And laughed!'

Knowing I had flown Mosquitoes, Doug asked if I could trace the pilot responsible for the mayhem. It happened somewhere north-west of Berlin, near Wittenberge, in March 1945, and almost certainly the aircraft responsible came from one of the intruder squadrons on 100 Group. But although I tried no-one ever put their hand up for it.

And who can blame them? With today's rampant compensation culture and the way the politicians are trying to weasel their way into Europe, any day now I half expect ex-RAF aircrew to end up in court under a pile of compensation claims from a disgruntled mob of former Nazi Party war criminals. And I wouldn't lay long odds against them winning, either.

CHAPTER THIRTEEN

Anchovy Airways

Not many people get the chance to run their own airline. We called ours Anchovy Airways, after the squadron's callsign at the time, and I was its chief (and only) pilot.

We set up the organisation following my one and only war-wound. Which meant that I flew our one and only plane (well, it belonged to the RAF, which also paid our wages) with my one and only left arm – my one and only broken left arm – set in plaster.

Firstly, about the war-wound. After flying some twenty operations over Germany, shooting at and being shot at by all and sundry (or should it be *Alles und* sundry?), I remained in fairly pristine condition, untouched by human hand, as it were. Then, on New Year's Day, my luck ran out. It was because there were eggs for breakfast – real live eggs I mean, none of your powdered rubbish, and they were a rare wartime delicacy. I was late up (when wasn't I!) and I was running from the billet to the mess for my share of the rare treat, when I skidded on some ice and fell heavily on my left arm, promptly breaking it. To my utter disgust I was sent off at once to the nearest RAF hospital, which was at Ely, and they obligingly slapped the entire arm in plaster and sent me back. They didn't even save me an egg.

The CO looked at my plastered arm disapprovingly. He was short of pilots, but even he grudgingly admitted that there were limits. 'We can't send you over Germany like that!' he complained. 'It's probably against the Geneva Convention.' (It was also, though he didn't know it, against the Cotmanhay Convention, and in case you're wondering, I'd just made that up because that's where I was born.) Then, being a busy man, he suggested dismissively, 'Make yourself useful – try flying the old Annie. You'll have a job killing yourself on one of them, and you need to keep your hand in.'

True. The 'Annie', or Anson, was a rather crude old aircraft, used as a general runabout, that bumbled about the sky at around a steady hundred and twenty miles an hour, happily absorbing all the pain and indignities that we pilots heaped on it. If you dived it at a hundred and seventy or thereabouts and then pulled out sharply you could make the wooden wingtips flap up and down rather alarmingly. Great fun. But, like the amiable old Labrador that it resembled, it didn't like sitting down – coming in to land it seemed to go on bouncing on down the runway for ever. I couldn't bend my left arm, but with a little squirming of the left shoulder, and using the fingertips poking out of the end of the plaster to maximum effect, I found I could manage the throttles fairly well. Not that there was any question of doing ops on an Anson, of course – not without an overnight stay in Berlin – but I could wander round the countryside, fetching and carrying people quite safely, under the blanket excuse of 'Navigational Exercises'.

The trouble was that the plaster on my arm kept working loose, giving the broken bone no support. So every time I went back for a check-up at Ely the medics declared that I needed a new plaster and proceeded to tear the old one off the ingrown hair on my arm, to my shrieks of pain. Then they would slap on a new plaster and take the old one away to read.

To read? Well, yes. It had quickly become a regular feature of squadron nights out to pour beer down the inside of White's plaster and write rude jokes down the outside, making it at the same time uselessly loose for its purpose and highly prized for its reading material among the Ely nursing staff. (I had four plasters on in all. They are probably still stored, somewhere in the depths of Ely hospital, like the Dead Sea Scrolls awaiting rediscovery on a Channel 4 documentary.)

Into this situation came Jake Baldwin. He was a navigator and the nearest thing to Private Walker of Dad's Army. In Civvy Street he sold perfume, and in the RAF somehow he had picked up a commission (someone suggested that it had dropped off the back of a Lancaster). He quickly saw the commercial potential of a one-armed spare pilot whom no-one bothered about, wandering round the sky giving lifts to people. Why not put it on a proper commercial footing and charge members of the squadron a flat ten bob to fly them home on leave anywhere in the country. (To the impossibly young I would explain that ten bob was all of fifty pence, apparently the bargain of the century, but it did represent at least half a day's pay at the time.) Jake intimated that he would organise everything, and all profits would go to pay for the next squadron party, awesome affairs held in the gym.

So was born Anchovy Airways, and it quickly proved popular. We were careful – we never charged the CO – and I learned to discourage requests like, 'On your way to Southampton, Chalky, can you drop me off in Glasgow?' I flogged my way happily round the shires as the prospects for the next party brightened.

Then one day I was asked to pick up a new squadron leader with his kit, at Lichfield (we were in East Anglia at the time.) The only spare navigator I could find was a very young and inexperienced sergeant, but no sensible Anson pilot ever took off without a navigator of some sort. This was not because you needed them to find the way, you needed them to wind the wheels up. One of the drawbacks of the Annie was that it had no hydraulics, and so you had to wind up the wheels physically with a large handle. (It took 127 turns, and by the time you got them up it was just about time to let them down again.) Anyway, we could hardly pretend it was a navigational exercise without a navigator.

The day was hazy, with the tops of church steeples sticking up out of the white mist as if we were flying over a drowned world. I flew due west while my companion strained to wind up the wheels, and then, as he returned to his navigating (and his normal colour) I waited patiently for him to give me the course to fly. For a long time his finger moved rapidly and confidently across the map, but no directions came.

Sarcastically, I pointed out that according to the speed his finger was travelling, we had apparently just broken the sound barrier, whereas an Anson couldn't catch a bishop's belch. Whereon he cheerfully admitted to being utterly lost. One church steeple looked very like another and he had been too busy winding up wheels to follow the map properly from the start. Disgusted, I looked around, and when a 'drome suddenly appeared below us in the mist, I decided to take over the navigation myself, using the tried and tested method used by pilots since the year dot – I would sneak down quietly and ask where we were. Preferably in a whisper.

But as we circled to come in to land, the sun suddenly shone on the mist below, hiding the runway in a blinding pool of light, and I lost sight of the entire airfield, which slid off to the left somewhere. Undismayed, I climbed back up again and set a new course, loftily explaining to the navigator that there'd been no need to land after all, I'd recognised where we were, and Lichfield was ten miles due south. Bang on time and course, a new 'drome showed up, and as I touched down and taxied up to the control tower, I advised my companion to watch and learn from my expertise.

A bored flying control officer appeared on the balcony. No, he'd never heard of the squadron leader, and yes, he'd heard of Lichfield, but this wasn't it – Lichfield was ten miles north of there, and would we mind taking off on the right runway this time, we were making people nervous. I don't think the sight of my arm in plaster allayed his worries any.

I found Lichfield again, this time landing without trouble, and as I taxied round the perimeter track a tiny figure hurtled out of the control tower with a pile of luggage and waved imperiously at me. In my innocence I took this to mean that my potential passenger wished me to cut across the airfield directly to him. A hundred yards further on I found that he didn't, because the Annie had stuck firmly in an un-suspected mud pool. The squadron leader had to hump his luggage all the way across the 'drome and then help unstick the aircraft by pushing on the Anson's tail while I revved the engines, meaning that the propellers deposited much of the mud on his best uniform.

As he climbed wearily in the now freed aircraft I made my second mistake – or was it my twenty-second? – who's counting? I didn't realise that he was rather buck-toothed, giving the impression that he was constantly smiling. The language that followed my cheery answering smile soon disillusioned me.

The flight back was made in icy silence, and my offer of a lift to the officers' mess for his kit in my little Austin 7, known as Shambles, was dismissed with one withering look at my plastered arm. The last time I heard of the squadron leader, he had strayed over Switzerland during a daylight sortie, and a bunch of Swiss fighters had invited him to 'Come on down!' What became of him subsequently I don't know. Maybe they used him as a spare part in a cuckoo clock.

Mind you, seen from his point of view, you had to have some sympathy for the man. He'd seen his transport arrive, and carried all his luggage out, only to see the Anson change its mind and disappear in the distance. No sooner had he humped the gear all back into the control tower than the plane returned and he had to rush it all out again. He had waved desperately to the Anson in case it vanished once more, and the fool pilot had then deliberately taxied it into a mud pool, then grinned like a maniac when he had climbed aboard spattered with mud.

On the other hand, we got back to find Jake Baldwin had craftily moved to another squadron, taking all our party funds with him, so what had he got to complain about? I mean, it's not as if we asked him for the ten bob.

So just remember, as you doss down on the airport lounge floor this summer, waiting for a long-delayed flight to Torremolinos or wherever, things could be a lot worse. You could have been travelling by Anchovy Airways. And you'd have needed that holiday after winding those wheels up and down.

CHAPTER FOURTEEN

Show Me the Way To Go Home

One of the first lessons you needed to learn when flying in the RAF was, 'Never Volunteer for Anything'. Fate tended to get very irritated when you mucked up all her carefully laid plans, and trouble came quickly enough without sticking your hand up and waving to it. Not only that, but it usually came sneaking up on you when you were least expecting it, and ninety per cent of the time when you were on your own. It was on such an occasion, when I ignored such sound advice, that I once ended up making my sole contribution to the science of flying – I invented Hot Breath Emergency Navigation.

It happened when we were in Norfolk and there was a slight lull in operations. The flight commander detailed a recently arrived pilot, Paul, to go and fetch a 'new' Mosquito from a place called Colerne, down near Bath. The squadron were a bit short of planes, having lost one or two on ops, and it was the custom to cast around the other RAF squadrons for any new ones going spare. Except that new they were not. You didn't give your best machines away.

Another pilot was needed to bring back the second plane, so I offered to go. I'd just retired, hurt, from a rather vicious poker school, and had nothing better to do, 'better' translating as 'more profitable'. Paul intended taking his own navigator down with him to tell him which way to point the plane for home. As they do, when asked nicely. However, this threatened to pose a small problem. The Mosquito cockpit was notoriously tiny for two people, being about the size of a phone box and fitting tight round the backside. By the time they had also stuffed it full of radar sets and electronic equipment plus all the other gear you carried, there was barely enough room for a fat fart, but it was just possible to shoe-horn a third person aboard, providing he wasn't too tubby and you weren't in too much of a hurry to get out again at the other end. Of course, the pilot had to have a seat all on his own to work the controls, and if the third person sat on the navigator's lap the only way that worthy could get a peek at his map was by getting downright personal. The phrase, 'I'm just trying to catch a glimpse of Bolsover' could raise all sorts of dark thoughts in a deeply suspicious mind. So the navigator usually tended to sit on the spare pilot. There was certainly no question of taking along a second navigator as well, and, anyway, unlike me, Dagwood was doing rather well in the poker school and would have been rather reluctant to part company with the pasteboards.

Mind you, I did hear once of four people somehow crowding into the cockpit for a trip from Manchester to Norfolk, though how they did it no one quite knows to this day, but no doubt all will be revealed in some future edition of the *Kama Sutra*.

The afore-mentioned problem was this. I've never been one for sitting with some fella on my knee, particularly when he's between me and the only way out. Still less did I fancy being chauffeured by a new pilot, nor being told where to go by an unknown navigator, so I decided that a bit of fast talking was called for. Tricky place to land at, Colerne, I observed, being on top of a hill like it was, with all those updraughts. Luckily, I knew the place well – it might be best if I were to fly the squadron plane down there. On the other hand, I wondered what was wrong with the new plane that they were so agreeable to letting us have it. Well, they weren't going to give us one of their good machines, were they. You usually got one that had given them so much trouble and was so clapped out that they were glad to get rid of it. Bad aircraft tended to do the rounds a lot. Maybe it would be better, with my greater experience, if I flew the new plane back on my own, following the other two home. (Meaning that if I didn't have Dagwood in the cockpit with me, I preferred my own navigation skills to the unknown talents of a new man.) By the time I'd finished my spiel, Paul was more than happy to agree on both counts.

It seemed a nice, sunny day and we got there without incident. The new plane was ready and waiting, and I ran it up and checked it. No problems. However, Paul seemed a little unhappy with something on the plane we had arrived in – maybe it was the way I'd flown it – so, impatiently, I suggested I take off and wait for him over the 'drome at two thousand feet. I could spend the waiting time putting the new plane through its paces. So I took off ahead of him, but as I started to climb I passed through a patch of misty cloud at about eight hundred feet that hadn't been there when we came in, and I idly wondered where it had suddenly come from.

At two thousand feet I levelled off and looked round. The thin cloud had suddenly thickened, forming a white layer below me so that I could see nothing of the ground beneath. Soon, it had turned into a solid white blanket from horizon to horizon. This was awkward, and so rather uneasily I decided I'd better call up Colerne Control to see how long my companion would be.

It was then I discovered that I had no radio in the plane, or at least not one that worked. Obviously, they hadn't got round to fitting one in yet. Normally, a plane was tuned to the base it operated from, but this had nothing, not even the Emergency Band, Channel C. I had taken off after getting a green light from the control caravan at the end of the runway without bothering to call the tower, and now I was totally cut off from communication with the ground. A small nagging doubt began to form in my mind. Why were they getting rid of it so quickly that they hadn't bothered to fit up the radio? – it must be a right stinker!

For a while I circled in this silent white world, hoping the other pilot would suddenly appear, like some airy-fairy godmother. I could not go back down blindly through the cloud, I didn't know how low the cloud base was by now, and as I hadn't checked the barometric pressure before take-off – and I should have – I had no way of knowing the true height of the ground. I didn't even know if I was still over the 'drome.

After a little thought trying to work things out logically, I reasoned that Norfolk was flatter than Wiltshire, and providing I kept clear of Ely Cathedral, the most prominent landmark on the way, there would be far less risk going down blindly through cloud at that end than this. So I decided to go back home on my own, hoping for a break in the cloud on the way. The question was, which way was home? I had no map, they were all with the navigator in the other plane. I had no watch to time myself, and without a navigator I did not know what course to set on my compass, anyway.

Of course, there was a standard procedure to follow in an emergency such as this – there was a standard procedure for almost everything in the RAF. You were supposed to keep going round in steady circles until the radar boys noticed, and sent someone up to lead you back down. The trouble was, I had a limited amount of fuel, because I hadn't expected to need a lot. And who could tell whether the duty radar man was actually watching the screen and not the legs of that pretty WAAF sitting next to him. Short of dropping a message in a bottle, it seemed that I was up the creek with the crocodiles, and minus one paddle.

It was then that I thought up Hot Breath Emergency Navigation. There was a small bad-weather panel to the side of the windscreen, a piece of glass set at an angle so that it always stayed clear, giving you a very limited emergency view should your main windscreen be blotted out by driving snow or rain. I breathed on this panel, making the glass mist up (though whether from water vapour or beer froth I wouldn't like to say). Then I drew a tiny outline picture of England with my finger in the condensation, with tiny dots where I guessed the two 'dromes to be. From this I guestimated the angle to be about forty-five degrees from North, plus, say, twelve degrees for variation – call it fifty-seven. I turned on to 057 on my compass.

But hang on – how far was it? I recalled reading that nowhere in England was further than sixty miles from the sea. Colerne was around the Bristol Channel and our base was near the Wash, on the opposite side – that would be at least twice sixty, call it a hundred and twenty miles. The Mosquito cruised at around 240 mph so that meant half an hour's flying time. But I had no watch and there was no clock in the plane – how to tell when the half-hour was up?

But I did have petrol gauges, and when cruising the two Merlins used around ninety gallons in half an hour. So if I flew on my chosen course until my fuel supply had gone down by ninety gallons, I shouldn't be too far out – should I? The cloud seemed as impenetrable as ever, with no breaks in it. I used up the allotted amount of fuel for my journey seeing absolutely nothing on the way. Now it was time to see whether my mental calculations were correct. I crossed my fingers and dived into the top of the white blanket, hoping to get through it at around eight hundred feet. Instead, I was still in thick cloud and it was getting darker the lower I went. I went down to six hundred. Still cloud, and I began to have visions of a stone devil suddenly appearing up through the cockpit floor to a loud clanging of bells as I spiked myself on Ely Cathedral's tower. Ah well, it would make a change from them usually appearing in a crash of lightning and a strong smell of fire and brimstone. Then, at five hundred feet, I broke through into clear air.

I was right over a small town set on a large bay that looked towards the north, and I had no difficulty in recognising King's Lynn and the inlet as the Wash. I was barely ten miles from home! With a sigh of relief I followed the local railway line back to camp, then flew low over the tower and waggled my wings to show I had no radio. I was invited to 'come on down' with the green flash of an Aldis lamp.

Barely five minutes after I had landed Paul and his navigator followed me in. He seemed surprised to see me sitting there in the crew-room. 'How the hell did you get back so quickly?' he demanded. 'We looked everywhere for you.'

I'd got away with it, but I'd broken almost every rule in the book, and the flight commander was within earshot.

'Oh – I took a short cut', I said.

So far as I know, no-one has ever tried to patent the Hot Breath Emergency Navigation System since then, but be warned. Should you be flying out on holiday to Tenerife or Majorca and the captain comes round, huffing on the windows and drawing little maps in the condensation, look for the nearest Emergency Exit and try to borrow a very large golfing umbrella. I can't see anybody getting away with it a second time. But it taught me a valuable lesson: always come back in the same aircraft you set out in.

A few years later an almost identical situation occurred. This time I was on another squadron and I was going – again – with a new pilot, Bob, and his navigator, from West Malling, in Kent, to Tangmere, on the south coast, to pick up another 'new' Mosquito aircraft. I flew them down there, but the aircraft wasn't quite ready. This time the weather was clear so I told the two of them to hang on for the new plane, because I was going back in the old one! Well, it was only a short hop, surely nothing could go wrong in that short distance. Could it?

I had only been back a couple of hours when they told me to go and fetch Bob and his mate back again. 'Oh, and you may be needed to give evidence to the court of inquiry!' they said.

What had happened was due almost entirely to the local set-up. At Tangmere they were in the habit of parking all the spare aircraft along one side of the perimeter track – the narrow strip of concrete you taxied along to reach the runway – with a row of buildings on the other side. It didn't leave much room, and the only way you could steer a Mosquito on the ground was by using the brakes – there wasn't enough air movement over the tail to make any effective turns with the rudder.

Bob had followed me out, bowling merrily along the track to take off, when he suddenly realised that his brakes weren't working. The only way he could keep the plane going straight in the restricted space was by racing first one engine and then the other. The trouble was that each engine burst also speeded up the plane, so that he was soon hurtling along this narrow corridor at a faster and faster rate of knots. Ahead of him he saw that the track turned sharply to the left, leaving the flying control tower looming ominously dead ahead in his path, and he realised with a sinking heart that he would never manage such a sharp bend at such a speed.

Suddenly, he spied a gap between two aircraft on his right, and he slammed his port engine fully open in a desperate attempt to turn his plane through it and onto the open airfield.

He almost made it, but his wingtip caught on one of the parked aircraft and turned him into it. The trouble was that it wasn't just any parked plane – there were one or two rather important differences about this particular one. It was an Anson, the old reliable, plywood and steel tube general runabout. But not just any old Anson. I gathered it was a specially tarted-up version, with all mod cons and special fittings. (It probably had things like seats that didn't give you piles, a control column shaped like a beer pump handle and a stainless steel pee-tube – little luxuries like that.) And it had been tarted up for some-one rather special – none other than the group's air vice-marshal. It was his pride and joy. Bob's whirling propellers did a workmanlike job, neatly reducing it all to a heap of expensive firewood and bent tubing in about ten seconds flat, with the merciless efficiency of a salami slicer.

The air vice-marshal wasn't at all happy about it – you could tell by the way he favoured holding the court of inquiry alongside the shredded remains of his beloved aircraft, with Bob neatly skewered to the top of the heap with the mangled pitot tube. Heads must roll because his aircraft wheels were no longer able to.

Of course, Bob should have checked the brakes before moving off, so it was put down as pilot error. (Everything was put down as pilot error where there was the slightest chance of blaming it on him. Possibly they hoped they might be able to offset the cost of any broken aircraft against a pilot's pension, whereas we fly-boys always maintained that the only error a pilot ever made was in not joining the Navy instead. There, they blamed all their bent planes on the boat going up and down, giving you the simple choice of dropping in from fifty feet or landing in the hangar without bothering to use the lift. Then they just pushed the bits overboard and asked for another one. That way, everyone was happy except the Chancellor of the Exchequer – and he was never happy, anyway.)

Bob landed up with a Severe Reprimand – a bit hard considering his rather skimpy training on Mossies. As a result he lost his confidence, and asked for a transfer to a less powerful aircraft. Preferably one made out of folded paper.

They also asked why, as the more experienced pilot, I hadn't flown the new aircraft back myself. I remembered my previous emergency, lost above the clouds, and I thought, 'Because I am more experienced, mate!' But I didn't say so. As I say, never volunteer. Especially a smart-arsed answer to a court of inquiry.

CHAPTER FIFTEEN

Shambles

Among the many perks handed out to wartime operational aircrew by a grateful Government was a minute petrol ration. Together with the other benefits we received, fresh eggs, chocolate ration, fresh milk, night-flying suppers, and a generous leave allowance of one week off in six, we must have seemed a right bunch of blue-eyed poofters to the rest of the people in uniform. Certainly we had to withstand the acid comments of the old sweats in the sergeants' mess about molly-coddled young boys.

Of course, today it seems little enough. But all those things were strictly on ration in wartime, and none so much as petrol. Tankers had to bring in every drop by sea – their crews risked a pretty grisly death from U-boats – and there was none at all for private motorists, whose cars were consequently laid up for the duration by the thousand.

Not that the authorities were exactly over-generous to us. They issued tables with the theoretical miles per gallon for each make of car, and you were allowed so many miles' travel per month, depending on how many operational trips you had flown, all calculated down to the last eggcup full. And you had to show your car logbook and licence before you got a drop. Of course, the squadron wide-boys bought both a car and a motorbike, then used the car's ration in the motorcycle, but few of us could afford such opulence.

My trouble was that although I had been flying for a couple of years in and over several countries, both friendly and unfriendly, I had never learned to drive. But I was tired of cycling everywhere – or rather cycling somewhere and walking back minus a bike chain – so that when the word went round the squadron that 'Jake' Jacobs was selling his car, I was more than interested. As a result of a little shrewd bargaining I shortly became, for the princely sum of twenty-eight pounds, the sole proprietor of a car named 'Shambles'. Incidentally, it didn't have that name when I acquired it, but got it shortly after the purchase when I asked a horny-handed garage mechanic to take a look at the vehicle.

'That's not a car,' he growled, after a contemptuous peek under the bonnet, 'that's a shambles . . .'

It was a 1933 Austin Seven, and looked like nothing so much as a large blue biscuit tin on wheels. (Come to think of it, it carried quite a few right little crackers in its time!) It ran on motorbike tyres, it had no self-starter or windscreen wiper, and it had lights that would have sent a nervous glow-worm scurrying to the nearest doctor. As the key was lost, I rewired it so that you switched it on by putting out the left indi-cator – it didn't actually have any indicators, so the switch wasn't doing anything else at the time. What it did have was a smart metal AA badge on the front. I did contemplate removing it, partly because I wasn't in the AA and partly to improve the mileage by cutting down the weight, but in those days AA men still saluted the badge and I rather enjoyed that. Well, mostly they did, in the case of Shambles they didn't so much salute as hold up both hands in surrender.

It didn't take long for the squadron comics to add their comments – just long enough for it to collect a layer of dust on its sides thick enough to write in. Soon, the body was labelled with the words, 'Chalky's chariot' and 'This way up – with care!' And it came into my possession exactly on time to make the trip to London for Dagwood's wedding.

Now it just so happened that Dagwood had inherited the post of Chief of the Chocolate Ration from another squadron member, Flying Officer Frank Clay ('Sticky' to his friends), and the job came in very handy for providing the nuptial nosh.

Along with all the other goodies ladled out to operational aircrew was a generous supply of chocolate bars. In wartime, chocolate was slightly harder to come by than gold-dust, and the bars were strictly doled out according to the number of flying hours undertaken by the squadron on operations. These goodies were stored in a strong locker, multi-padlocked against thieving fingers (not always successfully: it was not unknown for raiders to unscrew the back and help themselves), and possession of the keys rapidly raised Dagwood to the status of a minor Mafia mobster.

I have known the hint of a couple of extra chocolate bars in the back pocket to work miracles. You wanted the same week's leave as the flight commander? No problem, Dagwood – off you and Chalky go! In particular, the manager of our local NAAFI (known as the Never-'Ave-Any-Fags-In lot), through whose hands all this mouth-drooling bounty passed, was so closely checked up on that he could never manage to purloin so much as a single tiny bar of Cadbury's plain with which to curry favour with the local ladies. And without such a bribe how could a humble civilian like himself hope to compete with so many dashing blue-uniformed Brylcreem Boys? Accordingly, heavy hints were dropped that perhaps there was something –

anything – in the NAAFI Stores that might be profitably exchanged for a few samples of Mr Cadbury's or Mr Fry's noble art.

Which was the reason why the two of us set out for London and Dagwood's wedding in a tiny tin car stacked to the gunwales with all manner of highly unobtainable drink and confectionery, hidden beneath a pile of suitcases.

Our journey to the Big City would have done justice to a Charlie Chaplin epic. It was only the second time I had tried to drive a car of any kind, and the first time hadn't been too encouraging. I had bought Shambles the previous week and flown my first solo in her just once before, two nights previously – a mile-and-a-half trip to the local pub – so I was relying heavily on Dagwood's expertise. True, he didn't actually own a car, or a licence either, come to that, but someone in his family had driven one pre-war and told him all about it. This we considered adequate training for the journey. After all, we were a skilled night-fighter crew, and when the navigator said 'Turn left' you turned left and all was well. It seemed to work OK in a Mosquito, so surely it would work on the ground on a simple little thing like an Austin Seven. Wouldn't it?

All went well for the first half of our journey – apart, that is, from a couple of small incidents. Like the sunroof blowing off into a farmer's field. (It was a light wood frame with fabric stretched across it, and the wood had rotted at the corners. It seemed to be labouring under the delusion that it was the starboard wing of a Tiger Moth, and a breeze little heavier than a butterfly's belch was enough to send it sailing merrily skyward.) But the farmer seemed quite friendly and didn't mind a bit when we asked if we could get our car roof back from his field, though I did notice that he kept poking a finger in his ear as if he was not sure he'd heard correctly.

The second incident occurred soon afterwards, when we were unlucky enough to come to a level crossing. Not only that, it was a closed level crossing, a situation I had not come across before in my short driving career. And not only closed, but before it stood a police sergeant, standing by his bicycle, waiting patiently to go through. Now normally, Shambles' brakes would have thought about the situation a little, and then gradually slowed the vehicle to a halt in a reasonable distance. But we were not only heavily laden, we were running on (I confess it!) some high-powered 150 octane aircraft fuel, a liquid that carried a lot more oomph to the splash than your ordinary petrol. Almost too late, I jammed on the anchors, and watched in horror as we bore down on the police bike. It was lucky that Jake Jacobs hadn't painted the car before he sold it, or we would have hit him. As it was, the sergeant gave us a look that must have scratched the windscreen, moved his bike to safety, and without a word started to walk slowly to the back of our vehicle, giving it a close eyeball as he went.

I suddenly remembered the rear number-plate. Oh, we had one all right, no worry about that. It's just that it wasn't actually bolted to the car right then, we had lost the bolts. So at the last second I slapped the car into reverse and backed until the sergeant was level with the front seats once more.

'Is this the way to London?' I asked innocently. 'Yes', he snapped, biting the word in half, and resumed his walk to the rear. Still the train didn't come, so I swiftly repeated the manoeuvre, backing until he appeared once more in our side window and some frantic horn-blowing from the rear told me that we were within a gnat's spats of another vehicle. 'Is it far?' I enquired earnestly.

The sergeant was beginning to get annoyed. There was now no room for him to pass between Shambles and the car that had pulled up behind us. However, he kept his temper and gave it as his opinion that the distance would be a tad over twenty-five thousand miles if we persisted in going backwards like that, but he would much prefer it if we pulled forward instead.

At that moment a train rattled through and the gates swung open. I took him at his word, put my foot hard down and kept going. A few miles further on we stopped and hung the number-plate back on with some baling wire we found in the hedgerow and went blithely on our way. But the strain of the long journey was beginning to tell on me, and with the prospect of London traffic looming ever closer, we both agreed it was time that Dagwood took over. I think my trouble was that I kept trying to pull back on the steering-wheel and soar over the top of any vehicle that got in my way.

Some miles further on Dagwood noticed that a police car was following us, and while we were debating whether the level-crossing sergeant had phoned ahead, the cop car slid smoothly past and signalled us imperiously to pull in. There followed the usual barrage of questions that you get at such times. Is this your car, sir? No, conceded Dagwood, it's his – he pointed me out, and I tried hard to remember the newly acquired vehicle's number, without success. All right, then, said the patient copper, he'd settle for Dagwood's driving licence. I offered my own, pointing out that it was the same colour, but the constable thought his request was reasonable, seeing as my navigator was the one actually sitting at the wheel.

Dagwood did his best. He indicated the pile of luggage behind us. 'It's in the back,' he said, 'under that lot.' No doubt he hoped that the mammoth task of unloading and searching so many cases would put the constable off. No such luck.

'Better get started, then', he said affably.

I suddenly had a disturbing thought. Our very dodgy hoard of liquor for the wedding was about to be revealed, and awkward questions asked as to its origin, questions for which we had no legal answers. In desperation I added, 'So long as it doesn't make us late for the wedding, Constable.'

The copper gave me a quizzical look. 'So who's getting married?'

'He is. I'm the best man.' I decided not to bother him with minor details, like the fact that the wedding wasn't until the next day.

'All right,' he said, slowly, after some deep thought, 'I'm letting you go.' He looked hard at Dagwood. 'But fifty years from now you'll curse me for it.' He insisted I got back in the driving seat and sent us on our way.

We were now entering the outskirts of London, and even in wartime, London traffic was horrific to my untrained eye, but we struggled on.

'Straight across this next road junction!' advised Dagwood. Now as a trained night-fighter crew, when your navigator said 'Do this!' you did it, without hesitation.

The policeman on point duty leaped back to prevent me running over his boots, the oncoming bus jammed on frantic brakes, the taxi swerved onto the pavement, and I dodged between two traffic bollards onto the wrong side of the road. Dagwood refused to uncover his eyes until everything was far behind us. 'I meant when the copper waved you on!' he moaned. He should have said. Thankfully, everyone was too startled to take our number.

And then, in the middle of High Holborn, during the rush hour and in a raging torrent of vehicles, the engine finally died on us. What we didn't know until later was that the broken match had dropped out. Now for those not of a mechanical bent, let me explain. There was a hole in the engine manifold where you attached the suction tube that operated the windscreen wipers. That is, if you had windscreen wipers. Shambles didn't possess such luxuries, so it was necessary to block the hole with a broken match or the excess air meant that the mixture was too lean and the engine wouldn't slow run. Sorry to blind you with science. Of course, we didn't have a starter motor either, so Dagwood had to push-start the car while I desperately vroom-vroomed the engine, trying to keep it going, not realising the car was going as well. When I finally looked back I saw a tiny figure in the far distance in this ocean of traffic, belting along trying to catch me up, while angry car horns tooted furiously at him. When he finally made it, flopping back, exhausted, into the passenger seat, all he said was, 'It'll be nice to get back on operations.'

Still, in spite of everything, we made it to Dagwood's wedding. Which is more than the parson did. A covey of aircrew came down from the squadron for the ceremony, and we all sat there in the church, waiting for the ceremony to begin. After a long and fruitless pause and an organist rapidly getting repetitive strain injury fifty years before it had been invented, Dai Rees was sent in search of the missing prelate.

'Oh, is it today?' asked the Reverend in surprise, when finally run to earth in the local pub. Eventually he turned up with plimsolls peeping from under his surplice and an amiable smile on his face. After the service he chatted to me while the photos were being taken.

'So hard to get hold of suitable provisions for a wedding in wartime', he observed. For a moment I thought he was going to offer us a load of off-the-ration loaves and fishes that had fallen off the back of an altar, but he was referring to more liquid provisions. When I incautiously admitted that we hadn't done at all badly in that direction, he beamed and said he really must call in on the reception, just to jolly things along.

But I hadn't done the bootleg run from Norfolk for the benefit of our reverend friend. The word was quickly passed round: 'If you spot the God-botherer, hide the booze!'

After the service we went drive-about round the Hounslow pubs, treating each delighted tavern to a rousing impromptu concert of RAF songs. I carried a total of eleven people in – and on – Shambles, five inside, four on the roof, and two on the bonnet. It was Shambles' finest hour. Of course, with that load aboard, it would have been quicker to walk, but who cares! We only ran over one person on the way, and he was one of the gang – Arthur Briggs – so that didn't really count. Arthur fell off the starboard mudguard when I put the brakes on a bit too sharply, and passed under the front wheel. Not that anyone would have noticed, especially not Arthur, if his wife, Irene, hadn't mentioned it rather forcibly.

There was only one small worry when we eventually returned to duty. Flying is a jealous mistress, and unless you gave her your full attention at all times she was likely to turn vicious when you least expected it. More than once we had seen crews, where one or both members had become engaged or newly married, suddenly fail to return, or inexplicably crash. Whether their new status had taken the edge off their sharpness or otherwise distracted their attention we didn't know, but it had always seemed best to carry no spare baggage in the life that we led.

Would the jinx persist in our case? We were soon to find out.

Yet when things did start to go wrong it was mostly on my side of the job. We returned from leave to find that we had a new mark of Mosquito on the squadron. It had some alterations in the cockpit layout, but before we learned what they were we were sent off on operations. We climbed into the cockpit in the dark, and, as usual, I started up the engines by touch, and then pressed the button for the ultra-violet lighting to come on. Instead, the drop-tanks fell off. The CO wasn't at all pleased. They dragged the plane back out of the great puddle of petrol in which it was standing (why a spark from the engines didn't turn us into a couple of kebabs I'll never know!) and he gave us the choice. Either we go anyway, and in the next two minutes, or we face an inquiry. Put like that, we opted to go, on one of the longest trips we'd ever made, one where we needed all the fuel we could get. Over Lübeck, we got into a dogfight in the dark, and then, fearful of our rapidly dwindling engine juice, I broke off the action and dived into the top of a cumulonimbus cloud, which was a bit like taking a short cut through a tiger's cage to avoid a rottweiler. We were thrown around like a piece of paper in a whirlwind, and we got back with just about enough petrol to clean the stain off the back of my underpants.

But there was more to come. The pitot head was a metal tube with the open end facing forward, and the pressure of the air in it was used to show your forward speed, while the static pressure was used to operate what was basically a barometer to show your height. Both were vital to your staying in the air, and to discourage any bumble-bees from claiming squatter's rights and bringing up a family in the tube a cover was kept on it when you weren't flying. If you forgot to remove it before take-off you could be in big trouble. I had already done this once, but rather than suffer the em-barrassment of calling for someone to lead me in, I landed blind, relying on the feel of the aircraft to judge the speed and height. We got down all right, but it was risky and not calculated to do the nerves a lot of good. This second time, however, was different.

As we took off I suddenly noticed the wildly gyrating clocks and thought, 'Oh no! Not again!' I pointed out to Dagwood that according to the instruments we were travelling backward at high speed fifty feet below ground and he agreed that this was fairly unlikely. This time we did call for a lead-in plane and followed it in to land safely, only to find that someone had cross-connected the tubes and I was getting my speed on the altimeter and my height in miles per hour. Tricky.

There were a couple of other incidents. My automatic pitch control suddenly went crazy and one propeller raced out of control, threatening to get back home long before we did. Fortunately, we had been given a lecture on this only the week before, so I recognised the symptoms and cut the engine just in time, landing safely on the other one.

'I think someone up there is trying to tell us something', said Dagwood. 'Yes,' I said, 'and I think it's Goodbye.'

Then came Friday the thirteenth.

The war was slowly drawing to a close. The Allies had taken Brussels and were moving up to the Rhine, and Lancaster bombers were starting to sneak over in daylight under an umbrella of Spitfires. But there was still work to do at night. The rats were beginning to run. Nazi high-ups were slipping over to Norway in Heinkel bombers, tickets to South America in the top of their jackboots, seeking an escape route. Extra patrols were mounted along the north German coast to inter-cept them.

Strictly speaking, we had completed our tour of operations and were due for a rest, which meant us moving to an operational training unit, instructing new pilots on the superb but somewhat touchy Mosquito, or as ground instructors. But such postings to training schools were not always welcomed by the veteran crews. For one thing, it meant being split up as a crew, and Mossie crews in particular became closely bonded. Life on a front-line squadron was heady and exciting, a mixture of tense operations – which could sometimes amount to three nights in a row – mixed with squadron parties and dances, together with generous home leave. For months we had shared a room, a game of cards or snooker, and a pint. There were only two squadrons of Mosquitos on the 'drome, and you knew everyone. Nicknames abounded, and every crashed or missing aircraft meant the loss of friends.

So when the CO suggested we might just as well stay on the squadron now, we agreed. It was almost a fatal mistake.

Reporting to the crew-room on Friday 13th of April, we found ourselves one of eleven crews on operations that night. Chiefy West, the NCO in charge of aircraft maintenance, told us that our aircraft still needed some work, but would be ready soon. Our night-flying test passed without a problem – these days we went through the motions almost automatically.

At briefing the blue ribbon marking our route went straight as a die across the map to Kiel and Heligoland. It looked like a quiet and trouble-free trip – boring even. We called these trips 'beacon-bashing', as it involved circling German night-fighter assembly points, waiting, like Micawber, for something to turn up. These days not much did.

Our particular patrol was due to start just after dusk from Kiel, and we took off into the last light of a fine evening. The Mosquito's virtues never included crew comfort. The pilot and navigator sat side by side in narrow seats. (Talk about Deep Vein Thrombosis – we almost took it in turns to cough.) Our seat was the flat pack of the emergency dinghy – a collapsible rubber boat – on top of a tightly packed parachute. It also contained a metal gas cylinder for inflating the boat and a telescopic aluminium mast. Four hours on such a delightful cushion tended to encourage a rich crop of piles, and a tremendous urge to stand up, which was physically impossible. Our only relief was regular and skilful wriggling.

We crossed the Norfolk coast at Cromer, climbing to twenty thousand feet over the North Sea as the sky turned a deep blue in the nautical twilight, the last phase before complete darkness. Ten miles from the Dutch coast, just off the island of Texel, the German jamming cut in on the Gee navigation system, but we were expecting it. The little green blips on the clock face suddenly multiplied, rendering it useless, but it had been a useful check on the course and wind speed so far. We were on oxygen, but I liked to fly with my oxygen mask unhooked, as the rubber mask felt cold and clammy after a while and the gas leaking from the top of the mask blew into your eyes. Outside it was bitterly cold. Dagwood passed me a barley sugar to keep the face muscles moving, and then worked out our new course on the calculator strapped to his knee, while flicking over to the backward radar occasionally to check that no *Luftwaffe* dachshund was sniffing up our tail.

What caused the first feeling of unease I couldn't say – I just felt that something was wrong. I was checking the engine revs – often the first sign of trouble – when Dagwood suddenly said, 'I think the starboard engine's on fire.' I looked past him through the perspex canopy and saw in the darkness a long streamer of oily black smoke trailing back from the engine, and then a sudden flicker of flame from the exhaust shroud.

They say that fire at sea is every sailor's nightmare, but at least you are surrounded by oodles of the right stuff to put the flames out. We were brimful of petrol – with inner and outer wing tanks, belly tanks and an extra couple of hundred gallon drop-tanks hanging from the wingtips, we were carrying some seven hundred gallons of the stuff. The original Mosquito weighed in at fifteen thousand pounds, but our version was up to twenty-five thousand pounds, an increase of some seventy per cent, mostly made up of extra electronic equipment and fuel. It was like sitting on a bomb.

Whatever you do in flying you don't waste time doing it. First, we had to contain the fire. I reached across Dagwood and pressed the starboard Graviner fire extinguisher. There was no going back now, you couldn't restart the engine, and you could no longer use the outer fuel tank on that side. Nor could you use the drop-tanks any more, so they were quickly consigned to the North Sea, dropping away silently beneath us.

Then, because the milling propeller was acting like a brake, I feathered the blades on that side, turning them edge on to the airflow. It was unnerving to see the one propeller standing ramrod stiff and unmoving in the darkness, but the other hummed happily on. We watched the silent engine warily – you only got one go with the Graviner. But we were out of luck; there was a spurt of yellow flame along the engine panel and the black, oily smoke streamed out again.

There was only one thing to do. If you dived, at the same time slipping sideways with your control column over one way and your rudder hard the opposite way you had a chance of starving the fire of oxygen and blowing the flames out. Happily it worked, though we lost a lot of height doing it. I did a slow, flat turn (always into the live engine, never into the dead one!) until we were facing west, pointing back to England.

Now it was decision time. The nearest 'drome was Melsbroek, the newly liberated Brussels airport, but I didn't fancy landing at a strange 'drome at night on one engine, as it would be hellish difficult trying to go round again should anything go wrong. (Unknown to us, two others from the squadron had to land there that night, short of fuel.) There was an emergency runway at Manston, on the tip of Kent, but that involved a lot of time over enemy territory in a vulnerable condition. Instead, I opted to go back the way we'd come, risking a crossing over the North Sea on our single engine to get back to our own base. We'd been on radio silence from take-off. This was an emergency but there was no point calling from here at this height; the only ones to hear us would be the German Y-service, controlling the *Luftwaffe* night-fighters.

I gave it twenty minutes on Dagwood's hurriedly calculated new course, losing height steadily to maintain a reasonable speed without overheating the remaining engine, and then I called, keeping it short and simple.

'This is Driver Two Three. Are you receiving? Over.'

There was dead silence. It seemed as if we were the last people on the planet, going nowhere, and the others had switched off the lights before they'd left. I don't think I've ever felt so lonely. Another twenty minutes passed as our single prop beat a steady path through the black hole in the direction of home, and then we tried again.

'This is Driver Two Three. Are you receiving? Over.'

The surprisingly loud and clear voice of a controller came out of the darkness. 'Driver Two Three, this is Elflight. Receiving you loud and clear. Over.'

I kept the message short. Returning on one engine, fire in starboard one now seemed to be out. Request assistance.

'Roger, Two Three. Stand by to transmit for a fix.'

They needed a longer call for three stations to take a cross bearing on us. I dutifully obliged.

'Mary had a little lamb,' I intoned slowly, ' and a little bear; I've often seen her little lamb, but I'd sooner see her bare . . .' I finished enough of the verse for them to track us, and then waited.

'Stand by, Two Three', said a female voice, swallowing a giggle, and then, 'Two Three, steer two eight nine degrees.'

'What does she think we've been steering!' said Dagwood with a smug grin on his face. She'd repeated the course he'd given me forty minutes previously.

'Maybe I'd better ask for a doctor to meet us,' I told him, 'you're going to have trouble getting that helmet off.'

A few minutes later the controller came back on. 'Driver Two Three. Do not return to base. I repeat, do not return to base.'

'We come all this way,' I complained to Dagwood, 'and it's early closing!' But he had a different suggestion: 'Maybe they're afraid we'll crash on the NAAFI and destroy the beer stocks', he said. 'Then the country would be forced to surrender.' But we realised that we were being diverted to the big emergency 'drome at Woodbridge, in Suffolk, and we could guess why. Recently, the other squadron had started to go low level, dumping drop-tanks full of napalm on German barracks. One aircraft had managed to drop only one tank, the other had stubbornly refused to budge, and all the way back the pilot had frantically tried to shake it off, without success. However, as he touched down at base the tank had dropped off of its own accord and bounced along the runway beside him. He had hurriedly taken off again, leaving behind a sea of flame. All subsequent returning aircraft had had to be hastily diverted as far away as the south coast, on dangerously low fuel.

As we crossed the coast – even in the darkness you could make out the faint pale strip of the shoreline – they gave us a new course to steer. We didn't care, we'd made it to dry land. We always did our dinghy drill religiously, but there were few Mosquitoes that didn't break their plywood backs and sink like a stone when ditching in the water.

Below us, a searchlight suddenly shone out parallel to the ground, pointing the way south, followed by a string of others, a back-up system in case of radio failure, and soon we saw the unusual lighting system of Woodbridge coming up. Uniquely, out of all the 'dromes in the country, it copied the Continental Visual Lorenz system, a long row of lights with cross-bars at intervals. (Some months previously a German pilot had set his compass wrong, flown west instead of east, and landed there with all the latest radar, under the impression that he was near Berlin. The RAF said 'Thank you', but not loud enough for the *Luftwaffe* to hear. They thought that their man was at the bottom of the North Sea.)

Normally the 'drome was used for the battered US Eighth Air Force to creep into after their savage air battles or broken Lancasters from their terrifying night maulings. As a precaution I brought it in a little high and a little fast. Landing on such a vast runway with one engine there was no problem with overshooting, even with one wing still full of unusable fuel, and the superb facilities and organisation swung automatically into action. The blood-wagon and the fire engine were running alongside us while we were still rolling to a stop. It was a slack night for them, and they told us to leave everything in the cockpit, they'd see to it, though Dagwood took his precious charts with him.

They soon found the trouble: the flame-traps had burned out on the starboard engine, allowing the exhaust flames to set fire to our fuel lines. They fed us and put us to bed in clean white sheets, and we were tired and soon out to the world.

Next day the squadron sent along an Oxford to fly us back for debriefing. They seemed quite pleased to get their plane back, and they wrote a little note in the back of my logbook in green ink, saying as much (green ink was good, red ink was bad.) They even gave us a night off the following night. You couldn't ask for more. You wouldn't get it if you did.

* * *

There was a rather curious little postscript to all this, just a few years ago, when I was finally persuaded in my old age to apply for my campaign medals. They only sent four, instead of the expected five.

'No Defence Medal?' I asked.

'Oh, you don't get that', they said. 'You were on operations for too long. That's for people who spent their time doing other things, like instructing and training, and washing dishes.' And they were right. I was just short of the necessary length of home service when I went overseas, and I returned just that little bit too soon to count that instead. Then I went on operations, and stayed on them. Had we gone on our rest when we should have done, I would have got the medal and none of this would have happened!

'Ah,' they explained, apologetically, 'but you can add on any Home Guard service – that would count towards the medal – if you can prove you did any.'

I thought back to my time in the Home Guard, when we spent nights patrolling the grounds of Kingsway Mental Hospital with empty rifles, listening to the terrifying screams of the inmates. I don't know who the tortured souls were who were incarcerated in those grim buildings, but I know who should have been in there.

'Oh, forget it!' I said.

CHAPTER SIXTEEN

One of Our Aircrews is Missing

We knew him as Teg. He was a warrant officer pilot, transferred, with his navigator, to our squadron from one down south. He had the dark, curly looks of an Irish tinker, and he told outrageous – and mostly unprintable – tales of his amorous exploits with the ladies, spraying words at you like a well-oiled sub-machine-gun. Such as the one about his cavorting with a lady of the night in a darkened London park, the only repeatable bit of which was the ending, where she refused any payment, saying that she 'managed well enough on her old age pension, thank you, dearie'. The fact that we didn't really believe him didn't stop us laughing.

On the other hand, his navigator, Toby, had the slightly pained, supercilious air of someone who couldn't quite work out how he'd ended up among such riffraff.

Teg was soon a regular in the poker school, seeming to do quite nicely. Even though he didn't win all that many times, he never seemed to run out of money. It took us a little while to figure out how he did it.

Our favourite variant of poker was called baseball. You were each dealt two cards, face down, followed by four more, turned up for everyone to see, and then a final card, again face down. You made your best hand of five cards from the seven. As each round of cards was dealt out to everyone there was a spate of betting, varying on how good a hand seemed to be developing before your eyes. You settled to final rounds of betting as you tried to bluff the others that, say, the two kings showing on the table in front of you were backed up by a couple more hidden in your hand.

This could build up into quite a large kitty as you added to it with each round, even when playing in pennies, as we often did, and if you were temporarily short of the readies at some point you were allowed to 'drag' your contribution. That is, you took a coin out of the kitty and placed it in front of you, to show that you owed it that amount. At the end of the game you settled your debt by replacing the small pile of coins in front of you into the kitty, together with an equal amount that you begged or borrowed from the winner.

Teg had developed a technique, when he was 'dragging' a small pile of coins from the kitty, of suddenly starting to feed them back into the kitty again as if it was still his own stake money, under cover of his machine-gun chatter, He even 'dragged' the same coins out again, for a second time round!

After we made our displeasure known, his fortunes began to fade somewhat and he had to raise money in other ways to maintain his place in the poker school.

Did anybody want to buy a car? he asked.

Now, at this time (it was before my purchase of Shambles, my little Austin Seven) both Dagwood and I were interested in obtaining some sort of petrol-driven vehicle. However, we did point out one small point to Teg – we had never actually seen him with a car.

Well, no, he said, he didn't have it with him, he'd had to leave it back at his old 'drome, near Basingstoke in Hampshire, stored in a farmer's barn. It was a beautiful little car, a Vauxhall. There was petrol in the tank and the engine would leap into life at the first touch. He was asking a paltry thirty quid for it, as he was a bit short, but we would have to collect it ourselves. We had a better idea. We suggested he go and fetch it and then we'd talk business, but he said ah – there was this slight problem. A young lady down there just happened to be crazy about him. Whereas her husband wasn't crazy about him at all, he was just plain mad with him. In the circumstances, he'd rather not go back down there right now. But his navigator, Toby, knew where the car was stored and would be happy to go with us. We could scrounge a flight down there and drive the car back the same day before anyone knew we had gone.

The trouble was, you were never quite sure whether you were going to be on operations that night or not. The planners up at Bomber Command were apt to change their minds about how many aircraft were going to be needed on any one night. Unlike the Army generals, Bomber Harris had to commit a large part of his entire front-line bomber strike force almost every night, against a determined and well-prepared enemy. So different orders would filter down to the groups throughout the day as conditions changed.

Times would be put back, the number of aircraft could be increased, or a thousand-bomber Armageddon reduced to a small nuisance raid. This was partly in response to the latest intelligence, but a lot more was dependent on the weather. Would they be able to find the target if they went, and would they be able to find their own base when they got back again? So you could never be quite sure whether you would be needed or not, so opportunities to slip away were scarce, and the practice strongly discouraged. However, a few days later, one did occur. The weather forecast over Europe was grim for that night, with the cloud as thick as treacle. A proposed raid on Düsseldorf was put off, and anyway we'd flown the previous night, so we were fairly low down the stand-by list.

Furthermore, the wing commander would be away – he was flying down to Kent with a couple of others to attend the funeral of a squadron pilot who had been killed on an exercise with a Lancaster bomber near Newark. Just to clinch the matter, our squadron's light aircraft, the Oxford (the old Oxbox) was going down to Tangmere, and the pilot would be happy to drop us off on the way. It was barely mid-morning: we could be there and back by late afternoon and no-one the wiser.

Everything seemed to be falling into place. But just in case, we persuaded Teg to do our night-flying test if we were called on and we were late back. Then Dagwood, Toby and I hopped into the Oxbox just as we were, without flying gear or parachute.

The flight down was smooth enough, a short walk took us to the farm where the car was stored, and we quickly located the farmer. However, he seemed a little vague about things. You left a car here, you say? When was that, then? You don't mean that thing in the barn? We began to feel a little uneasy. 'That thing in the barn' wasn't the most comforting of phrases.

We found the barn, and in it, under a thick layer of hens and hay, we found the car. It was not a pretty sight. For a start the battery was as flat as a whore's pillow, and the four tyres were suffering from acute deflation. As for the bodywork, the only thing holding the dust to the rust was the chicken manure. Of the alleged petrol there was no sign, even the rag stuffed in the filler tube in place of a cap was dry.

Anxiously, we sorted out the starting handle and inserted it. It was as solid as a rock. We kicked it, we stood on it, we jumped on it, we swore at it – all to no avail. The only way we were going to turn that engine over was by tipping the car on its roof.

Finally, exhausted, we sat on the running board (they had them in those days) and thought things over. Time was getting on, and we had to get back to Norfolk before we were missed. We would have to abandon the car and resort to hitch-hiking back to base, and from long experience we knew that if you tried going across country on minor roads you might never be heard from again. The best way to go was via London.

By then, after messing around with the car, we must have looked a pretty grotty sight, because the only thing that would stop for us on the London road was an ancient flat-topped lorry. It appeared to have recently carried some very worried cattle judging by what was caked on the floor, and we soon found what had made them so worried. We had to cling desperately to any projection to stop us sliding off as the would-be Stirling Moss at the wheel bounced his way up to 'the Smoke'.

He dropped us in the suburbs on wobbly legs, to make our way by tube to the centre of the city. By now we had missed the last train to Norfolk that would connect to the Fakenham Flyer – the superannuated single-line puffer that wandered vaguely round the shire trying to remember where it was supposed to be going, like some old uncle with Altzheimer's. We weren't supposed to be out of camp at all without a leave pass or a movement order, and we had neither. Certainly we didn't fancy being discovered dossing down for the night on King's Lynn railway station by the service police who haunted the place.

So we'd have to stay overnight in London. We carefully pooled what little money we had, and it was just enough for the cheapest double room at the Strand Palace hotel. The clerk booked Dagwood and me in reluctantly – we had no hint of any luggage – and then looked enquiringly at Toby.

'He's not with us', we said.

We let him in later through a toilet window and dodged our way up to the room, where we rang the sergeants' mess at camp. The news wasn't good. There was a bit of a flap on, a wandering Mosquito had found a hole in the cumulonimbus that looked as if it might drift over the target during the night, with cloud cover all the way there and back for the bombers, so the Düsseldorf raid was back on. The wing commander had hurried back from the funeral and they were trying to round up eight crews for the night's work. Our names had been mentioned.

But there was nothing we could do about it, so we pushed the two single beds together and flipped a coin to see who was going to sleep on the join. Toby lost and complained bitterly, possibly because most of the money for the room and all the money for the coin-flip was his, but we pointed out that most of the fault was his, too, or at least his pilot's. Anyway, we were probably all going to be shot for desertion when we got back, so to stop moaning.

At intervals during the night the two beds rolled slowly apart and Toby would crash to the floor between them. In the end he gave up and stayed down there, still complaining loudly. Somehow, we got the impression that the thought of a court martial and solitary confinement for several years in a cosy prison bed was beginning to sound attractive.

Next morning, Dagwood and I went down to breakfast – we hadn't eaten for almost twenty-four hours – and took it in turns to consume as much as we could before going to the toilet, where Toby was hiding. He then swapped places with us and went back and finished what was left. Nobody seemed to notice.

We did much better getting back to camp. This was because we came across a WAAF on the edge of London, who was trying to hitch her way to Great Massingham, the next 'drome to ours. We three hid in the bushes while she smiled sweetly at the passing traffic, then when a leering rep. in a company car screeched to a halt, we all dashed out and climbed aboard before he could protest. He spent the journey muttering darkly into his toothbrush moustache.

Once at the 'drome, scruffy and unshaven as we were, we decided to go in through 'the hole in the hedge' – every 'drome had one. We would go straight down to the crew-room and pretend we'd been there all the time. It was a pretty forlorn hope, but we couldn't think of anything better. But we needn't have worried. To our surprise, the place was pretty well deserted.

We found Teg chatting up some WAAF driver round the back of the flights, and asked where everybody was. Oh, you won't see the officers yet, he told us. What with flying on ops last night, and the party afterwards, they wouldn't surface for a while yet.

A party after an op? That sounded a little unusual – how come?

100 Group was first set up at the end of 1943 in an attempt to cut the savage bomber losses (ninety-seven downed in a single night's massacre over Nuremberg, each with a large crew), and its work had necessarily been kept highly secret. We were a combination of heavy bombers and long-range night-fighters. The bombers were mostly Halifaxes and Liberators, crammed with radio gear, that blasted out an electronic screen of interference across the North Sea to cover the approaching bomber stream, while the Mosquito squadrons – low-level night intruders that haunted the enemy night-fighter bases, shooting at anything that moved, bomber escorts patrolling the flanks of the bomber stream, like sheep-dogs, and Free Rangers, fitted with the latest Yankee radar – scoured the night sky like pirates looking for plunder.

The result was remarkably effective. As the enemy night-fighter losses mounted, so-called 'Moskitopanik' set in among the Luftwaffe crews, sending their morale plummeting. It was decided to increase the effect by publicising the work of the new group on the BBC.

So the previous night a group of radio reporters (would it be termed a wave band?), headed by the redoubtable Richard Dimbleby, had turned up at our base, ready and eager to reveal all, or at least their tarted-up version of all, to the world. The CO hurried back, and the raid on Düsseldorf was reinstated, almost as a show-piece of our work.

The prospect of being associated, in however small a way, with a BBC broadcast had drawn a rash of volunteers, like wasps to a jam-pot. We weren't even missed.

Afterwards, the Squadron Diary recorded the event thus:

> . . . a party of journalists arrived on a goodwill visit towards sundown, headed by Richard Dimbleby. The party spent the evening observing the working of an operational station, dining in the officers' mess with the station commander, enjoying the inevitable noggin or two in the bar, and finally getting red-hot stories from the crews returning from the Düsseldorf raid. Unfortunately no one came back on one wing or with no engines, but the precise efficiency of flying control, the unfailing accuracy of incoming aircraft and the unassuming attitude of crews were all inevitably transmuted into

something gay and glamorous under the eager enthusiasm of those who trade in superlatives . . .'

'So where's the car?' Teg asked us, 'I thought you were going to bring it back with you.'

We kept our tempers, until we could find something hard to hit him with. 'We couldn't get it going', we told him.

'I knew I should have gone down myself,' he said, disgustedly, 'I'd have got it started at the first touch.'

CHAPTER SEVENTEEN

None But the Brave

Late in 1944, when the bombers weren't doing much, we tried out a new idea, called the 'Net'. A group of Mosquitoes flew over Germany at night in line astern, and fifteen minutes apart (at least you assumed you were in line astern, you never actually saw the others). A second line flew on the same course but on the other side of Germany. Then, at an agreed moment on our co-ordinated watches, we turned inwards and flew towards each other. In theory we should have trapped everything in the German night sky between us, and any plane fleeing from one line would run slap into the other. It was a wildly hopeful, rather daft idea, so far as I know producing nothing more than a glorious mixup when the two lines met in the middle of the Reich. The trouble was that the era of free-ranging Mosquitoes was almost over. They had been free to wander where they liked, looking for 'trade', like blood-thirsty cut-throats roaming the high skies in search of booty. It had resulted in the ruthless destruction of the *Luftwaffe*'s night-fighter force, and there were now too few victims left.

We ourselves had been intercepted by one such free-ranger a few weeks before. We were trying a low-level intruder trip, cruising at random, looking for things to shoot at – the tell-tale white smoke-plume that gave away the position of a train (sometimes with a hidden sting of flak-guns aboard) or an incautious light from a car speeding along the road. We had gone in low over the North Sea – a few hundred feet in the dark – climbing up to seven or eight hundred just before reaching the enemy coast. Then we dived fast over the shoreline where the flak guns were waiting, and in over the flat Dutch fields and away in the darkness before they could pick us up. We usually went in at Ijmuiden; it was reputed to be swampy ground that couldn't support the heavier guns. Although we maintained strict radio silence, everyone listened out on Channel C, the Universal Channel; and for good reason.

It was late at night, Christmas was coming up and maybe we weren't keeping quite as sharp an electronic eye open as we should have. Suddenly, a Scottish burr in our earphones snapped out a challenge, 'Bogey, bogey! Turn starboard!' 'Bogey' meant unidentified aircraft, and this was a warning call. A free-ranger was behind an unknown aircraft close by and making a final check before opening fire. Aircraft hearing this would immediately turn sharp right, showing that it was British.

A couple of dozen planes must have hurriedly, and simultaneously, turned right in response to the challenge. So how did we know that it was us he was behind?

Because, momentarily surprised, I turned left.

Our earphones crackled with Caledonian indignation: 'I said "Starboard", you prat!'

'Sorry!' I hurriedly turned in the opposite direction.

'Okay!' he called, 'Happy Christmas!' and went on his way. Or presumably he did – we saw nothing from start to finish.

Only Christmas wasn't all that happy. We got back to find a dozen Lancasters had been diverted to our base due to fog – eighty-four thirsty aircrew, unexpected and uninvited, ready to drink the mess bars dry.

But to our flight commanders any easing up on commitments was a golden opportunity to catch up on their list of 'Things To Do Before The War Ends'. This included sending crews on courses. Our gallant leaders were continually pestered by Group to fill squadron quotas on different training stints. It was a case of 'Never mind the war, send someone on to so-and-so course at once, you've got a quota to fill.'

So I was chosen to go on a night-vision course.

You might have thought that as I'd already done thirty operations at night over Germany, it was a little late to start worrying about things like that. After all, on night-fighting, you not only had to locate a small plane in an empty wilderness of night sky, but also confirm its type and origin – in fact, almost everything but the pilot's nickname – before you could dispatch its crew to an early hell, so a little instruction on how to see things clearly at night might have been more useful rather earlier on in life.

Because, despite all the special equipment we carried – the forward-and backward-searching radar, the Serrate that homed in on German sets, the Perfectos unit that picked up their identification signals, the infra-red scope that showed the exhaust heat from their engines – that vital final check still had to be made with the Mark I British Eyeball. But although Dagwood had done some basic training at Harrogate, there had never been time to send me on such a course before. Now the war was almost over there was all the time in the world.

A little extra impetus had been given to the idea of such training by a recent incident involving Jamie. He and his navigator, the dour Geordie, Tom, had come up behind an aircraft over Belgium one night and couldn't agree on what it was. Orders were strict, no opening fire without positive identification. So for long minutes they hung in the sky below their quarry, arguing whether it was an enemy or friendly. It turned out to be neither. It was a very unfriendly Martin Maryland of the 'Yewnited' States Army Air Corps, and its rear gunner eventually put down his comic book and coke long enough to spot them there and send over a personal greeting of a few hundred rounds of Browning point five ammunition.

The Yanks had few qualms about opening fire; they tended to shoot first and apologise afterwards, usually for missing. But this would-be Wyatt Earp didn't miss. He wrote his name in classic gunslinger style along the side of the Mosquito, and our two intrepid birdmen returned with a few more bullets in their aircraft than they started out with.

Group wasn't happy. Not surprisingly it wanted to know why the squadron quota on the night-vision course persistently remained unfilled when its pilots obviously couldn't tell the difference between a friendly (?) ally from a witch on a Mark VI broomstick. So they plugged up the holes in the Mossie and hastily dispatched me to the eyeball-polishing school.

Why me and not Jamie? I admit it, for once I volunteered! The course was on a 'drome within easy reach of home, being near a small mining town in the Nottinghamshire Coalfield. No beauty spot, but a place full of warm pubs, strong ale and friendly people. And being an official duty run, I wangled a gallon or two of extra fuel coupons for Shambles and tacked a few days' home leave on the end of the course.

On the way there, just outside King's Lynn, I gave a lift to a young Army private thumbing his way home to Doncaster. He was a bright lad, frustrated in his attempts to join the RAF, and an avid listener to my tales of flying and operations. However, during a pause for breath in my line-shooting patter he suddenly asked, 'But aren't you ever frightened?'

His question caught me rather by surprise, though I don't know why it should. I suppose I hadn't really thought about it. Fear is a bit like booze, a small amount could sharpen your awareness and your reactions wonderfully, whereas large amounts could destroy you.

But then there's fear, and there's fear. Like, there's 'Ooer!', and there's 'AAAAAAARRRGH!'

Everyone felt a certain amount of trepidation at times, as when you flew your first solo and you desperately tried to remember which bit to wiggle to make some other bit waggle before you got stuck up in the clouds for ever. And later on there was always the odd moment in your life when you felt like standing up in briefing and saying, 'Look, mate, we realise this raid could shorten the war by a good three minutes fifty-five seconds, and guarantee you a second bar to your VC, but the weather forecast for tonight is ten-tenths solid cumulonimbus from three inches above my left boot all the way up to thirty thousand feet, which is considerably more than an airborne eagle's anus. It's been steadily raining brass stair-rods for a month now – Noah's lads have been on overtime since the Second Sunday in Advent – and the ground crew are using guide dogs to try and locate the aircraft. So what say we settle for half a jar down at the Red Lion instead of having our arses shot off over Düsseldorf?'

As I say, you sometimes felt like saying it, but of course you never did – if only because the CO would have used your guts as a slingshot to launch his aircraft into the night for calling him 'Mate'. So instead, you just went ahead, and did what you had to.

I suppose what the Army lad was really asking was, had I had any moments of sheer trouser-staining terror, with an acute attack of the screaming lurgies and a hysterical refusal ever again to step onto anything higher than a well-worn carpet.

And the answer to that was . . . no.

There was no deathless heroism involved on my part. It's just that things happened so fast in flying. With a hundred and one controls, instruments, switches and levers to constantly monitor and adjust, there was just so much to do to get us into the air and stay there that somehow I never got round to feeling afraid. (I remember once noticing with some surprise an odd sound in my earphones during take-off. It turned out to be my own heavy breathing, gradually increasing as we picked up speed. In my intense concentration I'd never noticed it before!)

So you learned to look ahead for trouble and made sure you knew what to do if it came. You took the right decisions and you took them fast. Because if you didn't you were dead, it was as simple as that. Anything beyond that was out of your hands, you were at the mercy of an unpredictable – either malevolent or benign – Fate, and as you could do precisely seven-eighths of sweet sod all about that, there was no point in worrying.

There were cowards in aircrew, of course, in spite of the official line to the contrary. The RAF simply gave it another name, calling it LMF, or 'Lack of Moral Fibre'. Swift action was taken to isolate and remove a highly infectious condition, and anyone suspected of approaching the limit of their courage was moved, often, in the case of NCOs, to lowly and degrading ground jobs. (One specific unit for such people was at Leysdown, a pre-war holiday camp on the Isle of Sheppey.)

It was hardly surprising that some cracked. Lads of seventeen went straight from school and were pushed to the limit through intensive training in a highly skilled trade in a strange dimension. They moved halfway round the world, from RAF camp to troopship, from desert sun to freezing darkness. They learned bewildering skills in ever faster and more complex aircraft, and they struggled to survive training where the Fickle Finger of Fate picked off the stragglers – the incompetent, the unwary and the unlucky.

The RAF had barely two years to train them before they were thrown headlong into the bloody cockpit of war – in Bomber Command's case repeated night after night, with their chance of ultimate survival about one in two. In our case to be turned into trained killers, (which is what we were), able to fight a skilled enemy over a hostile continent in pitch-black darkness.

Yet everyone in aircrew was a volunteer – nobody was forced to be there. What kept most people going was pride and fear. Pride in what they had achieved, and fear of their mates' contempt should they fail, with the shame of being declared LMF.

I can recall only one out-and-out coward. I remember the white face spouting pathetic protestations that he suffered blinding headaches when he flew. But they began only after he completed his training and went on his first operation. The Doc didn't believe him and neither did anyone else.

There were lesser degrees of fear, of course, and they showed in small ways. Like the incredulous gasp of horror of a new pilot when faced with a seemingly solid wall of flak on his first low-level intruder trip at night. 'They don't expect us to go through that, do they!' Yes, they did, his more hardened navigator assured him, matter-of-factly.

Or the sudden rush to the bar or the bus when operations were cancelled, to ensure, should flying be reinstated, that they were long gone, either to town or in their cups. But this was done in rather shame-faced bravado by an embarrassed few.

But there were those who kept up a careful pretence. Like one particular crew on the squadron, whose actions drew deeper and deeper frowns of disapproval from the others.

The pilot had a keen eye for the ladies on the camp, who dubbed him 'the Timberwolf'. He probably thought the name rather dashing, with echoes of a lean, lone killer stalking the German night skies. Perhaps it's as well he didn't know that, privately, the girls added, 'Timber from the neck up, wolf from the waist down.'

His navigator was known by the sardonic nickname of 'Fearless Fred', and collectively the pair were more usually referred to simply as Timber and Fearless.

They confidently assumed the air and talked the lingo of 'Wizard prang, old boy!' and 'Jolly good show, chaps!', but it was noticed that they seemed to find many more faults in their aircraft during their night-flying tests than other crews, rather nebulous faults that were hard to trace. And when they did finally set out on their way to war, as often as not they would return early with a problem so minor that it occasioned increasingly funny looks from their companions.

For instance, we used the system known as 'Gee' (the name stood for Graph Navigation.) to find our position on the first and final legs of our trips. It consisted of three transmitting stations, situated on a base line approximately two hundred miles long and labelled A, B and C.

Station A was known as the 'master' station. It originated a wireless signal and at the same time sent it by landline to B and C, the so-called 'slave' stations, who retransmitted it.

The difference in the time taken by the three transmissions to be received by the aircraft were displayed as two scales on a cathode-ray tube behind the pilot's seat. The AB and the AC line values could then be checked against a specially marked chart showing these readings as distances in curved lines from the transmitters. You could locate your position fairly accurately from where the two lines crossed (depending on the angle of the crossing). The system was very useful until the Germans unsportingly jammed it by transmitting false readings on the same wavelength. Fortunately the jamming was effective only up to about ten miles off the coast of the Continent. So at least it helped you on your way and checked your windspeed, and it proved invaluable for re-establishing your position on your way home.

Timber and Fearless would return early, for instance, well before reaching the sound of gunfire, with the complaint that over the North Sea 'they had received a rather faint C signal on the Gee set and thought it best to turn back'. The rest of us were more than happy to get any kind of a C signal at all.

In the end the CO had a quiet word with them, and the word was somewhat stronger than their erstwhile C signal.

Timber, for some reason, chose to reveal this fact to me in the hushed and horrified tones of a curate who had caught a choirboy peeing in the Sacramental Cup.

'You won't believe this, Chalky,' he declared, indignantly 'but he as good as hinted at cowardice on our part . . .'

I believed it.

The Night Vision School was a pleasant enough place. Set in a corner of an old airfield, it shared the 'drome with an aimless mob of Commonwealth aircrew, half trained and too late to go anywhere. There was no flying taking place there, it was simply somewhere to keep them until the war ended.

My fellow night visioneers on the course were a goodly bunch, drawn from different commands and doing quite varied jobs, though all of them were on operations of some kind. It wasn't long before my little car, Shambles, with its newly won petrol ration, was in popular demand as a free taxi service for a small gang wishing to sample the delights of the local town after school was over for the day.

Normally, when you moved to a new place, the friends you had made simply moved out of your life for good – you never came across them again (not all that unlike your fellow aircrew failing to return from operations) – but in this case I had met one of them before.

He was known as Yorky, nicknamed for his frequently boasted-about home county (he actually came from near Dewsbury, but you couldn't have a nickname of 'Dewsbury', now, could you!) and he had been with me during training at Slaughter Hall. He had gone on to fly the Mark X Beaufighter – the TFX version – on anti-shipping strikes along the coast of the Continent – a fairly fearsome trade.

He came up to say hello while I was unpacking my gear from Shambles, and he gave my little car a quick eye-ball as he approached – he hadn't seen it before.

'Great little passion-wagon you have there!' he observed, approvingly. 'That'll come in reet handy.'

I remembered him of old. He had the Yorkshireman's sublime confidence in the superiority of everything that lay within the boundaries of England's largest county, and an equal though amiable contempt for everything that didn't. Women he didn't rate highly, not even those who knew one end of a cricket ball from the other, but he thought them an excellent invention, and for some reason they seemed to find his amiable arrogance attractive.

Yorkshiremen were never famous for their sublety or finesse in the Seduction Stakes – it was said that their idea of foreplay consisted of taking their flat hats off before getting into bed – and Yorky was a fully paid-up member of the 'Jump-em and Dump-em' school. Yet he enjoyed considerable success, and his transparent and cheerful honesty about his motives left most of his victims more rueful than wrathful.

He seemed totally without nerves, and, like Mac, another Shambles regular on our sorties into the Nottinghamshire bundoo, displayed lip-curling scorn for anyone showing the slightest weakness. Mac was a rather peppery-tempered pilot from a home defence night-fighter squadron. The fourth member of the Shambles Dragoons (you couldn't waste precious petrol taking less than the little car could hold) was Stan, a rather quiet sergeant navigator stationed down at Tempsford. He was the only married one out of the four of us.

Our days were spent in lectures, exercises and tests to try and help us to see better at night. And because the idea was for us to pass on our acquired knowledge to the rest of our squadrons we had to learn how to give a lecture to the small group. So we each took it in turn to give a little talk on the work that we did, and our efforts were then critically assessed by our instructors.

Stan was the first up, telling us about Tempsford. They carried out delivery and collection of agents and supplies to the Resistance in occupied France, and for this they used two types of aircraft. One was the angular-looking Lysander, a peculiar plane capable of landing on little more than a flattened French stick alongside a row of matches at midnight. Desperately dangerous – the pilot never switched off his engine – this was more often used to snatch returning agents back to Britain. It was easier to deliver men and equipment by parachute from a 'Halibag' – the Halifax bomber.

That was Stan's job. After navigating the plane to the right patch of garlic-scented darkness, confirmed by last-minute flickering signals from the ground, he went back to supervise the drop from the open hatch. It was not always an easy task. On their last trip the pale young French agent and would-be patriot they were delivering had apparently realised the enormity of his undertaking at the last moment and hesitated, looking down on the raging gale blowing through the dark hole at his feet.

'Hasn't the silly bugger gone yet?' demanded the pilot irritably over the intercom.

'Not yet. He's standing here shouting '*Vive La France*' to get his courage up.'

'Well tell him to *Vive La* bloody *France* on his way down. I've got to *Vive* this flaming Halibag back to base before the Jerry night-fighters come sniffing round.'

'So we gave him a helping hand,' said Stan, simply. 'or rather a helping boot.'

Whether that young Frenchman, falling involuntarily through the night air, survived I don't know, but if he did he had learned a salutary lesson. The time to chicken out is before you leave the chicken run, not after you've got airborne with the eagles.

Yorky's talk, a day or two later, was fairly brief and to the point on the subject of attacks on coastal shipping. Basically, it amounted to 'There's nowt to it. Just stick your nose down wi' your engines flat out, your thumb tight ont' trigger so they don't shoot back and keep your eyes skinned for t' one nineties. And don't be t' last man in a fiord, 'cos there's nobody following you to keep their 'eads down and there's nowhere to turn outa trouble.'

But it was Mac's dissertation that interested me, or at least the last bit of it. He talked about night patrols along the east coast, under the guidance of a ground controller, intercepting and identifying returning aircraft in case a German intruder tied to slip in under cover of the returning bomber stream. And he mentioned how he had recently come across a Mosquito, flying low over the North Sea, below the level of the home radar coverage.

Mac's radar was the latest version, the American Mark X, and he was able to follow the aircraft at very low level without it apparently being aware of his presence. He hung under its tail, following as it aimlessly circled, until he was convinced it was harmless. Then he left it there, without mentioning the incident to his controller.

A few days later he came across the aircraft again. At least, it was in the same place, circling in the same slow manner, so he presumed it was the same aircraft. By now, the dark suspicion was forming in his mind that its crew was sitting out the war, when they were supposed to be operational over Germany, by circling safely, low over the North Sea, until their time was up.

'You should've shot the booger down', said Yorky, calmly. 'I would have. Say it were a Ju 88 – who's going to know t' difference when it's at t' bottom of the North Sea!'

'Dinna worry,' vowed Mac darkly, 'next time I catch that skiving basket ah swear ah'm going tae do just that. Ah canna stand cowards!'

The instructor hurriedly changed the subject, but my thoughts immediately turned to Timber and Fearless. Were they the culprits? And was Mac serious in his threat? If so, should I give them some sort of veiled warning – and how, for God's sake?

The trouble was, there was no way of checking where we had been, we were entirely on our own. When a bomber dropped its ten-ton death tin or its load of fire-balls on a target an automatic flash photo was taken of the view below the aircraft. Anyone returning with the claim that they had smashed the heart out of downtown Cologne when their camera showed two broken deck chairs on a deserted beach that looked suspiciously like Skegness out of season (one wonders how they could tell the difference) had to repeat the operation *ad nauseam* until their picture corresponded with their story.

With us, no such check was possible, providing the right amount of fuel had been used and the story sounded feasible. That circling plane could have been anyone.

What was funny about our talks, though, was how each of the four of us thought we had the easiest job in operational flying.

Around midweek, we decided to try out the local dance hall. It was Yorky's idea: possibly he wanted to try scoring with something other than a piece of chalk on a dart-board. The rest of us were willing enough – I was no Fred Astaire, but thanks to my youthful apprenticeship over the printworks I wasn't exactly Freddy Starr, either.

There was an Army camp nearby, so the town was full of Brown Jobs, and a goodly bunch of them were already stomping round the dance floor – Army boots were not the most elegant of dance pumps – meaning that we were considerably outnumbered.

I was in the bar with Mac, trying to pump him further on the subject of errant Mosquitoes, when a young ramrod of an Army sergeant major broke sharply in on our conversation.

Would I calm my men down before everyone was thrown out?

My men? Then I realised that my warrant officer's badge made me the senior RAF man in the place. Ramrod explained that there was some sort of fracas building up between the Army types and the RAF lads, and unless he and I stopped it in its tracks we would all suffer by being banned from the place. I tried explaining that my rank was mainly an authority to let me fly a plane, and my experience of yelling orders at stroppy underlings was woefully inadequate, but his curled lip of contempt at what he considered my cowardice persuaded me to take a stab at it.

Out on the dance floor we found that Yorky and Stan had cut in on the dancing partners of two Army types in an 'excuse me' dance and refused to release them when tagged in their turn. It seemed that the two young ladies – they were friends and both wore wedding rings – preferred the occasional graze from RAF shoes to steady toe mangling by Army boots. We quickly retreated from the battlefield to the bar, leaving Ramrod to quell his rebellious and glowering troops.

The two relieved girls joined us for drinks. Beth was the more talkative and outgoing – her friend, Maisie, was quieter with a sort of calm wide-eyed innocence – and they had ventured warily out for the night to relieve the otherwise monotonous existence of a 'khaki widow' with a husband abroad.

At intervals we sallied out onto the dance floor, without incident, though there remained an undercurrent of hostility in the hall, and at the end of the night Yorky persuaded me to give the still nervous girls a lift home. Shambles resembled a tightly packed sardine tin as its little engine bravely laboured its way to the outskirts of town to a chorus of muffled giggles from the back.

They seemed to take an age saying goodnight, while I waited impatiently at the wheel. Without the benefit of a working petrol gauge my only way to assess Shambles' fuel state was with a thin wooden stick that I carried. We were running so short that the dipstick probably soaked up more than it left behind each time we took a reading, and I was worried.

Disaster struck on the way back. Two miles short of camp the little engine gave a sad little splutter and died of thirst. We pushed it into a corner of a nearby (and closed for the night) garage and walked the rest of the way. There was no key to lock Shambles, but confident that my highly eccentric wiring system (you will recall that you had to put out the non-existent left indicator to switch on the engine) rendered the little car impossible to steal, I didn't bother to remove the rotor arm.

My confidence was fully justified next morning when I returned with some of my rapidly dwindling petrol coupons and found the little car still there. No-one had bothered to try and steal it. I had refilled the tank and all but unwound my arm on the starting handle before I realised the truth. They had stolen the rotor arm instead. Shambles lay as lifeless as an empty and discarded biscuit tin.

Locating replacement parts in wartime was like looking for gold in a blind fiddler's hat, and without wheels the little group soon disintegrated. Yorky and Mac continued to cadge a lift into town each evening, and wearily hoofed it home very late after a night's dancing, while Stan had an attack of conscience and stayed in camp. I spent my spare time scouring the local scrap yards for miles around in search of a second-hand rotor arm.

Eventually, I haggled a replacement out of an ancient but rapacious motor trader for an arm and a leg, and thankfully Shambles spluttered back to life just in time for me to reload my kit into her at the end of the course.

Yorky said he was going down to London for a bit of a reunion, and could I give him a lift into Nottingham on my way. I didn't see why not. For the resuscitated Shambles it was very much of a test run, and in the event of trouble a spare pusher to the nearest garage while I steered was worthwhile insurance.

Maisie was waiting in White Lion Square with a packed suitcase. I wished Yorky a happy reunion and drove home.

I did meet him again, although many years later, well after the war. It was at some reunion or other; his belt was straining hard to contain a swelling beer belly, and his haircut had a pink hole in it, but it was the same old Yorky. By the time we got round to chatting most people had gone off to bed, and he was well into his cups, his eyes like pee-holes in the snow.

He was a little vague about who I was at first, and asked if we had met at another reunion somewhere? Sardonically, I suggested maybe he was talking of the one with Maisie.

'Remember Maisie?'

He remembered her all right. It all came spilling out like beer from a tipping tankard. They had gone down to London, but it hadn't exactly been the conventional dirty weekend. He really had been meeting up with others from the squadron, and he'd calmly dumped her in some slightly grotty hotel near Euston and said he'd be back later. She'd accepted this without complaint – not that she had much choice – and he had compounded his behaviour by staggering back late from the party, very much the worse for wear. Oddly, this served to convince the originally dubious land-lady (they were more convential days!) of the pair's married status: only a husband would treat his charming companion in such a cavalier fashion!

Yorky then collapsed across the bed, half in his pyjamas, and happily snored the night away. His throbbing head next morning owed less to the previous night's alcohol intake than his inamorata's left jab. Finally boiling over in frustration, she had pounded his head with flailing fists in a vain attempt to wake him.

'So you blew it!'

He denied this indignantly. Not at all – he had made it up to her. 'And that night were magic! I don't remember owt like it, not wi' any of t' others.' I didn't say so, but I bet he couldn't even count t' others, let alone remember them. They had several days of mind-blowing bliss together before Maisie had to go back home, and he took her by train as far as Nottingham. But she didn't want him to leave, in tears she begged him to go back with her to her home town, and stay in a hotel there. Yorky started to feel vaguely worried. It was all getting too serious, and he began to feel that he was walking into a trap.

From her talk, it seemd half her friends knew about the trip, and the envious Beth had even said 'she'd always wanted to do that herself'. (I was a bit amused at his shocked tone.)

'I suddenly thought, she wants to show me off to everybody – like some prize bloody bull. Maybe she wants to give her husband a reason to divorce her.' The idea alarmed him. 'I thought, no way! So I put her on t' bus and walked off.'

He was silent for a moment, and then he added, 'And I've never stopped regret-ting it from that day to this.'

He stared down into his empty glass. 'After t' war I got demobbed and went back home and married a girl I'd known since Sunday School.

She's a great gel, my missis, and we've had a good life. We've three grand lads – I'd be surprised if one didn't play for Yorkshire, one day . . . But I still think about her.'

'Maisie?'

He nodded. He had a faraway look in his eye. 'There was summat about her. She were real special . . .'

'So why didn't you try to do something about it? I mean, instead of getting married?'

He looked at me pityingly. 'You didn't know my mam, I wouldn't have dared. She were no more than five feet in her wet wellies, but she was as hard as a blacksmith's best hammer. The local church was her life, and if I'd ha' got involved wi' a married woman she'd ha' died of shame. But not before nailing me to t' pantry door.'

I suppose when it comes down to it, we're all dead scared of something. Or someone.

'But surely,' I persisted, 'if you felt that strongly you'd have done something about it?'

He hesitated, and then he said, 'I did write her once, just before I got wed. I didn't say too much, I didn't know who might read it, but I felt I had to do it. She sent a little note back, very pleasant and friendly. In it she said she'd enjoyed meeting me, but we'd known each other for such a short time. We knew so little about each other really and she supposed it had just been lust.'

He brooded for a few seconds. 'You know what? I reckon she were just like her pal, Beth. She'd always wanted to do something like that. It just happened to be me . . . And that were about it.'

He walked off unsteadily to bed. I never saw him again.

Back at camp after the Night Vision course, the CO's quiet word seemed to have had some effect on the intrepid Timber and Fearless, even if only temporarily. And the two continued to turn up for debriefing at the end of each trip, as bad pennies seem to. So I decided against trying any subtle warning, telling myself that maybe it was someone else, or maybe Mac had just been talking big. I suppose I chickened out.

In fact, on their next trip they marched into debriefing triumphantly proclaiming that they had 'been involved in a twenty-minute chase!' From somewhere in a bunch of returned aircrew, clutching tiredly at their tea-mugs as they awaited their turn at debriefing, an anonymus voice enquired sardonically, 'Where were you – back or front?'

After the war, a young sergeant navigator came on to our squadron. He was a quietly shy Northern lad who didn't mix well – he was seldom seen at the bar or joined in any rough-and-tumble, but hung around the edges of any communal activity, like a dog at a dinner table. He flew with an officer pilot – a friendly enough type but somewhat irritable at times – and he was known among the rest of the NCO aircrew as Weewee Watkins.

Weewee must have been absolutely terrified of flying, because he seemed physically incapable of getting airborne, even for the shortest trip, without requesting his pilot to pass over the pee-tube. Whereon he would immediately proceed to relieve himself of any excess liquid in a nervous reflex. The tube, together with its accompanying metal cone – the 'fearsome funnel' – was stored under the pilot's seat, and passing it over was both awkward and acutely embarrassing when wearing flying gear. I can't ever recall using it myself, even on the longest operation (although the WAAF driver meeting us on our return sometimes had to avert her gaze diplomatically when we clambered out).

We teased Weewee unmercifully about his habit, making out that the ground crew had threatened to mutiny unless they were issued with sou'westers and umbrellas before opening their cockpit door.

In fact I must confess that, as an outsider to the gang, he was very much the butt of our humour at times. I recall, once, when we were in Northumberland doing our biannual air-to-air firing stint between the Farne Islands and Holy Island, and down in Newcastle for the weekend we decided to give him a treat for his birthday.

Blame it on an excess of the local Newcastle Brown Ale if you like, but we planned to take one of the ladies of the night who plied their lusty trade round Newcastle Station back to camp to give him a birthday treat that we were fairly certain he had never experienced before. Rather fortunately for us, perhaps, we couldn't persuade any of the Geordie Jump Brigade that the trip would be a financially satisfactory one.

Yet despite our unmerciful teasing, and despite a delicate bladder that collapsed with fright at the sound of an aircraft door closing, and the irritation of his pilot at being asked for the nth time to pass over the fearsome funnel in the middle of take-off, Weewee quietly carried on doing everything that was asked of him, his fears screwed down tight with tiny bolts of determination, while dreading every minute he spent in the air. Maybe he was the bravest coward of us all.

Of course, I had no way of knowing how he would have coped with the stresses of flying on operations, because by then the war was long over, but I often idly wondered whether he could have become Britain's greatest secret weapon.

I had this great vision of a Germany at the war's end with long, silent corridors across it, where every flak gun, every Tiger tank and every V2 rocket was seized up solid with red rust, marking where Weewee had flown low over enemy territory.

A fascinating thought – even if it was probably against the Geneva Convention.

CHAPTER EIGHTEEN

The End of the Line

After winning our wings in Arizona, we had to hang around for a few days while we waited for a train back up to Canada and then home. The rest of the camp carried on with its normal flying training, as if we weren't there – we were no longer part of it.

You soon got tired of walking round trying to catch a glimpse of the new badge on your chest in the nearest shop window. We had achieved what we had been working so long for, yet the elation soon died, leaving an empty feeling inside, as if you'd just been retired from your job or thrown out of your favourite club. We felt like a spare drain-cock at a plumber's wedding – we had nothing to do.

There was much the same feeling in 1945 as the war in Europe drew to its close. Thirty-five times Dagwood and I had set out to patrol the edge of the bomber stream in the enemy night skies for three or four hours at a time, sometimes more. We rarely knew what day of the week it was, because to us there were only two kinds of day: there were days when we flew and days when we flew and they paid us. But it was a life we had got used to. Now, the enemy territory left for us to prowl was shrinking rapidly.

The Second Tactical Air Force (2nd TAF), clearing the way in front of the ground troops, had been allotted an operational zone ahead of the front line that we weren't allowed to enter. We were left with few places to go. We did a few low-level night intruder attacks on enemy barracks and airfields, or patrolled the Danish coast for Nazi bigwigs fleeing to Norway in Heinkel bombers, on the first leg of a desperate journey to seek some South American dictator's grudging sanctuary. Or there was an occasional trip covering Lancaster raids in support of the advancing Russians. Almost our last operation was one of these, the longest trip we had ever done. It was April 1945, and we went off to Plauen in Czechoslovakia, a weary (and uneventful) five-hour round slog of over one thousand two hundred miles, that took every drop in the extra hundred-gallon drop-tanks we carried on each wing.

At Christmas in 1944 the Germans had made one last despairing effort to throw back the advancing Allied armies in the Ardennes, when they tried to cut their way through to Antwerp in the Battle of the Bulge, but it ground to a halt. Their petrol and their luck ran out at about the same time, and they pulled back behind the Rhine, their final frontier.

The British losses at Arnhem – when an ambitious attempt to leapfrog across the Rhine into Germany failed – had left the British airborne troops desperately short of glider pilots for the coming attack across this last great river barrier.

But the RAF training system was still churning out more pilots than they could ever hope to use, so a call went out for aircrew volunteers to move over to the Airborne Regiment and fly their gliders. One of those to put his hand up was an ex-workmate from my old drawing-office, John Ramsden. He and I had last met on leave, a short time before, when after a few pints of Dutch courage we decided to call in on our old workplace. We were warmly welcomed by the other 'drafties', but I got a sour reception from the boss myself. Back in 1941 when I first volunteered for aircrew, the RAF wouldn't take me until I was seventeen. He had tried to sack me while I was waiting, but, tipped off, I beat him to the punch and gave in my notice at the last moment. Now he made me about as welcome as a fart in a spaceman's helmet. He made it very plain that he would be happy to take John back when the dust had settled, but I should seek fresh fields and pastures new, and not expect to nibble at his haystack. We parted with bad grace, my contemptuous farewell to him ensuring that he would never change his mind. (As it happened, John didn't return there after the war, either, but joined the family catering business.)

It was not long after our controversial sortie to our old workplace that John found himself crash-landing a Horsa glider, containing a jeep and a batch of Airborne troops, across the big river and onto a rail junction on the far side of the Rhine. They were badly shot up by the desperate defenders, and heavy fighting ensued. John received severe injuries, and for forty-eight hours he lay there hurt in a ditch as the battle surged backwards and forwards over him, his wounds being treated first by one side and then the other.

And then, quite suddenly, it was all over, and the Allied armies were racing across the West German plain to keep Denmark from the clutches of the advancing Russians. They just made it by taking Lübeck and its port of Travemunde, on the Baltic coast. I was to come to know both places well, later on.

I flew down to see John when they brought him back to a ward in Aylesbury Hospital. Among other injuries, I found him with a broken jaw and a nose split open by a bullet. The few teeth he had left were cemented together and the jaw was supported by a crane arrangement carried by a plaster band moulded round his head. He was fed by a straw through a gap in his teeth. His youthful good looks were badly mangled, but he gave me a welcoming gurgle through the cemented teeth in place of a hello and we found something to chat and chuckle at.

I had gone down there with Pete, an Aussie pilot from the squadron. He was off to see his mate, 'Honest John' Bridekirk, a fellow Aussie who had finished upside down in his Mossie when he tried to land at Brussels Airport.

Pete and I agreed that I should fly the plane down and he would fly it back. It was an arrangement I regretted pretty quickly, because a short while after leaving the ward I found myself hanging upside down over the hospital at zero height, with a great waggling of aircraft wings. 'Just saying "G'bye" to John', said the Aussie laconically. I could think of a no more certain way of saying goodbye to everybody.

So that was it, the war in Europe was at an end. The expected Last Stand in the Bavarian Mountains just didn't happen. Hitler committed suicide and the German generals caved in and signed the surrender on Lüneberg Heath. It was all an anticlimax, and, as in Arizona, we were suddenly out of work, with nothing to do. They allowed us to fly on a sort of Cook's Tour of the Continent by way of a small celebration. We flew in loose squadron formation low over Holland and Germany, in rather nervous triumph at the unaccustomed daylight, while the Dutch people below came out to wave their thanks. We inspected the remains of the Eder and Mohne dams, the bombed and fire-scorched remnants of Hamburg, and the fiercely-fought-over bridge over the Rhine at Remagen, now forlornly collapsed into the water (an event that is the regularly shown subject of a feature film of the same name). And then we went home.

But we had our own private festivities to come. Certain cities had been known during the war for their friendliness towards servicemen, and Nottingham was high on the list. So we celebrated VE (Victory in Europe) day by 'borrowing' Toby's car, and his precious petrol ration – rather unwisely he happened to be on leave at the time – piled it high with bodies, and careered off to the Midlands.

Nottingham's White Lion Square was full of cheering people with a posse of bigwigs preening themselves on the town hall balcony. We found an open window at the back of the building and climbed in, cheekily joining them in taking the plaudits of the crowd below. Our presence drew a few sourly disapproving but puzzled looks from the assembled dignitaries; nobody quite knew who we were or what we were doing there, but they daren't chuck us out with that great crowd watching. We had a high old time, finally driving happily back to Norfolk in the early hours to sleep

Nottingham City Hall on VE (Victory in Europe) Night. White Lion Square is crowded with people celebrating. Our small group of RAF aircrew can just be made out in the centre of the lower balcony, where we commandeered the microphone!

it off. Of course, there was still the small matter of the war in Japan to finish, but no one cared too much at that moment.

But our euphoria at the war's end in Europe didn't last long, because the Cook's tour was about the only generosity handed out by a grateful service. Our small, highly secret group of Mosquito night-fighter and intruder squadrons, along with the electronics-mangling bombers, had been hurriedly set up at the end of 1943 in an effort to stem the horrific bomber losses. The group had succeeded in cutting those losses by a fabulous eighty per cent, knocking the *Luftwaffe* out of their own night skies. But we had the feeling that some air marshals' noses had been put badly out of joint – they had had to hand over their best aircraft and equipment to the fledg-ling group, and they wasted no time in grabbing it back again. Within days our own squadron was disbanded without ceremony or even so much as a pat on the back. The swift and total dismemberment of the remainder of the group soon followed. Airfields were reclaimed and aircraft commandeered by other command groups with indecent haste. Our pioneering work on long-range all-weather night-fighting and electronic warfare was carefully researched in a final combined exercise with the defeated German air controllers, called Operation Post Mortem, to see what lessons could be learned. Then it was all hidden away from the public gaze for thirty long years. It was as if we had never existed, and today few people know about it. We were moved to the one remaining squadron, whose CO hankered after action in the Far East, and there we began low-level flying training over the Cumbrian hills in readiness for the jungles of Burma.

But if the war in Europe had ended, not with a bang but a whimper, the one in Japan now finished, not with a whimper but with the biggest bang of all time. The Yanks dropped the atom bomb on Hiroshima, virtually vaporising it, and the war was finally over. It was VJ Day – Victory in Japan.

I can't say that we were sorry – there had been scary tales of the cassein glue that held the Mossies together coming apart in the tropical heat of the Far East. Of course, the victory produced a second celebration, but this time one that was held in camp. It was a fair enough party, but muted. Somehow it didn't quite have the carefree joy of the VE wing-ding. We did consider another trip to Nottingham, but there was little real enthusiasm for it. Still, the home-grown celebrations were wild and joyous enough, with unexpected consequences for some.

Terry was a WAAF driver on the camp. One of her jobs was to drive aircrew out to their aircraft and later bring them back again, modestly averting her gaze as returning crews emptied bulging bladders on climbing out of their planes after the long flight. She was a friendly and pleasant girl, buxom in a cuddly way, possessing a wicked twinkle in her eye, and known for the long leather gauntlets that she wore for her job. In those gauntlets, so it was said, she kept a record of her 'kills', much in the manner that fighter pilots adorned their Spitfires. But instead of being marked down as swastikas, they were listed in rows of either ticks or crosses.

If asked, would-be Lotharios on the camp would airily claim to be 'fourth row down, three along, left-hand glove –', but no-one could quite work out the difference between a tick and a cross. Did it refer to competence, speed, satisfaction, how big an ego he had, or what? Certainly Terry wasn't letting on, she simply gave her serene little smile and said nothing. Let's just say that she was a very popular girl, and ordi-nary gloves would have been inadequate for keeping her score.

On the other hand, Paul Parrot was a young, likeable but reserved young pilot officer who came fairly late to the squadron. Quiet and friendly, he never raised his voice in either anger or excitement but stayed calm and precise. Yet there were hidden fires below that placid exterior, which, fuelled with alcohol, flared up in a brief but intense passion when the two of them came together at the camp's celebration. And not long after the VJ Day party word went round that the two were engaged to be married.

His navigator (a flight-sergeant, and one of the gang) told us the unbelievable news, and it came like a bombshell.

'To Terry! Are you sure? Doesn't he know about her?'

Apparently not. Someone, we decided, had to do something. The only question was who, and what? We voted to draw straws to decide who would have a quiet word in his ear.

But trying to tell a man that his bride-to-be was very much a bride-already-had, and quite often at that, could be a hazardous occupation in those days, likely to earn anyone who tried it a buy-one-get-one-free smack in the mouth.

In particular, his navigator refused to join in the draw, feeling that there was a strong possibility of Paul unscrewing the control column at thirty thousand feet and beating him over the head with it, before baling out, taking both parachutes with him.

As it happened, our problem was resolved by a sudden but unexplained cancellation of the engagement, almost immediately followed by a swift shutdown and scattering of the squadron. Which is why I did not learn the full truth of the matter until almost fifty years later, when I happened to meet Paul's daughter.

It seems that despite her encyclopaedic experience, Terry's unbridled night of passion had quickly become very bridalled. She ended up with a full bomb-load, looking for a target. Not surprisingly she informed Paul, and he, like the gentleman he was, 'Did The Decent Thing' (a phrase virtually untranslatable these days) and promptly proposed marriage.

What caused the cancellation of the proposed nuptials, however, is unclear. Possibly a warning hint from a more senior member of the Officers' Mess as to the unsuitability of such a match – Terry's hand-in-glove accounting system covered a wide clientele. Anyway, Paul flatly refused to go ahead with the ceremony though, later, he succumbed to Terry's pleadings to inspect the by-product of their passion, and discreet financial help was given by Paul's family.

Paul spent his final years until his death in 2001 locked in the silent world of Alzheimer's, unaware of his surroundings. This young fair-haired pilot, to whom flying was the breath of life, ended his days a still trim, grey-haired man with puzzled eyes, remembering neither his present-day family nor his long-ago love. As for Terry, I have no idea what became of her, but if I did I would probably send her my fond regards. I'm sure she made a splendid mother and would have made someone a warm and loving wife. After all, they say practice makes perfect.

In those young and foolish days, when the ultimate sin was being found out, such a happening would earn you the moral condemnation of an unforgiving society. Today, it would get you nothing more than a priority flat and a lavish handout of benefits.

After the local celebrations, we made a swift dash in Shambles down to London to join the crowds cavorting round Buckingham Palace, cheering anyone who appeared on the balcony, and cheekily calling, 'We want George!' to our beloved monarch. Later, when the euphoria had faded, people began to think about getting demobbed and finding jobs and going home for good.

But if we felt a little let down at the sudden wiping-out of the squadron, the aircrews of Bomber Command had far more reason to feel bitter at the ingratitude they were shown.

Bomber Command had lost over half its flying men, more than fifty thousand casualties, predominantly in the savage night battles over Germany after D-Day. They suffered one of the heaviest casualty rates ever borne by a still cohesive force, yet they alone were refused a campaign medal. To this day they have never received one, and it is utterly shameful. Instead they were grudgingly given the France and Germany Star, which was for the forces liberating Europe and a totally different campaign.

The reason for this was the bombing of Dresden.

The town lay in the path of the advancing Russians and was an important rail centre, crowded with troops and refugees. The Russians requested the bombing, Churchill ordered it, Bomber Command organised it and the squadrons carried it out, as they had on other targets many times before. But once the war was safely won and the danger past, all kinds of bleeding-heart critics came out of the woodwork, with their condemnatory voices raised in pious protest against the conflict in which they took so little part. It was claimed that Bomber Command had 'blindly bombed innocent civilian targets' and destroyed 'the unique baroque capital of the north'. Among the high-ups there was suddenly much washing of hands and denial of complicity in the affair, and the bomber crews (or the fifty per cent who were left) and their leader took the blame.

Well, in my book, there's no way that a population that cheered on a monster like Hitler in his subjugation of Europe, his blind raining of buzz-bombs and V2 rockets on London, or the slaughter of the helpless in the concentration camps, can lay any claim to innocence. And as Bomber Harris so succinctly put it, all the buildings in Dresden weren't worth the life of a single Grenadier Guardsman. Of course, the really ironic twist to it all is that Dresden was lovingly restored to its pre-war glory while we suffered post-war attacks on our old towns from crazed architects and planners that have left most of them looking like bomb-sites, and identical bomb-sites at that.

But now, with the coming of peace, a lot of airmen were in a vulnerable position. Many had entered the service straight from school, and had no trade to return to, so to help them the RAF started its EVT, or Educational and Vocational Training programme, to teach them new civilian skills.

Dagwood hoped to return to university sometime, but realised that it wouldn't be easy to settle down to studies after so many years' gap. Until his future prospects became clearer, he decided to try his hand as an instructor on the programme, and subsequently moved into teaching, as did many aircrew. But for me, 'civvie street' offered no future half so attractive as flying, and although I got a half-hearted interview with BOAC as they started recruiting for post-war operations, there were too many ex-bomber pilots around with experience on the big four-engined planes, experience that I lacked. I decided to stay on in the service, and having flown at the top level, I preferred flying on a front-line squadron.

I was posted back to Fighter Command, to a night-fighter base on the south coast, so it was time for Dagwood and me to say goodbye. In the short two years since we had first met we had experienced a lifetime of excitement and danger, and shared both happy times and tremendous, adrenaline-charged experiences together. Like almost all Mosquito crews, we have remained firm friends to this day.

I moved to No. 85 Squadron, down at Tangmere, a famous Battle of Britain airfield that still bore the scars of that conflict in the bullet-flaked walls of its hangars. But little by little life began to change as the service settled back into peacetime mode. Experienced crews began to leak away into civilian life, to be replaced by fresh green pilots with no experience of action. The old camaraderie between commissioned and non-commissioned aircrew began to change to a more formal and disciplined approach, and the latest mark of Mosquito that we flew started to suffer from a shortage of spares, especially for the American-built radar. The new Government refused to spend its dwindling dollars on replacements, so our aircraft were steadily cannibalised, and our 'state of readiness' was compromised accordingly. Tension was rising between Soviet Russia and the West, yet there were nights when we had barely a dozen night-fighters ready for combat.

But the life was still fascinating, and there was plenty happening. The High-speed Flight arrived at Tangmere to make a patriotic attempt on the World High-speed Record. It was commanded by Group Captain Donaldson, together with Flight Lieutenant Neville Duke (who later broke the record in a Hawker Hunter) and a Canadian squadron leader. The high-speed run was to be made off the coast between Bognor pier and the one at Worthing, and the aircraft making the attempt were not allowed to dive onto the first pier but had to approach it flying straight and level at a thousand feet. They used Gloster Meteor jets and our squadron aircraft had to fly

above them to check. After landing we had to sign that the Meteor had stuck to the rules as laid down by the International Aeronautical Society. The team eventually achieved a wafer-thin increase in the record, and went away satisfied, but it didn't stand for long.

The prickly General De Gaulle, the new prince of Paris, was trying to re-establish his air force. French Air Force officers came over to purchase some of our spare Mosquitoes, and I was detailed to show one of the Gallic air captains over the plane. The conversation between us bordered on the farcical, sounding more like a routine between a couple of stand-up comics.

I took him out to the aircraft. 'This is the latest Mosquito night-fighter, the Mark 36, with the American Mark X radar –'

'Vare ees ze guns?' he demanded.

'Oh – they're right here, in the nose. Now, the aircraft has two Merlin 113 engines–'

' 'ow many guns?'

'Four Oerlikon or Hispano-Suiza cannon, there's no room for the three oh three machine-guns because of the radar. As I was saying –'

'What size ees ze guns?'

'Twenty millimetre. Now the aircraft carries a one-hundred-gallon drop-tank under each wing –'

' 'ow you fire ze guns?'

'With the bloody firing-button!' I was beginning to get ratty. 'Right, to start the engines you plug in the –'

'Vare ees ze firink bouton?'

'On the top of the control column – here. OK? Now the fuel cocks are on the bulk-head behind the pilot's seat –'

' 'ow many bullet in ze guns?'

I gave up. I left him sitting in the cabin, staring dreamily through the perspex and caressing the 'firink bouton' as if it was a scantily clad member of the *Folies Bergère*. He seemed to be dreaming that he was in a twin-engined Spitfire, awaiting the call to scramble in the Battle of Britain.

Sadly, he was about five years too late.

The sudden end of hostilities had taken the RAF by surprise – it had expected a long haul out in the Far East, as winkle-picking Japs out of forest foxholes was not an easy task. So like some mad mechanical midwife, the RAF training machine continued to churn out batches of inexperienced aircrew who were no longer needed. A few of them started to trickle through to the squadrons, but they were woefully under-trained. The experience of one of them, Johnny Wakefield, was typical.

'Wacker' Wakefield was a solidly built flight sergeant navigator from Birkenhead, who played rugby like a master butcher's bulldog. He did his basic training out on the Canadian prairies, where map reading was almost a lost art, because there was nothing much to put on the map to read. The towns were so widely spread that if you came across one there was no argument about its identity – there was only one it could be. Anyway, who cared where it was – you'd found a town!

So when he returned to the UK with its intricately tangled landscape he first needed to go on a map-reading course on Tiger Moth aircraft at Cambridge. While there, he was asked by a Canadian flight lieutenant pilot to go up with him. John had already been airborne three times that day but he was persuaded to go for one more 'quick flip'. Back home in Canada, the pilot had been a flying instructor, but like many long-time instructors, he was eager to get onto a front-line squadron for the few remaining (and reasonably safe) weeks of the war, if only to make the future war tales he told his grandkids sound more interesting. To accomplish this, he needed to amass as many flying hours as he could in as short a time as possible in order to qualify for an operational training course.

Unfortunately, the Canadian had chosen the wrong man to join him in his leap into the bright blue yonder, because old Wacker was still prairie-happy and rather good at losing himself in a country where towns overlapped one another and roads couldn't make up their mind which way they wanted to go. They were soon hopelessly lost, dusk was falling and they had no radio and no navigation lights. So when they suddenly found themselves tangled up in a great gaggle of Flying Fortresses wearily making their way back from a late daylight raid, they decided the best thing to do was to follow them home to their base. There they announced their presence by beating up the Yank control tower, completely failing to notice the signals area's warning sign indicating 'Land on runways only!'

John's pilot decided it might be safer to leave the concrete clear for the big bombers, and land on the grass. Unfortunately, the thick, globby mud on which the grass was happily growing stopped the little Tiger Moth in only slightly less distance than if they had hit the brick wall of the control tower itself.

It didn't help matters that thick fog rolled in as soon as they touched down, trapping them there for the next two days. Most of those two days were spent trying to prevent slap-happy Flying Fortress pilots from taking that 'cute lil' Tiger Moth up for a quick flip in the fog.

Soon after, John moved on to the standard radar training course at Ouston, but in a Wellington bomber (not the old Anson of my day). This was a steady aircraft with plenty of room to move around in, and he thoroughly enjoyed the experience. Sadly the war came to an abrupt end right in the middle of the course, so together with hundreds of other half-trained aircrew, he was moved to Kirkton-in-Lindsey to be made redundant.

But he had a hidden advantage over the others. He was a regular serviceman, not one of your 'hostilities only' or 'just in it till we win it' types. He had joined up as an aircraft apprentice (known throughout the service as a 'brat'), and the RAF tended to have a soft spot for its lads. It was like being in a blue-uniformed branch of the Freemasons or having a cousin in the Cosa Nostra.

After four months' leave he was allowed to continue his training, and ended up at Charterhall – dear old Slaughter Hall itself! – on the Night-fighter Operational Training Course.

There, things were in an even more shambolic state, with people suddenly being demobbed halfway through the course, so in desperation the RAF decided that it would be better for crews to complete their operational training flying on the squadron itself. Which was why, incredibly, John had never even sat in a Mosquito cockpit until he arrived at Tangmere!

When he did sit – and even take off – in one, there followed a sequence of mishaps that was to damn for ever in his eyes the cramped 'wooden wonder' that we veterans revered so much. To us, when handled right, the Mossie was a superb near-faultless machine, a thoroughbred that could take on, outfight and outrun anything in the night sky, while to him it was a plywood potential death-trap, to be avoided at all costs.

With his brand-new pilot, the couple made their very first solo flight in a Mossie soon after arriving at Tangmere. It was eventful enough to warrant a swift change of laundry. They had to take off in a hurry because a squadron formation (including myself) was returning from a fly-past rehearsal over London. Now, a Mossie getting airborne in a hurry can be a bit like a lurcher who has just seen a rabbit in full flight, crossing his bow swiftly to the left. You had to catch that swing fast with your port engine while it was still thinking about it. John's pilot, Dicky, didn't, and swerved wildly to port off the runway. Instead of throttling back and starting again, he then carried on bouncing across the grass, hitting a notice-board on the perimeter track as he was getting airborne. They managed to land safely by staying cool, no doubt helped by a rather strong draught through the new hole in the side of the plane.

As if that wasn't enough, on a later trip John was flying with Butch Baker (the same Butch Baker who had been at Charterhall with me, and later had cut off all communication to the isolated desert emergency landing strip in Africa). This time they collided with an aircraft of 29 Squadron and lost their wingtip. The other crew lost their elevator, their height and their lives, in that order. Small wonder that John didn't share our enthusiasm for the plane, and looked on it as more a 'wooden blunder' than 'wooden wonder'.

In their turn, the ground staff, too, were beginning to have problems with the new crews coming in. One of the pilots was asked to do a flight-test on an aircraft, but refused to pass it 'because it didn't smell right'. The incredulous ground-staff sergeant suggested that the smell might possibly have some connection with the nervousness of his navigator.

In wartime, such apparent ham-fistedness would have been enough to get you discreetly removed from a squadron with such an eminent history as ours (indeed, I had known of a pilot being 'moved on' because the CO found out he was teetotal!). But it didn't always need fancy split-arse flying for you to be looked on with surprising favour in the peacetime RAF.

It was decided to move the squadron to West Malling in Kent, together with two other night squadrons, to form a night-fighter wing. Accordingly, we subsequently landed at Malling and lined up in front of our aircraft to be greeted and inspected by our new station commander, Group Captain Ramsbotham-Isherwood, a veteran who had commanded a wartime Hurricane wing.

After meeting our CO and giving the rest of us a cursory glance, he suddenly called out. 'Right, where's Wakefield?'

A group captain calling for a flight sergeant? It was unheard of! John quaked in his shoes, wondering what he had done wrong, as the beribboned officer with more rings round his arm than a zebra's pyjamas bore down on him.

'You're the rugby player, right?' barked the group captain. 'Well, there's no rugger team at this station, so you are to form one within three weeks. Do nothing else!' John's face split into a huge grin – three weeks away from the dreaded Mossies!

He was given a corporal physical training instructor to assist him. The first time Dagwood and I had been at Malling, during the war, there had been no proper runways, for even as a prime Battle of Britain 'drome it had been merely a large grass field.

Now, there was a concrete main runway, but still grass only on the shorter and little-used cross-wind runway. So John decided to lay out their first rugby pitch on the end of this. What he didn't know, though I could have told him had I known what he was about to do, was that immediately under the grass was a metal reinforcing grid. In the rush to make the 'dromes fit for take-off in bad weather they had laid down Somerfeldt tracking, an interlocking metal grid system dreamed up by a certain Czech, Karl Somerfeldt.

This metal reinforcing was still there, by now just below the surface of the cross-runway's grass, as they were soon very painfully to discover on their first practice matches. The newly formed station rugby team were all very close to being hospitalised before they had played a game.

John produced the team and went on to play for the station, the group and Fighter Command. It didn't get him any further up the promotion ladder but it ensured that he stayed on that squadron (and more importantly in one of their new married quarters!) for five long years. The station commander saw to that. It just went to show the RAF's priorities in peacetime – aircrew were ten a penny, but a good front-row forward was rarer than gold dust in a workhouse Hoover bag.

The reason for the station commander's interest in rugby was simple – he was a New Zealander, with all the Kiwis' love for the game. He was a tough little character, untainted by the British public school system (he had led a fighter wing to Russia), and as he was fairly new to the camp the junior officers were quick to curry favour with him.

So when he announced that he would be personally supervising rugby team training, the officers' mess bar lizards turned up in force to demonstrate their keenness. Flaccid muscles were unaccustomedly flexed and beer bellies sucked in.

They had a shock. The first thing he did was to lie on the pitch and invite everyone to run over him. This they managed, but then he led everyone else in a run over each man in turn. It was to toughen them up, he explained. The stud-pocked bar-proppers promptly decided that it was rather a rough game.

I happened to cross him one day. I and my navigator, Andy, passed without saluting, thinking he wouldn't notice. His back was turned and he was busy talking. But he swung round and collared us. I was a warrant officer and Andy a flight sergeant, and he quite correctly gave Andy the dressing-down. But it was meant for me – I knew it and he knew it. And as we went off, chastened, I heard him say to his companions, 'Because I'm a little bugger they think it doesn't matter. But it does.'

But like many a desk-bound station commander before him he missed the flying and was tempted into taking short flips into the sky. He took up a Meteor – at that time a new-fangled jet – and was seen to dive into the heart of a black cloud during a snowstorm. He came out of it vertically, hurtling straight into the ground. You can't be a part-time pilot in a plane like that, not in a cloud like that when your instrument flying skills are a little rusty. He was a sad loss to the RAF.

CHAPTER NINETEEN

The Mighty T-Bolt

There was a slack period on the squadron and they needed someone temporarily at No. 10 Maintenance Unit who had plenty of experience on different types of Mosquito, so I was seconded to Wiltshire for a time.

I found five other pilots already there, and they were a great bunch of old sweats. There were two parts to the job. Firstly, we had to collect all shapes and sizes of Mosquito from where they had been dumped – all over the country and in all kinds of condition. We would bring them down to 10 MU in Wiltshire, where they carefully inspected them and put right anything that was wrong. Then we flew them up to West Freugh, a small 'drome near Stranraer in Scotland, where they proceeded to crush them under a bulldozer. It seemed an almost criminal waste, because if we had managed to get them up there, there couldn't have been too much wrong with them!

But crazy as it seemed, there were an awful lot of spare aircraft lying around the country that nobody wanted, and they had to get rid of them somehow. (It was rumoured that more than one quarry was quietly filled with old Lancaster bombers and then grassed over. I even heard of unused railway tunnels filled with unwanted equipment and the entrances blocked up.)

We had an easy-going life. Early in the morning we would toss a coin, and whoever lost the toss had to follow the other five up north in the slow old Anson to fetch us back. They wouldn't let us have navigators, we had to find our own way round the country. But it wasn't difficult, we just followed the River Severn up to Shrewsbury and kept going north until we saw Liverpool. Then we followed the Lancashire coast round Morecambe Bay to the Lake District – the Cumbrian mountains were an impressive sight from the air. Finally, we cut across the Solway Firth and turned west until we ran out of land, and there on the end of the Mull of Galloway was Stranraer. We were all old Mossie hands and rarely needed to glance at the map.

But the trip back in the bumbling old Anson was much slower. We could barely make it by dusk, and the nights were getting shorter. We would soon be coming back in the dark.

Fly at night without a navigator? No way! decreed the Air Force – that is against regulations! You must land at the nearest 'drome and seek accommodation for the night. We gently pointed out that there would be six pilots on board who had been finding their way back home from every corner of Europe at dead of night for quite a while now. And this time we weren't expecting any flak, not even over Liverpool. A short flip down the Severn Valley after sunset would not exactly be an Odyssey.

That was wartime, they said loftily, this is peacetime and you will adhere to peacetime regulations.

But it so happened that one pilot's sister ran a small hotel in Blackpool. So guess what! By a remarkable coincidence, from then on we were always exactly opposite Blackpool tower when night fell. And regulations being regulations, we curled straight into Squires Gate airport, Sis fixed us up with beds, we had a night out on the town in Blackpool, and the RAF picked up the bill. And serve them right.

Back on the squadron again, I found the ground staff still bemoaning the lack of spares for both the planes and the radar. 'Has anyone tried ringing Stranraer?' I asked. 'We've just taken loads of Mossies up there. There must be plenty of spares around. There might even be a few that haven't had the bulldozer over them yet.'

'That's Maintenance Command for you,' they grumbled, 'they never tell us a thing.'

But things had been happening while I was away. I had managed to miss a Big Panic. And I wasn't the only one. Johnny Wakefield had narrowly missed World War Two by a gnat's spats, and now he also missed the possible advent of World War Two and a Half because he went to the pictures with his missis.

At the time, Britain was still running Palestine from the end of the First World War, under a League of Nations Mandate. Understandably, the survivors of the Holocaust, realising they had long worn out their welcome in Europe, yearned to return to their ancestral homeland and began to flood into the country in anything that would float for more than five minutes. We had, they claimed, promised the land to them, or at least a British politician named Balfour had. The trouble was that it wasn't his (or ours, for that matter) to give, but when did politicians worry about small details like that?

We were caught up in a nasty little war between the Arabs who already lived there and the Jews who wanted to move in. The Jewish extremist underground group, Haganah, did what extremist underground groups routinely do, and began setting off bombs and shooting soldiers.

While I was away (Haganah was obviously trying to lessen the odds against it!) a light aircraft belonging to the group was found in France with a light bomb on board. The intention, apparently, was to drop it on the Houses of Parliament as a calling card. (They probably tried to rent the cellars first, but found they were still full of Guy Fawkes's gunpowder.)

Fearful that there was a back-up plane, the night squadrons were put on emergency alert, under orders to clobber any Tiger Moth type trying to invade Westminster's air space, though whether with a butterfly net wasn't specified. The trouble was, it was a long weekend and they couldn't rustle up enough crews. John and his pilot, Dickie, were the only ones within reach as they were still living in married quarters down at Tangmere and had gone home for the weekend. So an old Oxbox was panicked off down there to fetch them back. Dickie was soon found, but with a visiting granny on baby-sitting duty, his navigator had taken his wife off to the flicks without saying exactly where. In the end, Dicky had to fly back on his own and John followed next day to find the panic over. Haganah had apparently had similar problems finding a crew. One wag suggested the RAF change its motto to 'Per Odeon Ad Astra'. But it all goes to show that the only thing that changes in life is the name of your enemy. Everyone returned thankfully to normal duties.

Some years back I watched the fly-past on TV to celebrate the Queen's Jubilee. Six Red Arrows and a borrowed Concorde – superb flying, as ever, from the Red Arrows, but, frankly, as a demonstration of Britain's air might it was pathetic. In our day, you wouldn't call that a real fly-past.

One of our jobs after the war was to take part in such events over London – and elsewhere – and there were a lot of them. Celebration of the Battle of Britain, VE Day, the King's birthday – you name it. A great armada of aircraft took part, and it required meticulous planning to get it right. Many hours of practising tight ceremonial formation flying were needed to get our positioning correct in the aerial parade.

On one such fly-past the Yanks joined in. They flew in from Germany, with half a dozen Thunderbolt fighter aircraft – the mighty T-bolt, as they called it. It was big for a fighter, with a cockpit roomy enough for two people who weren't talking to each other, and luxurious in its electric fittings. There were buttons to open the canopy and switches for this and for that. We waited for the horde of ground crew who would be needed to service such complex machines, but only five master sergeants turned up. They all seemed to have more stripes on their sleeves than a tiger's waistcoat, and when we asked about their men they explained that one master sergeant looked after one plane – hydraulics, electrics, armament, and engine, one man did the lot – all, that is, except for poor old Hank, who had to look after two!

But of course their system was totally different from ours. Anything that didn't work they didn't mend, they threw it away and bolted on a new bit. It was Meccano maintenance. The master sergeants were brought in by Tex, a long lean character wearing cowboy boots, who flew in aboard his Dakota aircraft, with a mass of spare parts. Tex flew the big silver plane on his own, piloting it, navigating it and, when on the ground, living in it, in a small cabin in the tail with every mod con.

The master sergeants moved into the sergeants' mess, but had no English money with them. An unbelievable order came down from Air Ministry: 'Look after them well,' it said, 'we'll pay all the bills!' We didn't need telling twice – we didn't expect another message like that in our lifetime.

The party that followed was historic. It was the custom, at intervals, to invite the officers over for what was euphemistically called a Games Night, when officers and NCOs challenged each other at various so-called 'sports'.

This usually started quietly enough with contests in snooker, darts, shove-ha'penny and the like, building up through a beer-drinking contest to mess rugby, and ending up with the deadly confrontation of Hi-cockalorum.

This was a wild and violent game, with each mess fielding a captain and a team of six men. The captain stood with his back to the wall while the team formed a line snaking out from him, bending down as in leap-frog and clutching the man in front to form a chain. The other team would then vault in turn onto their backs as violently as they could to try and make the chain collapse under their weight, crashing as many vaulters as possible onto the weakest man in the chain. Naturally, the captain put his weak links furthest up the line, so the finest vaulters in the opposition led the charge.

I was the sergeants' mess captain, and we were soon doing badly. It was quickly becoming a needle match, with the officers trying their hardest to impress the CO with their fitness. One officer in particular seemed determined to hammer us into the ground. We quickly decided that unless we could nobble him in some way we would stand no chance.

He was a large, loud, athletic chap, with so many bulging muscles that his brain needed repotting. He came thundering down the room and launched himself off the first bent back high into the air with the ease of Superman coming out of his phone-box changing-room. This was the moment of truth.

'Right!' I called, and our entire chain took a step to the right. I don't think I will ever forget the look on that man's face as he found himself flying through the air six feet above the ground with nothing below him but a hard wooden floor. Seconds later he crashed, knocking himself out cold and being carried unconscious to sick bay. He soon came round, with nothing broken but his nerve, but the CO, realising things were getting a little out of hand, called a halt to hostilities and took his team back to the officers' mess. We celebrated our triumph by hauling the station warrant officer's bicycle to the top of the flagpole ready for the morning parade.

Next morning we crawled ruefully out into the daylight to be greeted by the already emerged master sergeants. Tex had been sent post haste up to the American Embassy in London, and returned with a fistful of money for each of them. 'You paid for last night's party,' they told us gratefully, unaware of the Air Ministry's generosity, 'so tonight's party is on us!'

Tex's Dakota was due back in Germany but he said, 'Hell, I ain't missin' this!' and reported two flat tyres on his plane. And he should know, he let them down. He finally got back a week late, and I am the first to admit that the quality of the fly-past on that particular anniversary was not quite up to Red Arrows standard. The mighty T-bolts had been put on the outside of the turn for the fly-past but couldn't keep up and were switched to the inside. My guess is their noisy engines were throttled back deliberately to help ease a few throbbing heads.

Still, we made up in quantity what we lacked in quality.

CHAPTER TWENTY

Death in the Afternoon

But not all these occasions were happy ones.

In preparation for the next fly-past event, I was in one of three aircraft sent up to practise formation flying. I was in number three position in the formation, which meant I flew on the left. The leader, a flight lieutenant, was short of a navigator, so he had asked me if there were any spare people around, and I suggested one of the gang, Albert, a quiet sergeant navigator from Newark, to go with him.

Our number two, on the right, was an arrogant young pilot officer, new to the squadron and usually referred to – rather contemptuously – as BH, which stood for Big Head. He considered himself a red-hot Mosquito pilot. Several of us would have loved to help him become one with the application of a blow-torch to his backside.

I soon slid into my position alongside and slightly behind the leader, but BH raced in on the other side too fast and far too close. The Mosquito had such clean lines that it wasn't easy to slow in time, and BH seemed to be flying like a circus clown. He surged backward and forward, lifting his wing over the lead aircraft as he overshot, then chopping back hard on his throttles in an effort to get back into line. I was appalled at such a slap-happy attitude and was about to call a warning when the leader suddenly shot up several feet above us and appeared to be struggling with his controls. I was fairly sure that BH had hit him, but I didn't know what damage had been done, so I yelled 'Break – break!' and we peeled away to leave him a free run in to land.

It transpired later that BH had forgotten to allow clearance for the radar aerials sticking out of his wingtips, and these had hit and bent the trim tab on the leader's control flap, the small metal strip that you adjusted to keep the plane flying straight and level. The bang caused the plane to keep trying to make a climbing turn, and the flight lieutenant had great difficulty forcing the stick forward to hold it level.

Because of this he came in to land too fast and too high, touching down too far along the runway to leave enough room to stop. He then made the fatal error of slamming open his engines to go round again for another try. Despite his rank he lacked experience on the Mosquito. He should have pulled his wheels up and flopped onto his belly – two bent propellers were a small price to pay. But with full power on there was no way he could hold the nose down, and he flipped over onto his back beyond the end of the runway and burst into flames. We saw the ominous, black, oily smoke as we came in to land. Neither the flight lieutenant nor Albert survived.

There was a court of inquiry, of course, at which I had to give evidence. Despite his denials, I gave it as my opinion that BH had flown recklessly and hit the leading plane, and the investigators agreed they had found two marks on the trim tab at the same spacing as his twin aerials. I had to repeat my evidence in front of him – which was only fair – but I ignored his malevolent glare, I was as much angry with myself for suggesting Albert for the flight. To my old rule of 'Never volunteer' I mentally added a rider, 'Never volunteer anybody else, either.'

In spite of everything, BH received only a severe reprimand, which may have slowed his promotion in later years but wasn't much for a couple of lives lost. He was posted away from the squadron and I never saw him again, which was soon enough for me, but Albert's two brothers, both aircrew like himself, came down to Tangmere to find out what had really happened. I told them everything I knew. They were enraged but there was little they could do about it.

Their short visit, however, did cause quite a stir in the mess. The younger of the two brothers was Albert's identical twin and held the same rank. When they had both been on the same 'drome they had played endless practical jokes, constantly swapping identities, until the baffled authorities had finally split them up. Now, all unwittingly, they played their final joke. To see the startled disbelief of the mess members as they came in to tea to find an apparently reincarnated Albert calmly sitting there facing them would have been funny if it hadn't been so desperately sad.

All, that is, except for one placid but puddle-headed sergeant pilot who always seemed a couple of clocks short of an instrument panel – we used to say he had to ask the way to the sky. He collected his meal, sat down at our table and beamed a greeting. 'Oh hello, Albert,' he said, amiably, 'have a good leave?'

But there was one final sad little duty we had to do for Albert. He had been spending much of his spare time with a local girl, a young widow with a couple of kids, who lived on the far side of the airfield. She was a dark, slim young woman – quite pretty – and Albert seemed very keen on her.

She was a regular at our dances, and she was known locally on camp as 'the Black Widow'. At first I assumed her nickname was either because she was so dark or because she was a bit of a man-eater. (After all, Black Widow spiders were supposed to eat their mates after consummation.) But I was wrong. I heard later that she had been married to an RAF pilot who had been killed in action. Then she had got engaged again, to another member of aircrew, but soon afterwards he too was posted missing on a raid over Germany.

Albert had arranged to meet her in the local dance on the evening of the day that he crashed, so we had the unenviable task of going along and telling her that for her lightning had struck not twice, but three times.

She listened slightly open-mouthed with shock as we stumbled through our news, and her eyes filled with tears. 'I'm just bad luck', she murmured, despairingly. It was hard to deny it. For a moment she closed her eyes and leaned against the wall. 'She looks as if she's going to faint. Take her out for a breath of air, Gordon', someone said.

Gordon promptly obliged. He was a fleshily good-looking pilot with an air of calm arrogance, a bit older than most of us, and despite being long married, he was a great believer in Equal Rights for Women. Every woman had an equal right to share his bed.

He was outside quite a while, and he returned alone.

'You took your time', said his navigator suspiciously.

'She didn't feel like coming back in, so I took her home.'

The navigator was a blunt Yorkshireman and he knew his pilot, especially that bland, self-satisfied smile.

'You're not seeing her again!'

'You don't abandon a goldmine after you've just struck a rich seam!'

'You didn't!'

'At a time like this,' Gordon told him loftily, 'what a woman needs more than anything else is reassurance.'

'And what you're going to need more than anything else is life insurance', said his navigator, bluntly. 'That woman's a walking death sentence. So either you pack her in or you find someone else to fly with.'

And, like every good night-fighter pilot planning on making an interception, Gordon followed his navigator's instructions.

CHAPTER TWENTY-ONE

Garrison Duty

In October 1946 the news came through – we were off to Germany.

The tension between Soviet Russia and the West had been building up for some time, and it was decided that, as well as the day-fighter squadrons permanently stationed in BAOR (British Army of Occupation on the Rhine), a garrison of night-fighters might add a little window-dressing to our deterrent. There weren't all that many night-fighter squadrons around at that time, so we were to go over twice a year for several weeks at a time. And we were to go to Lübeck. It was the city that the Army had raced for to cut the Russians off from Denmark as Germany collapsed (and, incidentally, the same city that had almost blasted me from the sky with anti-aircraft fire during the war), and it lay close to the border of the Russian Zone of Occupation. But just how close we hadn't quite realised.

We flew out in squadron formation. It hadn't taken the Customs Service long following the end of hostilities to re-establish its authority on everything going into or out of the country – probably all of thirty minutes – so we had to call in at Manston, an airfield on the tip of Kent, to go through a customs check on both our inward and outward flights.

We had been warned to stay clear of the Russian Zone, they got quite ratty if we overflew it, but this was easier said than done. Their Zone of Occupation was right at the end of Lübeck's runway, so if the wind was in the East no matter how tight a turn we made on take-off we went over their border by a few hundred yards. And each time we did so an angry note condemning our violation of their frontiers would be received from the local commissar.

Lübeck sergeants' mess was a luxurious building – the 'drome had apparently been built as a *Luftwaffe* show place by Hermann Goering just before the war, to outshine Cranwell. The rooms were triple-glazed and centrally heated, and in the biting cold of the North German plain it was both welcome and necessary. We met old friends in the mess who had been out there for some time, and wondered at their gaunt and lined faces – until we discovered the reason. The beer wasn't fit to wash your plane down with, but Steinhager, a cheap and potent German gin, was a shilling (five new pence) a bottle. The dearest drink was a rather fine Trieste brandy at 4p a tot. There were lots of German waiters around to serve you your meals, and to clean your quarters, and in Lübeck was a rather splendid club for NCOs, known as 'The WOs and Joes'. It had a small orchestra made up of ex-musicians from the Berlin Philharmonic, to play for you during your meal. All in all it left the average NAAFI looking like a tram-shed.

When you walked in the quiet, sullen city, grey men with nothing to do would follow you for miles in order to pick up the butt-end of your cigarette when you threw it away. They would reroll the remains into hand-made cigarettes that could be sold on the black market. We began to experience some of the feelings that the triumphant German troops must have had when they stormed through Europe. The life of a conquering army, cosseted by a subject people, was very easy to get used to.

There were one or two things that we found alarming. If you were walking in the black market area (it was closely monitored by the service police, on guard against illegal fraternisation) you were liable to be accosted by a furtive German who would suddenly appear in front of you and flash an open cut-throat razor in your face. When you jumped back in alarm, thinking it was the long-expected appearance of the German Resistance, he would hiss dramatically in your ear, 'You vont to buy a razor?' The only legal currency around was either the plasticised cardboard small change or Monopoly-style paper money, issued by BAFO, but a handful of cigarettes or a pound of coffee was the unofficial black market currency, and it would buy almost anything.

Typical of life over there was an incident when we took a trip to Hamburg, a burnt-out city struggling back to life. In the Services Club there we came across a queue and joined it, as you always did, without knowing what it was all about. Five minutes later we found ourselves clutching a couple of free tins of tobacco each, wondering what the hell to do with them. 'Take 'em to the front door', said a passing sergeant, with withering contempt for our naivety, 'There's a German buying them for a tenner apiece.'

The purchaser was young, blonde, and once handsome, but half his face bore a terrible wound from some tank battle deep in Russia. He was a typical *Wunderkind*, a child of the Master Race, hard and sullen, with eyes like blue marbles. I wouldn't have liked to face him over a Gestapo interrogation desk.

But the ultimate illustration of the purchasing power of the mighty cigarette came just before the end of our first stint in Lübeck. A small, cocky 'erk' – as the ordinary

airman was called – wandered into our crew-room (not a place they were normally encouraged to enter), plonked himself on a corner of the CO's table and delivered a short speech.

It was the custom, he informed us airily, for visiting aircrew to provide a small treat for the ground crew out there (that is – the inference was – if we wanted small favours in return, like engines that kept working). The treat consisted of hiring a large steamer on the River Trave and enjoying an evening's cruise to Travemunde, the small port on the Baltic coast. An orchestra would be playing on board, and there would be dancing, and all food and drinks would be free. But we weren't to worry about the details, he added loftily, seeing our startled looks; if we'd just pay him up front he would organise everything.

'Oh yes! So how much do you want?' we asked, warily, when we got our breath back.

'It'll cost you', he said, 'forty fags apiece. And that's Players, none of your bloody Woodbines.'

It was a great trip, all that he claimed it would be and then some. As we had been warned that the only drink allowed on board would be the desperately thin German beer, we imbibed deeply of the German gin, Steinhager, before going aboard. I remember – very vaguely, I must admit – a German spiv on the quayside asking me what I wanted for a tin of fifty cigarettes I had, and on a whim I told him I'd take his hat in exchange. It was one of those high-peaked German SS caps with the Death's-head badge carefully removed. I donned it and marched unsteadily up the gangway, doing the goose-step and giving the Heil Hitler salute, while the bare-headed spiv and his pals doubled up with laughter. On board, I announced to the captain that 've haf kom to take over zer ship.' He was a friendly chap, very forgiving of our eccentricities. In fact, he even let me steer the steamer for half an hour or so, without actually mentioning that it was still tied up to the jetty. As it turned out, there was no beer aboard, only fruit cup. But what fruit cup! It was the nearest thing to rocket fuel I have ever tasted. You don't get parties like that with Woodbines.

Although you could buy high-quality goods such as cameras and binoculars on the black market (providing you kept a wary eye open for the service police), the problem was how to get things back to England. We had to return through Manston – the watching radar saw to that. There we received the standard third-degree grilling and all our gear was checked, as was the inside of our aircraft. There were various fiddles going on in BAOR, and the Customs were determined to stamp them out. However, their net had a small hole in it. We were taken from our aircraft to the Customs hall by bus, and it was driven by a cheery ex-bomber pilot awaiting demobilisation.

'Right, lads!' he said to the aircrew on board his vehicle, 'If you have anything you want to slip through, just stick it under your seat and remember where you were sitting. I'll look after it while you're in there being searched.'

Not, of course, that we ever took advantage of his very kind offer, I wouldn't like you to think that.

One day, there was a newcomer on the squadron. I'll call him Barmy Barker. That wasn't his real name, but it's as close as I care to go until I'm quite sure he has shuffled off this mortal coil. And knowing him, he will be much more likely to have shuffled off with this mortal coil.

He was our new commanding officer, and he looked a typical dashing fighter pilot of 1940s vintage – fair haired, blue eyed, with a handlebar moustache and talking that strange language of the time with its idiosyncratic phrases, like 'Tally-ho, old boy', 'Whacko!' and 'Wizard prang!', and calling girls 'Popsies'. But Barmy was something more than just the epitome of Pilot Officer Prune. He was a cheerful, outrageous, and charming rogue.

When we first met I was rather at a disadvantage. My little Austin Seven, Shambles, was as dry as a camel's crotch and I was busy 'borrowing' just enough 150 octane petrol – the special fuel we put in our aircraft – from a barrel behind the crew-room to enable it to reach the nearest filling station. Caught red-handed, I half expected to be for the high jump, and sure enough, he commenced to read me the Riot Act.

Then I suddenly realised that he was telling me to go and find my own barrel, because he had only just pinched that one himself. From that moment on, I had a suspicion that life was about to get a lot more interesting.

He once gave us a talk about his adventures during the war, when on a bombing trip to northern Italy. On the way back his aircraft wouldn't climb over the French Alps so he tried going over one of the passes, only to end up in a blind valley where he crash landed in a French field. He and his crew were rescued by the Resistance and parked at a large and luxurious house on the Riviera while rescue arrangements were made.

But with excellent food, some luscious female company, and long lazy days of Mediterranean sun, sea and sand, Barmy and his crew decided that this was the perfect place to lie low for a year or two until the Allies could mount a rescue expedition for them via the Normandy beaches. The Air Ministry had other ideas. A stern message came via the Underground, pointing out that there was still a war going on in England, and they would appreciate a little help with it, so would Barmy and company kindly pop over the Pyrenees to Gibraltar and back home. Barmy said they didn't fancy the idea much (some wit suggested that they probably considered eating the note, but the chef couldn't decide what sauce to put with it). But in the end they reluctantly tagged onto a gang of Basque smugglers over the mountains, complaining bitterly about the steep goat tracks they were forced to use.

Barmy's basic instincts soon began to surface. There was a local car auction near us, cars being a much sought-after commodity just after the war. Barmy would purchase a battered jeep there and bring it back for the ground crews to repair. He then sold the vehicle the following week at a nice little profit. It didn't do much for our 'State of Readiness'.

Aircrew were taken on regular so-called 'educational' trips, supposedly to various places in the area connected with aviation, so that we might learn something of use to us in our trade. Under Barmy, these almost invariably became trips to local breweries, where after a cursory inspection of the general brewing process we were parked at the end of the bottle line and told to help ourselves, but to smash the bottles afterwards to keep the Inland Revenue happy. It certainly kept us happy.

Except on one occasion, when, mystified, we suddenly found ourselves driving through the main gates of the Martin-Baker Company, a small aircraft firm. We were met by Mr Martin himself, a genial Irishman, who welcomed us to lunch in the board-room, during which he explained the purpose of our visit. We were to try out the new ejector seat for aircraft. The food seemed to lose its flavour rather suddenly.

Baling out of a plane when in trouble was getting harder as air speeds increased. With the fast jets now coming along, it became almost impossible, as the slipstream increasingly became like a brick wall. A different method was needed, so Martin-

Baker produced what was in effect a gun, that shot your seat out through the roof – with you still strapped to it – by means of a couple of blank shells fired in quick succession.

Apparently, when they had first built the ejector seat they had needed someone to try it out. Instead of advertising for a stunt man, they wandered through their works and found a likely chap in their drawing-office, named Bernard Lynch. To their great delight everything worked well, so well that they never found anything to worry about, until one day they happened to take split-second photographs of the ejection. Then they discovered that Bernard was coming within a whisker of snapping his neck from whiplash at the point of explosion. To counter this, they made him a small blind to pull over his face, this serving the double function of holding back his head while setting off the charge and at the same time protecting his face from the slipstream.

Bernard joined us after lunch as we marched out and inspected 'the machine'. It consisted of a long steel girder, pointing up into the sky for almost thirty feet, along which moved an aircraft seat on runners. It had a steel gun barrel on the back. An old mangle wheel completed the somewhat eccentric structure.

At this point, one of the pilots remarked that for once the trip was certainly educational, it had already taught him how stupid he'd been to join the Air Force.

Another turned deathly pale when he realised there was no stop at the top of the girder, and he was the smallest and lightest man ever to test the machine. The unpurturbed Lynch proceeded to give us a demo. He was strapped to the seat at the bottom of the girder, and he pulled the blind down over his face. There was a loud bang, which made us blink – and there he was sitting at the top! Nobody remembered seeing him anywhere in between. We were very quiet as they wound him back down with the mangle wheel.

I decided there was only one thing to do: volunteer to go first, while my sense of self-preservation was still stunned by the blast. Then I could stand around laughing at the others while I waited for my knees to stop knocking.

It was a weird experience. You whipped the blind down and up as fast as you could, to find your companions had magically shrunk to tiny garden gnomes, and you sat there like a toffee apple on the end of a very long stick, waiting to be wound slowly down again. When you got off the machine you were half an inch shorter from where the discs in your spine had been compressed, though they soon stretched out again.

The trip back home was very quiet, a silence broken only when we dropped a hint to Barmy that, all things considered, we preferred the brewery trips.

The time came for our biannual visit to Lübeck, and Barmy called me into his office.

'Chalky', he said, 'You've been over there several times, what's the best thing to take as currency on the black market?' I suggested he try coffee – not the liquid extract with chicory, which they wouldn't touch with a barge-pole, but the genuine beans, which could command one pound sterling a pound (good money in those days). I assumed he'd be taking a couple of pounds or so to buy the odd souvenir, like everybody else.

Not Barmy. He scoured the local town, returning with every coffee bean for miles around. He brought two hundredweight of them back to the crew-room and the place stank of coffee. Even had there been room in his aircraft – which there wasn't – he would never make it through Customs. We looked forward to future developments with great interest.

Then, the night before our departure, Barmy announced that we wouldn't be calling into Manston after all. Instead, a pal of his in Customs would come and check our aircraft at our 'drome. We couldn't believe our ears! Next morning, his Mossie heavily pregnant with as many coffee beans as he could shovel into it, he revealed that his pal couldn't make it after all; instead we would fly direct to Germany. Oh, and on the way out we would do a bit of practice low flying. In other words, we were going to sneak under the radar screen!

He staggered into the air and we followed him at low level out to Lübeck, while Johnny Wakefield and his pilot flew at normal height to act as an emergency radio link for the squadron, none of us knowing of the furore that was building up. Then after a few days out there, Barmy claimed that there was something wrong with his aircraft that couldn't be repaired in Lübeck, and he would have to fly back home. We grinned to each other knowingly – he was going back for the rest of his beans!

When Barmy got back to England, he got a cool reception from the station commander. Hard questions were being asked, and Barmy was told that this time he was to go back through Manston, and no argument. Unperturbed, plane magically repaired, he flew there quite openly, leaving his coffee waiting at the end of the runway. There he passed inspection by Customs, then darted back at treetop level, for his waiting cargo. But bad weather had set in, and try as he might, he couldn't manage to land. Up in the control tower an irate station commander watched grimly as Barmy finally abandoned the attempt and flew out to Lübeck.

Soon afterwards, I had to return to England ahead of the others, to take a medical to confirm the extension of my service until 1950.

It was all arranged so hurriedly that I dropped into Manston clean of any contraband. This immediately made them suspicious – everybody tried sneaking in something! But when they learned what squadron I was on they went berserk. However, despite an inspection that would have got me through an SAS medical they found nothing on me and they had to let me go. I tried to pass a warning through the grapevine to the others in Germany, but there was no way I could manage it, and the squadron flew back straight into a trap. An army of Customs men lay in wait.

Everyone was strip-searched, and the aircraft all but dismantled in the hunt. And what a treasure trove they turned up! There were watches and cameras, typewriters, toys, champagne and binoculars. There was even a ceremonial sword.

They all had to pay fines, and the officers were made to write abject apologies to the Air Officer Commanding – all, that is, except Barmy. He appeared to be as clean as a whistle. Back at base there was a further search of his plane. Again nothing was found.

But it was there!

The main radar on the Mossie was controlled by a gubbins shaped like a small dustbin. It was kept under pressure and tightly sealed at all times, with a warning notice that it was not to be opened. Barmy opened it with some help from the ground staff, packed it with Leica camera lenses, and resealed it.

He was moved on soon afterwards and disappeared from our ken. Rumour had it that he also bought a Mercedes-Benz out there with his coffee beans, and shipped it back home through a friendly Navy man. I don't know the truth of it, but I can believe it.

For our part, the squadron's moral fibre was judged badly to need a wash and brush-up, and a new squadron commander was moved in. It was to start a chain of events that would prove disastrous.

CHAPTER TWENTY-TWO

The Great Escape

During the War the Air Force went to great lengths to supply us with various equipment in case we were shot down. To assist us in escaping from the enemy we were given maps printed on silk handkerchiefs, tiny compasses hidden in brass uniform buttons, combs with small files set in the plastic spine, and a batch of genuine money for the countries we were due to fly over. We carried emergency rations to sustain us while on the run, and even a .38 revolver if we wanted it (though nobody with any sense took it with him. We only heard of two people who did. One was Spud Murphy who tried to John Wayne his way home but lost a shoot-out with the German police. The other was a chap who was last seen hanging his revolver on the compass before take-off. Not surprisingly, no one ever saw him again). Above all, we carried a photograph of ourselves to enable the Underground, if we were fortunate enough to contact them, to produce forged passes for us. Apparently they could manage the printing but not an authentic-style photograph.

It was all very efficient. They even made us remove any moustaches that we were wearing (particularly the handlebar style) before photographing us, as they didn't wear such things on the Continent. The one thing they didn't give us was training on how best to evade the enemy. There wasn't enough time for that, at least not until the war was over, when the necessity for it was totally past. But that's the Air Force for you.

Speaking of handlebar moustaches, I had one once. It was a very peculiar thing, and I was very glad when they made me shave it off for the picture.

The trouble was, it wouldn't grow beyond a certain length. I took advice from people with such luxurious upper-lip growths that the ends threatened to curl round and clean their ears out as they talked. The secret, they said, was to grow hair on your cheeks to support the thing halfway along, rather like a flying buttress. Unfortunately, the hair refused to grow in the creases running from my nose to each side of my mouth, so that my handlebar had two distinct gaps in the middle. One large moustache was fair enough, three short ones side by side was like looking at Charlie Chaplin through somebody else's reading glasses.

Ah, said the hairy ones, try plaiting the main bit across the gaps and into the extensions on the cheeks. This worked fine, and the result, if not a true handlebar (you couldn't see both ends from behind and this was the test) was definitely a fair-sized bottle brush. That is, providing I didn't laugh. If I did the added strain produced an almost audible 'plink' and the moustache once more split into three sections. And I laughed every time I looked at it in the mirror.

Anyway, the subject of escape exercises came up when we got a new Fighter Command chief, after the war. He was an ebullient character, with the emphasis on the bull. He had risen swiftly through the ranks during the conflict, not least because of the notoriety he achieved from making an escape from northern France following his capture after Dunkirk.

He was fond of telling the story that the Germans had imprisoned him and threatened to shoot him as a spy, but he had escaped by strangling an enemy sentry 'with his bare hands'. Whether he was trying to insinuate that sissies like us would have stopped to put on gloves first, we were never quite sure. But he gave us a little pep talk on his arrival, telling us that 'The future of the RAF lies in Fighter Command!', and ordained that all aircrew in the command would go on an escape exercise. Nobody liked to point out that the war had been over for two years now, and such training was superfluous, at least 'Seven Ways to Strangle a Sentry without the use of Gardening Gloves' wasn't included in the training schedule.

They chose a bitterly cold January night, with several degrees of frost, and they planned to drop us in small groups all over Kent at midnight. We were given a map, a handful of raisins and a water bottle (which we promptly emptied and refilled with whisky) and twopence for an emergency phone call. We had to discover where we had been dropped and then make our way by any means we could to one of two secret addresses within forty-eight hours, where a hot meal and a bed would be waiting. Meanwhile the entire police force and a goodly part of the Army were set to hunt us down.

Which is how it came about that six of us were marooned at midnight from a blacked-out lorry on a cold and lonely country road miles from anywhere, and left to our own devices.

By a flickering cigarette lighter we read the nearest signpost. It said 'Faversham', and a check on the Pole Star revealed that we were probably due south of the place, somewhere near Charing. For the remainder of the long night we stumbled across the frozen countryside cursing our new boss and wishing that that German sentry had got his strangle in first. Daylight found us holed-up in a cold barn, trying to snatch some sleep, using a pile of frozen potatoes for a pillow, and huddled together for warmth.

I woke to find a farmer's collie dog nuzzling my face. His master wasn't so friendly and ran us off his land. We were supposed to talk to anyone we met only in broken English, to make it more realistic, but it was the farmer's English that was broken, cracked wide open and stuffed full of swear-words.

Meanwhile, across Kent various incidents were happening to the little groups of escapers. One lot got onto the main London railway line and walked back without seeing a soul, while another group was captured by police, but escaped by overpowering the desk sergeant and slamming him in the cell. They finally reached one of the secret rendezvous, looking forward to the promised hot meal, only to find that it had been discovered by the Army, who proceeded to lock them in their guardhouse. One escaper, dropped in a lonely lane, nipped round the other side of the truck, climbed back on the roof, and was driven back home again by the unsuspecting driver. A disgustingly healthy civilian, out for his customary Saturday hike, was picked up by a disbelieving policeman and locked up in jail for the weekend. He wasn't happy, but it served him right.

We fared no better. After accidentally climbing into a bull's pen, and climbing out again a lot faster, we were jumped by a gaggle of CID men, halfway to the rendezvous, and were too exhausted to outrun them. Slung into a Maidstone police cell, we considered emulating the exploits of our new boss by unhooking the lavatory chain with some wild idea of garrotting a policeman or picking a lock with it. But there are surprisingly few uses that a lavatory chain can be put to, and anyway the cops soon transferred us to Rochester. This was the centre for the second part of the exercise.

With capture came interrogation. We had treated the whole affair so far with a certain light-hearted contempt, but now they were starting to get rather vicious. Intelligence officers took over the questioning; they were mostly Polish and they were good, having honed their techniques on German prisoners of war. They were determined to locate the second secret rendezvous (an unguarded remark had already revealed the first, where military police sat happily arresting escapers as they staggered in, exhausted).

For some extraordinary reason they seemed to think that I was deeply involved in the planning somewhere – I wasn't, but I was locked, naked, in a freezing cell to make me reveal all, which wasn't a lot at that temperature. In fact, the only 'all' it revealed was the light blue colour a naked body will turn when deprived of covering at below zero. They tried yelling at me, ordering me, coaxing me and confusing me. They tried the hard-man-soft-man technique but they learned nothing, for the simple reason that I hadn't the vaguest idea what they were talking about. It was only when it was all over that I discovered what the fuss was all about.

We should each have been issued with a standard RAF map of Kent, but there weren't enough to go round, so I'd taken an old map that I'd been using for a quite different purpose. At that time, Whitbread, the brewers, had started a publicity stunt to attract new customers. Each of their Kent pubs handed out a small aluminium sign,

The Startled Saint

The inn-sign shown here is of the pub, 'The Startled Saint', that stood beside the famous Battle-of-Britain aerodrome in West Malling, near Maidstone, Kent. All aircrew on the 'drome knew and used the pub, and during the Battle it acted as a sort of makeshift Mess for the aircrew. It was affectionately known to the aircrew as 'The Strangled Virgin'.

The name – that is, the real name – is connected with St Leonard, who, legend says, landed on the south coast during the Christianisation of Britain and travelled north. According to the legend he rested for a while on the very mound on which the pub was built. The inn-sign is a humorous speculation by the artist on what the saint would feel if he returned to the spot during the Battle.

Whitbreads, the brewers, issued over fifty of these inn-signs for their pubs in this area of Kent, during the late 1940s. They are made of aluminium and measured three inches by two inches.

three inches by two, bearing a pretty picture of the pub sign, to each new customer. We were into collecting these inn-signs in a big way, and we planned trips to new pubs each week to increase our total. (I still have nearly forty of them, including one from our local at the camp gate, called The Startled Saint, and nicknamed The Strangled Virgin.) It so happened that the map I was carrying had several crosses on it marking our targets for the coming week.

The interrogators discovered the map and assumed that the crosses marked the positions of various secret rendezvous, and that I was some sort of co-ordinator. They had investigated, but found nothing but ordinary public houses, totally free of escapers. (I wonder if they collected any inn-signs while they were there!) Frustrated, they had tried worming the secret of the crosses out of me, without success. They wouldn't have been too pleased about all their wasted efforts, if I had told them the truth after it was all over. So I didn't bother.

Still, I'm glad the air vice-marshal never found out about it. He'd have strangled me.

CHAPTER TWENTY-THREE

Hopping Mad

It was hop-picking time, and we were in the middle of the Kent hopfields. Each year the East End would move en masse down to the green fields of Kent for the annual picking. They were a cheerfully garrulous race. London was the world, they owned London, and they looked on Kent as their back garden. Whole families, with the exception of dad, humped their belongings, in some cases including the iron bedstead, on the back of an ancient lorry and set off for what they took as a working holiday. (Dad stayed behind. He probably worked on the docks and considered that he could pick up a lot better things at work than the stuff they used to brew beer out of.)

Their accommodation was pretty basic. Windowless and often doorless brick huts were the norm, with primitive facilities.

The local pubs prepared to make a lot of money and prepared even harder to make sure they hung on to it. Wire-mesh screens with small serving holes were erected along the bar tops – it was not unknown for people to fish for their pound notes back from the till with long canes. You paid a hefty deposit on your beer glass and hung on to it all night, and landlords who had nailed everything down were mildly surprised to find they still had the nails next morning, if nothing else.

If there was a dock strike on father would come down and join the family in the fields – hop-picking was said to be the biggest strike fund of them all. In fact as the weather got hotter, reasons for going on strike got sillier, as the dockers began to envy their families in the open air. There was one occasion when they demanded 'embarrassment money' for handling a cargo of children's potties – this from a people who had stood up to bombs, doodlebugs and rockets a few years before!

We would cycle down to their noisy, crowded pubs at the end of the day's flying, to enjoy their laughter-swamped company, returning in the small hours on our rickety, creaking RAF bone-shakers, falling merrily and monotonously into the ditch at regular intervals. But though enjoyable, it proved to be a rather expensive hobby.

Jack Bromford – known to one and all as 'Brom' – was a sergeant armourer, and one of the few ground staff in the sergeants' mess to join the aircrew on our evening excursions. He loved the ladies to an extent that you suspected him of being an experienced harem-tester to some Eastern potentate in a previous existence. But a sergeant armourer's pay didn't go far in lavish entertainment – even less than a sergeant pilot's – and as he succinctly put it, 'You don't get much for a bag of chips.' Being a cheerful unremitting scoundrel, he devised a moneymaking scheme to improve his finances.

The RAF supplied everyone with a sturdy if unexciting bicycle, and on the pretext of repairing his, Brom would borrow the key to the bike store. There he would slap together enough basic parts to make a rideable machine. This he would ride to the pub at night, flog it cheaply to some unsuspecting hop picker and carouse the proceeds away, afterwards scrounging a lift back on someone else's cross-bar. Eventually his little market was flooded, and came the night that he had to ride back on the bicycle on which he came. But there was a slight drawback. He never had time to fit little luxuries like lights (or brake blocks, come to that!) and the night was black, so he rode back with John Paulikowski (an amiable Polish pilot) and myself. We did our best to shield him safely between us.

However, on the way back an approaching car suddenly blinded us with blazing laser-like headlamps. Indignantly, Brom swerved towards it and hurled imprecation-wrapped insults about certain details of the unseen driver's birth certificate.

To our horror, the car screeched to a halt just beyond us and began a hasty 180-degree turn. It was a police car. Brom suddenly surged out of sight into the darkness ahead, pedalling like a maniac.

I left the talking to John. His perfectly understandable English seemed to sprout lots of Polish Ks and Ws and Zs when he wanted, forming a mixture that even other Poles failed to recognise. I said nothing (was it my fault if they thought I was Polish, too?), but the gist of his reply seemed to be 'What other cyclist? We couldn't see anything for your przwczing headlights.'

Their eyes speared us in contemptuous disbelief and they roared off in pursuit of the absconding culprit. We wisely decided to take an illegal shortcut back across the 'drome.

Brom turned up an hour later and told us what had happened over a late-night cup from the mess tea-urn.

He had hurled his bike over the next hedge and dived after it. It turned out to be a cemetery, of all places, and he hurriedly dropped behind the largest headstone. The cop car drew up nearby and he clearly heard the driver's voice.

'No sign of the little sod, he must be hiding somewhere. You duck behind the hedge and I'll drive off, see if he shows himself. I'll come back for you in ten minutes.'

The car raced away and the second policeman climbed the hedge and settled comfortably on a gravestone only a few yards away. Brom scarcely dared to breathe as the longest ten minutes of his life slowly ticked away, while he tried hard to suppress all kinds of beer-fuelled bodily functions and sounds. It wasn't helped a bit by the hidden sentry noisily relieving himself against the hedge.

At last the cop car returned and the minions of the law appeared to give up the pursuit and race off, after a comment of 'No sign of the bugger!' Brom thankfully got back on his machine and set off for the 'drome once more. The last couple of hundred yards to the camp were uphill and he had to get off and walk. Hardly had he dismounted than the cop car roared up once again, to a triumphant cry of 'Gotcha!'

'Riding without lights?' he protested, in reply to their charge, 'No way! I've been at the girlfriend's all night. So, as it was dark, I walked home, pushing my bike.'

Oh yes! And the name and address of this girlfriend?

'Come off it, fellers!' he said, 'Her husband's over six feet tall and nasty with it!'

They had to let him go, of course, but they reported it all to the wing commander in charge of Admin. And that worthy was already looking into the odd discovery that the bike store was bare of both bikes and spare parts. Nothing was proved, but Brom's card was well and truly marked.

Not long afterwards, Bucky, a navigator on the squadron, was posted away. He had been on the camp so long he could not get all his accumulated gear into his kitbag. Did I, or anyone else, want to buy a raincoat that refused to be squeezed in? Sadly, everyone was broke.

Two days later Brom suggested a night out at the King's Head. Not to worry about money, he'd found the raincoat Bucky had abandoned when he left and he'd managed to sell it for a few quid. It all sounded reasonable, and we all became innocent – if somewhat gullible – accessories after the fact.

Then the man Bucky had, unknown to us, really sold the coat to complained that it had been stolen, and the balloon went up. Brom was court-martialled, and his defence officer asked me to speak for him. I said I'd tell the truth as I knew it, and confirmed on oath that I and others had been offered the coat but no-one had the money to buy it. We didn't know it had been sold subsequently. There was reasonable doubt, but they weren't after justice, they were after Brom.

He was reduced to the ranks, awarded fifty-six days in His Majesty's Glasshouse, a place where you routinely and quickly became sorry you were born. But people like Brom never get their just desserts, they take every one else's desserts followed by the cheese and biscuits. Brom was a great cricketer and the Glasshouse Cricket Club was badly in need of a good bowler. So before you could snarl 'You might 'ave broke your mother's 'eart but you won't break mine', he was put in charge of the officer's mess bar with orders not to risk straining his bowling arm by pulling too many pints.

On the other hand, my own evidence to the court martial was viewed with sour distaste. Junior squadron officers sitting in on the case to learn its ways were told by its president that my evidence was strongly suspect and I deserved to be charged with perjury. So my name was permanently blackened. I can't say it often enough, never volunteer.

Brom soon got his rank back, since the Air Force was nearly as short of armourers as it was of good off-spinners. Whether he ended up an air commodore or the opening bowler of Strangeways Cricket Club I don't know. Probably both.

As for John Paulikowski, years later I heard that two wives turned up to his funeral when he died. I bet they both knew the Polish for 'I love you'. I gather he used to proudly boast that he once slept with the 'Peggy O'Neil' of the old song. Mind you, he probably pronounced it Pritzi O'Nygorski.

It's a funny old world, and that's funny peculiar.

CHAPTER TWENTY-FOUR

A Matter of Conscience

There was no way you could call Taffy good looking, yet there was something about him that women found attractive.

Perhaps it was his soft, lilting Welsh accent, or maybe it was the self-deprecating, anxious little smile and the big, velvety brown eyes, like a puppy that had just been caught sitting in the middle of a large damp patch on the new Axminster.

Whatever it was, Taffy seemed to have an unerring instinct for recognising a wife bored out of her skull with a beer-swilling husband or one grimly determined on revenge on a straying spouse. This probably made things a whole lot easier for him, but there was no doubt that Taffy made the most of his inborn flair.

He was married himself, mind you, to a chapel-happy young girl in the Rhondda. There was also a small squawking young Taffy whose lusty bawling – in fluent Welsh, of course – was said to have almost drowned out the calling of their banns, but Bronwen, his wife, preferred to stay in the valleys, near her mother and handy for choir practice.

I met Taffy in Gloucestershire, just after the war. We shared a room in the sergeants' mess of a well-built pre-war 'drome I was temporarily attached to. The pair of us, along with four other pilots, were engaged in ferrying away redundant Mosquito aircraft up to Stranraer in Scotland, where they were broken up.

Being a pre-war 'drome, it was one of the first to reopen the married quarters (popularly known as 'Married Patch') that had lain dormant and unused during the war years. There was great competition for the well-built but rather old-fashioned houses – post-war accommodation was at a premium, if not non-existent – but managing to get hold of one could be a bit of a mixed blessing.

No sooner were you comfortably ensconced in there than the RAF had a nasty habit of sending you off to any far-flung fragments of Empire that were left – places such as British Guiana, or even Norfolk. And being a long way from a town of any size, as most 'dromes were, almost the only entertainment available (apart from the odd Saturday night hop in the local village hall) was the ubiquitous Bingo session on a Sunday night in the sergeants' mess.

And often it was a sergeants' mess full of young, hot-blooded airmen. More than one absent airman had won himself married quarters and found that, far from his new home being his castle, it was more a safety deposit box for his family that wasn't all that safe.

Taffy prowled the Sunday night Bingo game like a U-boat with a spare *Schnorkel* searching the shipping lanes, though he drew the line at actually participating in the game itself. He preferred to sit at the bar with a pint pot, checking out the runners through the bottom of the glass. As the monotonous calls of 'Two little ducks', 'Doctor's orders' and 'Kelly's Eye' rang out through the room, Taffy's eye was sizing up the talent, and many a cry of 'Bingo!' was softly echoed from behind his pint of bitter.

The station warrant officer's wife – the uncrowned Queen of the Patch – and other senior wives, watched his tactics with grim disapproval and resorted to an unofficial convoy system to get all the unescorted ladies back home again, herding them back to Married Patch after the Bingo like fussing destroyers. But then Taffy spotted Trudi.

Trudi was a lusty South African girl, dumped into married quarters with three young kids and a randy husband. He was a signals sergeant with an eye for the WAAFs under him. And they were under him quite a lot. Then he was moved to a neighbouring 'drome, some thirty miles distant, leaving Trudi alone, far from her sunny homeland and with a smouldering contempt for her absent spouse that was only equalled by her opinion of her nosy neighbours. She and Taffy came together like the opposite ends of two loose magnets.

I used to get the blow-by-blow details of their grapples each night before I was allowed to go to sleep. 'There's nothing between us, mind', Taffy would insist earnestly, and when I observed, 'And frequently, it would appear', he corrected me quickly. 'Look, boyo, she's nothing to me, and I'm nothing to her. If Bronwen was here it would be different, but she isn't. Trudi is and she says she hates all men, but she can't do without them. So it's a perfect solution for both of us. Nothing more.'

This rather mechanical arrangement went on for a while, mostly in the surrounding fields, but the nights began drawing in and getting colder, and when rain stopped play now and again, Taffy began to get frustrated. He tried to talk her into letting him stay the night at her married quarters, but she always said no, the local female Gestapo were on the watch. Besides, the youngest kid slept in her room. Eventually, though, she agreed to move them all into the back bedroom for a night, but she exacted a price. Taffy had to take her to the Saturday night hop in the local village hall, and dance every dance with her.

At first, he was delighted. But by Saturday lunchtime he was starting to cool off a little. I thought perhaps the potential cost of the outing was beginning to worry him, Trudi was a prodigious downer of pints and Taffy needed a guidebook to find the bottom of his pocket. But then some mail came for him, and he seemed to go very quiet.

One of those regularly eating at our table was a chap known as Brummie, due to his coming from that sprawling city. He was a bit of a dandy. Extremely fussy about his appearance – we swore he Brylcreemed his eyebrows – and fastidious about his clothes, he was utterly vain of his skills on the dance floor as he effortlessly pirouetted his partners round the room. Taffy asked him if he was going to the dance in the village that night, but Brummie said he didn't think so, there wasn't much talent locally, and the floor wasn't up to much.

'Pity,' said Taffy, 'I'd arranged to meet this smashing popsy there, from Married Patch.' (We called them popsies in the aircrew language of the day.) 'Only I can't make it, see. I was going to ask you to give her my apologies.' Brummie didn't look very interested. 'Mad keen on dancing, she is', added Taffy, temptingly, 'Dances closer than a sweaty shirt in a heatwave. A handy chap like you could Fred Astaire his way up her bedroom stairs faster than a coal-fired rocket. Still, if you're not going . . .'

Brummie said he hadn't finally made his mind up, and could he have a few more details.

Taffy and I spent a quiet night in the mess billiard room, playing snooker. When I quizzed him about it all he would say was, 'I changed my mind, that's all', and after a quiet pint or two and a leisurely potting of balls we went back to the room for an early night.

I was woken by the noise at about half past one in the morning, to find Brummie leaning over the sleeping Taffy, pummelling him hysterically. But it wasn't the immaculate Brummie that we knew; this wild figure was hatless and scratched and his uniform, soaked in mud, looked as if he had been dragged through a hedge backwards. Which, so far as I could make out, was remarkably close to the truth.

'You rotten swine, Taffy!' Brummie was yelling, hoarsely, 'You knew, didn't you – you knew!'

Between blows – fortunately Brummie seemed too breathless to put any force behind them – we both asked him knew what?

'You knew her husband was coming home this weekend. He was waiting for us – I've been chased over every ploughed field in Gloucestershire. Just look at me! I'll never get this uniform clean again!'

Eventually we calmed him down enough for Taffy to protest his innocence. No, he hadn't known: the reason he'd decided not to go to the dance that night was simple. He'd had a wedding anniversary card from his wife in the post that morning, reminding him of the occasion. 'I couldn't go after that, could I!' he said. 'I couldn't have that on my conscience.'

We talked Brummie back to his room and eased him into bed, little knowing that the story wasn't yet over.

Next day – the man must have risen early – the glowering hulk of Trudi's husband stationed himself at the door of the sergeants' mess dining hall, checking everyone going in to breakfast. Due to the previous night's uncertain light, he didn't seem quite sure of exactly who he was looking for, but he appeared to be searching faces for a guilty blush or a bloodied nose, and uniforms for a grass stain or a muddy tear. Taffy and I hurried through our meal and got back in time to warn the still sleeping Brummie that it might be healthier to give the porridge and toast a miss.

However the vengeful figure was back at his post at lunchtime, his eyes like beady blue lasers, raking the hungry hordes surging past him. Taffy made the excuse that he had forgotten something as we passed him, and turned back to warn the terrified Brummie once more. After the meal was finished, the brooding figure took to wandering round the mess corridors, and Brummie promptly locked himself in his room, and kept away from the window. Visits to the loo became bladder-bursting dashes of sheer terror, and he was pathetically grateful for our Redskin-style scouting patrols and hoarse whispers of warning through toilet-door plywood.

At teatime the grim sentry was back once more (by now the ravenous Brummie could have gladly consumed a scabby horse between two mattresses) and he only gave up and hurried off to catch the last bus back to his own camp when the mess cooks slammed the serving hatch shut.

Still fearing a trick, it took us a long time to persuade the fearful Brummie that he had gone and it was safe to emerge. When he did he made a beeline for the tray of sandwiches left by the catering staff for that night's Bingo players. An eagle-eyed station warrant officer warned him off. They were for guests only, he was told.

And who should turn up for the Bingo session that night but the redoubtable Trudi, as calm and unruffled as a millpond in a monastery.

'Oh, him!' she said contemptuously, when we asked after her fiery spouse, 'I sent him off with a right flea in his ear. He wanted to know why the kids were all in one bed in the back room. I told him, next time he came home without warning I'd be in there with them, then he could bring one of his fancy pieces back for the weekend.'

Once he was assured that Nemesis was receding rapidly on a far-off bus back to his own 'drome, Brummie began to relax. In fact under the influence of good Gloucester ale on an empty stomach he even began reviewing his options with regard to the shapely Trudi and certain unfinished business between them.

'Sorry I dashed off last night,' he told her, 'but I never expected your husband to come down the lane looking for you in the dark like that. I don't know why he was so upset – I mean, it was all quite innocent – nothing was going on, was it!' and Trudi said, no, not a thing, in a rather bored voice that inferred that nothing was coming off, either.

'I was just showing you a few dance steps, that's all – like that reverse cross-over backlock, for instance – everything was quite straightforward.'

Trudi suggested it might have been because the lesson was taking place round the cowpats in the middle of a field at midnight, and had her husband caught up with him things would have been far from straightforward, they were much more likely to have been bent backward rather forcibly. For all his wandering eye her spouse was insanely jealous and didn't take kindly to other people dipping their spoon in his gravy.

'We need to work on that reverse cross-over backlock while your hubby's away,' persisted Brummie, 'then you can surprise him when he's next home. We could go through it when I take you home tonight.'

Taffy broke in to say he didn't advise it. The station warrant officer had been asking rather pertinent questions about the previous night – all the shouting and chasing across fields had woken his wife, which was more than he dared do. Taffy guessed that he'd have half the service police patrolling the place for a while.

'It might be best', he added, ingenuously, 'if I took her – with all the others – and leave her on her doorstep so everyone can see it's all above board. After all, I can prove I was playing snooker all last night. Trudi can say she asked me to see her home tonight because she was nervous.'

Personally I could think of no one who looked less nervous than the unruffled Trudi, but, reluctantly, Brummie saw sense in his remarks. Even so, as Taffy grabbed the lady's arm he grasped the other one. 'All right – we'll both walk her home.'

It was Taffy's turn to sound indignant. 'He doesn't trust me! He thinks I'm going to check the place over, then sneak back later when everything's quiet! That's it, isn't it!'

In the end, they both escorted her back, each hanging onto one arm like two dogs after the same bone, under the watchful eye of the Married Patch Mafia. Trudi seemed bored with the whole thing.

I was getting ready for bed when Taffy came back to the room.

'You've been quick!'

Apparently they had walked her chastely to her door-step and Trudi had gone in without another word to either of them.

'Couldn't do much else. There were two or three rotten service police on the prowl and Brummie was watching me like a hawk all the way back', he said sadly.

He sat on his bed, unmoving, still wearing his greatcoat. Then he suddenly dived into his kitbag and produced a small porkpie. To my unspoken question he said it had come in the post, yesterday, with a wedding anniversary card 'And I got a bag of crisps here.' He dug the crackling bag out of his pocket. 'Could you drop them in to Brummie, he's had nothing to eat all day.'

'Why can't you do it – he's just along the corridor?'

He hadn't time, he said, he was off out again in a few minutes, when everything had quietened down. He'd try not to wake me when he came in. Oh, and if Brummie asked, I was to say he was having a bath.

Off out again, when everything was quiet! Where had I heard those words before? Then I realised. His protestations at Brummie's suspicions had been a coded message to Trudi, standing next to him! He had probably squeezed her arm as he said it.

'You're off out to see her again, aren't you! After all that bull about your wedding anniversary!'

The soft brown spaniel eyes took on a puzzled look. 'My wedding anniversary was yesterday.'

I said, oh well then, anything after midnight was all right. And I supposed a lump of Cardiff catsmeat in a pastry overcoat with a bag of crisps made up for poor old Brummie's dance with death through the Gloucestershire mud.

'It wasn't my fault, what happened', he said, indignantly. 'I don't know why her flamin' husband turned up like that. He must have been tipped off by someone.'

He thought for a moment. 'Look, being chased by her husband before you've done anything was rotten luck, but it happens. But I thought I was doing the bloke a favour putting him on to Trudi at the dance. Still, maybe I was stretching things a bit when I told him she was a good dancer. To be honest she's like a charging rhino – she not only trips the light fantastic, she trips everybody else on the dance floor. So I feel sort of responsible, in a way. I mean, putting up with all that, and mucking up his uniform and going without food all day . . . and nothing to show for it at the end – it's been on my conscience a bit. So I thought I'd try and make it up to him.'

I said, OK, I'd give Brummie the porkpie and the crisps, and he went off happy. After all, Taffy said it was from the best pork butcher in South Wales. And I wouldn't like old Taff to have anything on his conscience, now, would I?

CHAPTER TWENTY-FIVE

Dr Crippen

Most people have a rather stylised idea of a typical squadron leader fighter pilot, *c.*1940. He was always imagined as a dashing, steely-blue-eyed and granite-jawed figure in a sky-blue uniform, with lots of things that set him apart from other men.

For instance, he usually had a brain-challenged blonde hanging onto both his every word and his left arm – the right was retained for clutching a pipe, a beer glass, a sports car steering-wheel or a Spitfire's trigger. On his top lip he had a sprawling hairy appendage that, to earn the proper title of 'handlebar moustache' was required to have both ends clearly visible from the back at the same time. On his chest hung a gaudy display of medal ribbons, (known in the trade as 'fruit salad') topped by the famous wings badge. A shapeless peaked hat was jammed on his untidy head, and he spoke an unknown and largely indecipherable language, sprinkled with words like, 'Goodshowcheps' and 'Wizardprang, olboy!' And he invariably referred to the female of the species as a 'Popsy'.

The final accoutrement that he was popularly supposed to wear was, of course, a dog. And it had to be the amiable, concrete-brained, faithful Labrador, like a black or golden shadow attached firmly to the back of his heel.

And when his master roared carelessly off into the bright blue yonder, the faithful hound would sit waiting patiently by the side of the runway for his return, with only a pleading, sorrowful look in those soft brown eyes betraying his anxiety.

It's a nice picture, and certainly there were people like that. And there were dogs like that, as demonstrated by Guy Gibson and his immortal pooch, Nigger, though personally I've always had a sneaking suspicion that any faithful Labrador waiting anxiously by a runway is there because the daft animal has discovered this new row of street lights and is waiting for the lamp-posts to grow to a decent height so that he can relieve himself against them.

On the other hand, you sometimes got dogs like the one we had in the sergeants' mess down at Tangmere on the south coast, but fortunately not too many of them.

He was a Staffordshire bull terrier, and his name was Dr Crippen, or at least I rarely heard him called anything else. This was usually shortened to Crippen or Cripp, although occasionally he was referred to, rather irreverently, as 'pig-dog'.

I believe he actually belonged in the first place to the commanding officer of the Spitfire squadron that happened to be stationed on the base at the time. They were an élite mob who flew an elegant version of the aircraft – the Mark V – with contra-rotating propellers. But despite this Crippen wasn't considered a suitable candidate for membership of the officers' mess. Instead, he was given his own chair in the sergeants' mess, where he was generally welcomed by the sergeants, most of whom were also rated as a rabble equally unfit to enter those hallowed halls. All of which suited the lugubrious Crippen down to the ground, because being situated halfway between the officers' and the airmen's messes as it was, it admirably suited his favoured life style.

Despite the blatant snub of his being banished from 'Pigs' Palace' (as we were wont to label the officers' mess), Crippen used to go dutifully rushing up to his master's plane in the approved manner whenever that worthy came in to land, chiefly, we suspected, because he enjoyed the cooling air that came from those six whirling propeller blades, whichever way they went round. But then the squadron was converted to the jet-engined Meteor and they forgot to tell the pig-dog. So the first time Crippen did a duty run up to one of those flying stovepipes, there was a strong smell of scorching Staffordshire bull terrier as the low-slung jet engine gave him a quick ten seconds at Regulo 77.

Not surprisingly, Crippen took all this rather personally and thought, 'Sod that for a game of airmen.' He quickly gave up his pale imitation of a fawning Labrador, and instead retired to his favourite lifetime's occupation, which was eating. In this he quickly established a new daily routine that deserved an entry in the Guinness Book of Records.

As soon as he woke he would lumber off to the airmen's mess (which was usually the first to start operations), and there he collected breakfast number one. To help it down he then executed a brisk waddle across the parade ground to the officers' mess, where he consumed breakfast number two, which he rather hurried through because he didn't want to miss breakfast number three back at the sergeants' mess. He then slept the morning away until he started his rounds once more at lunchtime, followed by afternoon tea and ending with dinner at the Pigs' Palace. The rest of the evening he spent in the sergeants' mess bar, snoring loudly until the faintest crackle of a carefully opened crisp packet set him leaping eagerly to his feet once more.

Of course there were occasional variations to his schedule, as when he waddled onto the square in the middle of the CO's parade with the name ORDERLY DOG written in large black letters along his back. The station warrant officer, for whom such a ceremony bordered on a religious experience, expressed his deep unhappiness in a few original phrases, though he never discovered the culprit. But possibly Crippen's starring role in life came when he chose to bring his canine lady love into the sergeants' mess dining room at teatime and attempted to achieve fatherhood right there under the gaze of the mess members awaiting their evening meal.

As a cabaret act it was something else. But while the watching hungry sergeants (particularly the aircrew, I have to admit) at first enthusiastically cheered on the efforts of their hero, Crippen, they were soon made to pay for their enthusiasm. The WAAF waitresses flatly refused to serve the meal while the performance was proceeding, or, indeed while the dogs remained in the sergeants' mess at all. No-one was quite sure enough of Crippen's – usually amicable – temperament when engaged in his annual current workout with his inamorata to risk trying to eject them bodily from the dining room while in *flagrante delicto*. It was stalemate. 'Give us the tools,' Churchill had cried to the nation, 'and we will finish the job!' Patriotically, Crippen duly obliged, finishing the job, and then ambling off to the airmen's mess for his last meal of a memorable day.

Perhaps wisely, Crippen never repeated his performance. Somehow he seemed to sense that he had to choose between indulging in unbridled passion and eating his regular nine meals a day, to say nothing of the extra bags of crisps and pork scratchings.

To him it was no contest. He settled down each evening in the bar and waited for his supper. There was a round iron stove in the middle of the room set in a square hearth of concrete and usually glowing a fiery red. Crippen annexed this space for himself, curling his bloated body perilously round the stove so that his naked stomach roasted steadily within a hair's breadth of the cherry-hot metal. Winter was coming on, and while the mess members shivered as close to the fire as they could get, Crippen was ceding his fireside seat to no-one. He barely deigned to move for even an occasional replenishment of fuel, and there was a steady aroma of scorched flesh that easily overpowered the normal beery aromas of the bar. He steadfastedly ignored the pointed remarks of the bar customers about blocking the heat, only rarely lifting pained brown eyes in a mute 'Shift me, I'm burning' appeal.

It could only end one way. One October night during a high wind, a red-hot coal fell out of the bottom flap with the inevitability of Nemesis. It fell on the most vulnerable part of a male's anatomy, be he hound or human, and Crippen took off, almost literally, like a coal-fired rocket, on a three-lap circuit of the bar walls, at a gravity defying height, in a despairing attempt to cool it.

This was followed shortly afterwards by a rave-up in the mess when the squadron – almost unbelievably – won the Sports Day cup, and celebrated by filling the large silver-plated vessel with a sample of almost every alcoholic beverage known to man.

Whether the idiot who topped it all up with a dash of Ronsonol, causing considerable blistering of participants' lips, was the same idiot who persuaded the long-suffering Crippen to over-indulge, in the same celebration, in a considerable amount of that dark wine of the Irish peasantry, Guinness, I do not know, but life for him was never quite the same again. It was at this time that we moved to West Malling and we lost track of him. I did hear fitful stories of a daring last foray involving the gallant old pig-dog and a Great Dane on heat, and I believe he was posted as 'Missing on operations, believed died in action.'

So passed Dr Crippen, doggy patron saint of food and fornication.

CHAPTER TWENTY-SIX

Prang!

When I had first moved down to Tangmere, at the end of the war, the RAF had been in a great state of turmoil. It had been a long, hard war, but now it was over and the service, albeit very slowly, began to relax back into its peacetime mode. Slowly, because it still had hundreds of machines that it no longer had any use for and thousands of men who no longer had any use for the RAF. But you couldn't just hand each one a pay-packet and a railway warrant on the first Friday night after the last shot was fired, and say, 'OK, chaps, thanks for all your help in World War Two, and goodbye for now. See you again in World War Three. Try not to be late.' For one thing they all needed jobs to go back to, but the jobs had to be peacetime jobs, and it would take time to reabsorb so many people back into a peacetime community.

Of course, you were entitled to claim your old job back – if you'd had one. But you couldn't claim an automatic promotion or pay rise, and if you'd left behind a junior who had now risen to become your senior you couldn't claim his promotion. And the prospect of going back to a position below someone who had stayed safely at home during the conflict did not exactly appeal.

Indeed, many aircrew had come straight from school, in some cases from satchelled pupil to bemedalled squadron leader over the five years of war. Somehow they all had to be fitted back into industry in a position reasonably commensurate with their new status but lacking any experience. The prospects weren't good, and many with a new sense of self-importance were to be severely disillusioned.

So it was to be a long wait, a gradual demobilisation spread over many months. You were given a demob number, based on your length of service and married status. Meanwhile, the RAF had to begin the difficult task of forging a smaller but highly efficient peacetime Air Force from this unpromising mixture of war-weary veterans longing to go home and a new temporary influx of National Servicemen, unwillingly dragged from their apprenticeships to serve what they saw as a totally unnecessary and unwanted break in their career.

Down at Tangmere, I had met and married my wife, Phyl, a tall, fun-loving Canadian-born nurse from 'Dirty Dick's', as we called St Richard's Hospital in nearby Chichester. We met on the camp, at a mess dance, and suddenly there was a lot more to life than just flying. Each month we held a dance in the sergeants' mess, and she was one of the gang of nurses that regularly attended.

(And what a hungry bunch they were! Food rationing was still in force, and the NCOs would sacrifice a goodly portion of their rations for the month to put on a royal spread as a sort of bait, and the girls would descend on us from the Nurses' Home like a cloud of locusts! We would watch as they arrived and disappeared into the Ladies, then the door would ease gently open and long arms would reach out from behind it and steadily clear the nearest tables of the succulent goodies, down to the bare wood. And that was just the lot they could cram into their handbags to take back! When those same handbags were full they would start to demolish what was left. But their company was well worth our sacrifice!)

By the end of 1947 Phyl and I were living happily in a house on the coast near Bognor, in a winter let, but we were hoping to move into one of the newly refurbished married quarters.

I had changed my navigator once more, this time from Andy, who had come down from 100 Group with me but who was now leaving the service, to Larry, a happy-go-lucky Londoner, as tall as Dagwood had been, and we got on well. Life became a steady round of night-flying training and carrying out fly-pasts at any wartime anniversaries that happened to be going, such as Battle of Britain celebrations. And not only over London but also over places like Plymouth, Dover and Calais, and particularly over the Channel Islands to celebrate their freedom from the German occupation. We flew on co-operation exercises with the anti-aircraft lads and the searchlight units, and went on our twice-yearly garrison duty trips over to Germany. Interspersed with these were trips up to the Northumberland coast for air gunnery practice between the Farne Islands and Holy Island.

Oddly, we had done very little air-to-air gunnery practice during the war itself, although my pal, Bert, had lost his life target-towing on the very same ranges that we were now to use. The only previous firing I recall had been some air-to-ground practice at a range just to the north of King's Lynn. There, I had distinguished myself by pouring the contents of my 20 mm cannon unerringly into a long, thin, white, oblong target on the coast that they later informed me was a large canvas number one, indicating the position of the first target. They declined, however, to award me the sign as a 'destroyed' or even a 'probable' as no one else saw it – the markers were cowering for dear life in their bunkers.

Air-to-air firing was carried out by shooting at a canvas drogue, towed along the coast (at the end of a very long cable!) by a light aircraft, usually a Martinet, and like all firing ranges there was a strict procedure to follow. To save time, two pilots fired on the same drogue, one after the other, and to distinguish whose bullets had hit the thing, your shells were first dipped in different-coloured paints. Your camera ran automatically while your cannon were firing so that your firing technique could be assessed later.

But first you had to take a camera-only shot so that they could line up the picture correctly. Again to save time, the first man would take a camera shot on the towing plane itself, after which the Martinet would 'stream' (that is, let out) a fresh drogue on its cable and the Mossie would happily poop off at it. Then the second Mossie would arrive and take his camera shot on the drogue itself before, in turn, hopefully peppering it full of different-coloured holes. Finally the Martinet would fly back to the 'drome and drop the tattered drogue in front of the control tower before returning to the range for the next couple of airborne Wyatt Earps.

On this particular day, I thought I was number one on the target when I was actually number two. The CO had already had his go, and for once – he was not the best shot in the world – had managed to riddle the drogue with a fair number of hits.

I can only blame the Newcastle Brown Ale of the previous night for the error, but, thinking I was number one, I came up behind the Martinet ready to take my camera shot of the plane, only to discover a large cable snaking wildly through the sky a few inches above my starboard wing. I was between the Martinet and its drogue.

Desperately I stuffed the nose down, but too late, the cable curled suddenly into my propeller. There was a loud bang as the whirling blades chopped it cleanly through and the inoffensive drogue tumbled to a watery grave into the sea below. But not all the restraining cable went with it. A large piece still lay across my wing looking as if it had cut deep into the plywood. Had the wing been fatally weakened?

I called Control and said I was coming in on a wing, a prayer and about ten feet of drogue cable. The other wing, I added, would probably be landing before we did, but in the event the watching crowd was highly amused when the length of cable fell off harmlessly as we touched the runway, revealing an aircraft body without a blemish on it, save for the tiniest of scratches on one propeller blade. In fact, the only things to be damaged were my pride and the CO's chances in the scoring competition.

Mind you, he was pretty decent about it, considering that I had just sent his best efforts spinning down into the North Sea. 'Chalky,' he reproached me, wearily, 'if you run out of ammunition on air-to-air firing, you're not supposed to fix bayonets and charge!'

While we were up in Northumberland, enjoying the delights of Geordieland's countryside and capital – Newcastle – contact was maintained with our base by the occasional aircraft flying down to Tangmere, usually to pick up mail, information or aircraft spares.

A returning pilot was wont to be quizzed as to the latest local gossip down there, usually during a noisy teatime meal.

'Anything new happening down there?'

'Not a lot.' I remember one returning pilot reporting, through a mouthful of whatever-on-toast. Then he suddenly added, 'Oh, yes . . . Fontwell Annie's pregnant!'

The deathly silence that instantly descended on the mess dining room was as though a radio had suddenly been switched off in the middle of a noisy programme. Faces suddenly blanched, mouths fell open, eyes widened in shock.

The silence was broken only by the clatter of nervously dropped cutlery – sounding like a thin round of applause from a convention of metallic robots. More than one plate of food was pushed aside uneaten, appetite running out of its intended consumers like sand from a cracked egg timer.

The lady was a friendly Scottish lass, an ex-WAAF who had left the service but chose to continue to live locally. Whether she earned the nickname connecting her to the famous pre-war racecourse was due to her living near the place or because she chose to make use of its wide open spaces I do not know. Of course, these days DNA has taken all the fun out of gossip about such events – it's rather like knowing the winner of the Derby before you lay your bet – but in this case, I recall, there were a great many runners but no final winner was declared.

The reason I mention the tale is because of the remarkable effect that the announcement had. Any teacher facing an unruly class, any chairman attempting to restore order to a stormy meeting, even the Speaker of the House of Commons trying to calm down a House noisily debating pub-opening hours, is recommended to try using the phrase in a loud, clear voice: 'Order! Order! Gentlemen! Fontwell Annie's pregnant!'

Works every time. Mind you, they won't know what it's all about, but when did they ever?

Shortly afterwards we began carrying out the Met. flights for the weather boffins, a boringly dull job of taking temperature and pressure readings every five hundred feet up to forty thousand feet.

Up there it was a totally different world. There were no clouds above thirty thousand feet, and the sun was a cold brassy disc in a clear black sky. On fine days the view was superb, and you could see from Southampton in the west right round to Harwich, in the east. Of course such heights are commonplace in these days of pressurised cabins and jet aircraft, but then we were right on our flying limit, wearing only oxygen masks in unpressurised aircraft. The rarified air up there gave a false reading of our speed on the clock due to the lower air pressure in the pitot tube. Yet, because the aircraft wing was supported by that same air pressure, our stalling speed – the speed at which we would fall out of the sky – remained the same on the clock dial, one hundred and thirty miles an hour. Those last couple of hundred feet took an age to climb as your airspeed steadily fell away until it hovered on the edge of your point of stall.

Once, I decided to relieve the boredom by beating up the 'drome at zero feet, and was hauled over the coals by an irate flying control officer who stood on his balcony glaring down at me as I passed, several feet below him. What did I think I was doing?

'Taking the temperature and pressure readings at ground level', I said innocently, and was told rather sniffily that they could do that themselves, down on the ground, thank you very much, but I was let off for my cheek.

Then, suddenly, the squadron moved to West Malling in Kent, and, following the brouhaha over Barmy Barker's exploits, someone started checking up on aircrew records.

Puzzled, they rang through from Group Headquarters. My records were incomplete, there was no mention of my taking any rest in nearly five years of operational flying. Could I let them have the missing information?

I had to confess that I'd never been on a rest; I'd managed to change squadrons or 'dromes or wars enough times to escape their notice. What's more, I didn't want a rest, but despite my protests I was hauled off the squadron and sent to Flying Training Command to learn to be an instructor. And whom did I come across there? Our old friend, the air vice-marshal had taken over, and he gave us his little pep talk, but with a slight alteration in is script: 'The future of the Royal Air Force', he thundered, 'is in Training Command!'

Not for me, it wasn't. Housing was in short supply in the service, but they were starting to build new married quarters back at West Malling and I wanted the chance of one. I talked my way off the course, but instead of returning, as I hoped, to the squadron, I was sent to Pershore in Worcestershire. Britain had sold her spare Mosquitoes to Australia and New Zealand, and Number One Ferry Unit's job was to take them out there.

And what an itinerary it was! You flew via Marseilles, Rome, Athens, Habbaniyah (in Iraq), Karachi, Calcutta, Singapore, Darwin and Sydney, with, for some, a further leg across the Pacific to New Zealand. Then you came back by British Overseas Airways. It was a dream job, but it was no picnic.

For one thing, you flew in pairs, with the spare pilot doing the navigation. As pilots we could navigate – within reason – but going halfway round the world was pushing our rather rusty experience too far. There was no room for error, especially on the long sea crossings, so the training was hard. We heard of an old commanding officer of ours, back in our days in Norfolk, who had tried flying a light aircraft out to Aussie land and had crashed on a lonely beach somewhere in Indonesia. As he lay injured, unable to move, he was attacked by a horde of scavenging crabs. All he had to fight them off was a revolver, and he saved the last round for himself. I've never fancied crabmeat since.

Meanwhile, conditions at Pershore were not pleasant. It was out in the wilds of Worcestershire, difficult to get back home to the south coast for the weekend, and after the easy-going atmosphere of a front-line squadron, discipline was harsh: the drill sergeants had taken the Air Force back from the aircrew.

There was a further complication. Although the ferrying trips to the other side of the world would have been new and exciting, they were reluctant to let me go on them. I had never learned to swim. When I was young and my schoolmates were learning, I was in Derby Royal Infirmary with a broken leg, and I never got around to lessons. What difference it would have made in the middle of the Pacific or the Indian Ocean I didn't quite see – I preferred sinking without trace to swimming in the wrong direction for a week – but sadly, I had to give up the dream and put in for a transfer. To my surprise I was sent back to my old squadron again, where I quickly crewed up once more with Larry. So much for my rest!

However, we soon fell foul of the tightened-up discipline of the new regime, following the slackness of Barmy Barker's reign. We happened to turn up late for briefing one morning and copped a rotten job as a consequence. A new aircraft needed to be collected from the depths of Norfolk, a couple of miles from the end of the world. Thick fog threatened the whole of the country. What's more, it was a Friday and by that time the RAF virtually closed down until Monday morning. We'd be lucky to get back in a week, and bang went my chances of going home for the weekend.

We travelled up to Norfolk on a slow train that spent half its day wandering round East Anglia looking for stations to stop at, but finally we got there. The plane was ready, they said. Ready for the knacker's yard, we thought, when we saw it. We recognised it at once as C Charlie, a Jonah aircraft that had given so much trouble that the squadron had palmed it off onto another squadron months before. Since then it had gone from squadron to squadron, like a game of Pass the Parcel. Now the process had gone full circle, and the music had stopped with us.

'Of course, you can't take-off', said the Met. officer, 'Not today, the whole of England is clamped in.'

Was there nowhere clear at all? We'd take anything rather than endure a fog-bound weekend in the Norfolk bundoo. The Met. officer admitted that there was just one place, the last place open in the country – at Tangmere on the south coast, and that wouldn't last more than half an hour.

Tangmere – five miles from where Phyl and I were living! I knew it like the back of my hand, I could land a pram in a pigsty at Tangmere. I said we'd try it.

They were reluctant to let us go, but I talked them into it and we took off into the thickening fog before they could change their minds. Halfway down the runway, engines going flat out into the rapidly gathering fog, I felt a quick flicker of alarm – one engine seemed to miss a beat and gave the gentlest of stutters. It was no more than a discreet clearing of the throat of a butler entering the master's bedroom on a Sunday morning, and it was past in an instant, then we were climbing up and setting course.

I asked my navigator. 'Did you hear anything, then?' Larry thought he had but wasn't sure. Still, everything seemed to be running smoothly, and thirty minutes later we picked out the misty outline of Tangmere's runway below us.

If you lowered your wheels and flaps and chopped your engines right back, you could drop a Mossie in like a falling brick, a thousand feet right onto the end of the runway. The trick was to pull out of your plunging turn and slam on your engines at just the right moment to avoid a high-speed stall. I'd done it many times before, and we sailed over the hedge with the incoming fog hooked on our tailwheel. It had been a close thing.

I offered Larry a bed for the night, but he had set his heart on a weekend up in London. Could I get back to Malling on my own on Monday, if he caught a train directly back to camp? I said no problem, and went off to chat with the flight sergeant in charge of station flight. He serviced all incoming aircraft and he was an old friend.

Dismal Dan, as he was known because of his pessimistic outlook on life, was not the sort of man to encourage you to take to the air lightly. When you collected an aircraft from him, he would look at you sorrowfully, like a spaniel who hadn't been fed, and observe in a sepulchral voice, 'Well, I done me best with it, Chalky,' (here came a deep sigh.) 'but I can't say as I'm 'appy with it!' You had to get used to Dan, or you wouldn't so much as dare to stand on a low stool. Anyway, I told him of the slight take-off hiccup and asked him to take a look at the engines. Then I went home for the weekend, happy to have saved a rail fare.

On Monday, the fog was still around but not quite so bad, and for once you could say the same for Dan's confidence. 'Well, I done me best with it, Chalky – and I think you'll find it orlright, now.' I could scarcely believe my ears.

Take-off was smooth, I stayed at a thousand feet and set course for West Malling. It wasn't far, around sixty miles. But the fog was beginning to increase once more, and I came down to seven or eight hundred feet in my search for the 'drome. Malling

Prang – Wateringbury, Kent

was on a hill, and I caught a fleeting glimpse of it on my port side at the very instant that trouble struck.

The power suddenly cut out on the starboard engine and the rev counter needle swung wildly back against the stop. I looked across and saw raw petrol flooding out of the exhaust manifold. Something was very wrong.

The swift falling away of the Mossie's speed that had helped me drop easily into Tangmere now worked against me. My speed was plunging, but I was too low to bale out, I would have to stay with it. I had done single-engined landings before, but not while looking for a 'drome hidden in the mist, at the same time carrying out emergency procedures, and all on my own.

A dead engine's propeller windmills round, acting like a brake, so you had to 'feather' it quickly – that is, turn the blades edge on to the slipstream – or it would drag you down. I banged the big red button to set the emergency mechanism in motion to stop the blades spinning, then I dived to pick up speed and turned back to where I had seen the 'drome.

At last the propeller slowed to a stop. Then, to my horror, it began speeding up again. This sometimes happened if you didn't depress the button long enough. My speed started to fall away once more.

I was at little more than four hundred feet now. I yelled into my radio, 'This is Two Three – emergency!' to the unseen Flying Control, and pressed the feathering button once more. I knew the runway was ahead, and my only hope was to dive to treetop level and pray that I would gain enough speed to reach it.

As luck would have it, and I wasn't having a lot, at the bottom of my dive I couldn't avoid clipping the top of a tall elm tree. This finally stopped the faulty engine, but it also stopped the good one, and in sudden silence I began to sink slowly into the tree-tops in the world's most expensive glider.

I remember feeling very calm, and thinking, 'Ah well, this is it. It's my turn to go, and it's been a great life . . .' The trees began tearing at the aircraft and I was thrown around violently against my straps. Then, quite suddenly, my mind changed. 'No,' I decided, 'I'm not ready to go yet!' and braced myself. I remember the tail of the aircraft moving inexplicably across my vision, and then the world went dark.

I came to a few moments later. There was complete silence but for a soft hissing sound. I was still sitting in my seat, but the seat was no longer in the plane, it was several feet from it, or rather, from the pile of scrap wood that had once been a plane. Behind the pilot's seat had been a 15 mm thick bullet-proof steel plate. I was sitting holding part of this, it had snapped in half as it went through the roof, clearing the way for me to follow. Over all there was a tremendous stench of petrol – almost every crashed Mossie I had seen had burned up, and my first desperate thought was to get the hell out of there.

I pushed the plate away and tried to move, but couldn't, I was still strapped firmly in the seat, so I banged the quick-release box and fell sideways onto the ground. My left leg was floppy and pointing backwards; it was broken, as was my right arm above the wrist. So I crawled away like a crab, using my right knee and my right elbow, dragging the useless left leg behind me. As soon as I was clear of the wreckage I leaned against a tree, totally drained, and looked around. I had landed in an orchard and destroyed some sixty cherry trees, their small trunks acting as a crude brake, steadily smashing off chunks of the aircraft as it slowed. Lucky for me this included the petrol tanks.

There was shouting, and a farmer came running up. He was smoking a large pipe and with him were a landgirl and a German prisoner-of-war. All three started to search the wreckage. I called, in rather feeble anger, 'Put that bloody pipe out!' and they turned in astonishment. 'He's over there!'

I asked the farmer to pull on my broken leg and hold the foot upright, while the landgirl went all Florence Nightingale, kneeling down behind me and pulling my head down onto her lap. She suddenly saw my upturned face, which was a mask of blood from bits of broken perspex still in it, and for a moment I didn't know whether she would faint or be sick.

Then up raced the ambulance – the end of the runway was barely a couple of hundred yards away – and with it the RAF doctor. In no time I was lying on a stretcher in sick bay, my broken leg strapped in a Thomas's splint, while the medics cleaned me up and pumped me full of things to numb the pain. Larry looked in, but left quickly, ashen faced, and I was loaded onto an ambulance for the long drive to hospital.

The journey seemed to last for ever – it was twenty long miles, to the Guy's Unit in Orpington, and I felt every bump on the way – but eventually I was wheeled down the Accident Ward, hardly seeing the line of pale, curious faces watching on each side as I was gently unloaded onto a bed and the curtains drawn.

They eased me out of my bloodied uniform and asked me lots of questions, but I was too woozy to answer properly and they left me alone for a while. A woman visiting her husband in the next bed peered round a corner of the curtain at me for a long minute. Then I heard her say softly to her husband, 'I think he's dead!'

I tried to say 'I think so, too', but the words wouldn't come. Instead, I drifted away into a deep, dark sleep.

I came round from the operation at around three in the morning. For a long time I didn't know where I was, and I cared even less. The darkened ward was silent except for the gentle whiffle of heavy breathing from sleeping bodies, and the occasional night-nurse would slipper quietly past.

I could vaguely make out some sort of wooden scaffolding frame round the bed. Perhaps they had already found me guilty of breaking an aircraft while I was under the anaesthetic and this was part of tomorrow's preparations for a drumhead court martial and hanging? But so far as I could make out, the only thing hanging from the structure as yet was my left leg. It was heavily bandaged, and two cords came out just below my knee and went onto pulleys at the top of the wooden frame and thence to weights hanging over the end of the bed. A furtive exploration revealed that they had hammered a long stainless steel spike through my left shinbone and it was to this that the cords were fastened.

I lay on my back, unable to move, and everything hurt like hell, while my throat felt as if it had a broken hacksaw blade wedged down it.

The night-nurse noticed me stir and padded down the ward to ask if I wanted anything. And in a voice like a November fog I said, yes – a drink. It wasn't easy to take while lying on my back – half of it went in my left ear – but I managed to ease my throat a little.

Was that enough water? I said yes, for now, but I'd rather like to get rid of some as well, if that could be arranged, so she obediently padded off for a bottle.

When she returned we looked at each other for a long moment while we both tried to work out the mechanics of the operation. My right arm was encased in plaster to the fingertips, while my left one had a saline drip weeping steadily into it from a nearby stand. My left leg, of course, was strapped halfway up the scaffold, firmly held there by the weights, while a couple of drain tubes ran from the bottom of my lungs, one of which had collapsed

The only part of me free for any other business was my right foot.

Now, I was aware that certain gifted disabled people could paint infinitely delicate pictures using no more than a couple of toes and a near-bald loo brush, but I wasn't one of them. All they were likely to get from me if they didn't hurry was a large watercolour splashed on the opposite wall. No problem, said the night-nurse, and swished back the bedclothes.

She was a big, sturdy girl who didn't laugh a lot. She had seen it all. I'd say she was probably a farmer's daughter who was used to helping her dad sort out the bull on her day off, but she was quickly brought up short. Because there was a problem. They'd left my Y-fronts on during the operation.

She thought about this for a while, trying to work out a plan of campaign. But you know how women can't read a map unless they're holding it upside down? It's the same with Y-fronts – they can't fathom out which way they go unless they're actually wearing them.

In the end, she gave up. She pulled out the largest pair of scissors I have ever seen, and in a couple of swift strokes, like some latter-day Alexander cutting the Gordian knot, she reduced the offending garment to no more than a couple of lace hankies, while I closed my eyes in sheer terror. I fell asleep again before I could blush.

CHAPTER TWENTY-SEVEN

In Dock

Most of the patients in the Casualty Ward at Orpington Hospital were local civilians. However, at the far end was a small section that came under the control of Guy's Hospital in London and was consequently – and not surprisingly – known as Guy's Unit. Here, patients from the services were treated.

There were some half a dozen servicemen there, mainly from the RAF but also from the Army, and they were in for various reasons, varying from flat feet to – like myself – flattened everything. They ranged from a young airman whose father ran a cider press in Devon to a young Army corporal suffering from tuberculosis of the spine. That particular patient was being nursed in what was then a rather novel way. He lay in a large plaster mould shaped to him, so that his body was held totally supported at all times. The trouble was that he was unable to turn or twist to ease the pressure on his by now scrawny form, and the nurses spent a great deal of their time massaging life back into his bed sores. When things got too bad they put a sort of top plaster cover onto the base, leaving him like an oyster inside its shell. They then turned him upside down, removed the base for cleaning and nursed him for a time on his stomach. It seemed a rather painful and primitive system, but it appeared to be working.

There was even a German prisoner-of-war, named Hans, in a bed further down the ward. He was quiet and friendly, with none of the Nazi arrogance we had been led to expect, and like most of the POWs had been working on the land. He had a broken leg, which had confined him to hospital in this country while most of his companions had been sent home. He must have been very lonely, but he never complained.

I must confess that I was not too well disposed to him at first, and ignored him. I had lost too many good friends too short a time before to feel like forgiving my enemies, and he quietly observed to the others that ' Mister Vite, he does not like me', but I gradually warmed to his quiet and courteous manner and became as friendly as the rest.

But I was to spend many long and weary hours pinned to my bed by the weights hanging from my leg, the plaster on my arm and the saline drip into my other arm. The days passed agonisingly slowly and painfully. I tried not to watch the big ward clock, convinced that it had stopped as it moved so slowly. Every four hours, day and night, I was given an injection of penicillin. And in between times the nurses washed me and wiped me and shaved me, lifted me on and off bedpans and rubber rings, or massaged my backside with surgical spirits where it was rose-red sore from constantly lying in one position. Meanwhile my own spirits slowly sank to zero from sheer boredom. I felt like a large, helpless baby, particularly when the lights

went out at nine o'clock at night. For years I had been accustomed to flying into the small hours, and my brain became sharp and clear just as they dimmed the lights for us to go to sleep. When they woke us at six in the morning I invariably dozed off again, missing my breakfast. For a long time I couldn't read a book or a newspaper because I couldn't hold them; all I could do was talk to the other patients, which I proceeded to do in an unnaturally high and piping voice that I couldn't recognise as my own. After several weeks of suffering this I had had enough.

'How long', I squeakily demanded of a passing doctor, 'do I have to have these penicillin jabs? I feel like the treble twenty on a dartboard.' He asked what jabs those were, and I pointed out that I was now so full of penicillin that any bed-bug taking an unwary bite out of my backside would be instantly cured of everything from gout to gallstones.

'Oh, are you still having those?' he said airily, which did nothing to improve my faith in doctors. 'Yes, I am. And another thing, what about my voice?'

He looked puzzled. 'What about your voice?'

'You don't think I normally talk like Mickey Mouse in a diving suit?' I squeaked indignantly. 'Well, yes, I did', he confessed, then he frowned thoughtfully. 'I wonder whether we found all the damage.'

I assured him, so far as I could tell (and count), that nothing appeared to be missing from the original check by the midwife, and all I seemed to need was an Eezit oil sandwich.

The Ear, Nose and Throat specialist stalked down the ward and peered into my mouth. He was a man of few words, and most of them rude. 'You're talking too much', he snapped. 'Shut up!' And he went off again, leaving me with a small notepad and pencil with which to inform the nursing staff of any urgent needs I might have for the next week or so. It wasn't easy writing the word 'Bottle!' left handed, while trapping the notebook against the blanket with my plastered arm. By the time I'd succeeded in convincing the puzzled nurse that I wasn't trying to write 'bootlaces' it was almost too late, but the addition of several exclamation marks helped, once they grasped the fact that the number indicated the urgency of the request.

At intervals the Great Panjandrum himself puffed his way round the ward, towing a long tail of nervous nurses and obsequious students behind him. He was known affectionately among the hospital staff as Butcher Bill, from his habit of finishing an operation with a deep red apron when he had started out with a pure white one.

He was a kindly man, really, but his manner of talking to patients could be a little alarming. He would stand close to you, but ignoring you completely, while discussing your case with his houseman in a normal voice that you could quite plainly hear. 'Yers, I think we'll have that plaster orf the arm, but we'll give the leg another week.' Then he would turn and put his lips close to your ear and bellow exactly the same message at the top of his voice, as if convinced that God had forgotten to drill a hole in the middle of that particular organ. 'We're going to remove the arm plaster,' he would roar, 'but we're giving the leg another week!' At least the weights on my leg stopped me from leaping to the ceiling in fright.

Our ward came under the strict control of Sister, a stern young disciplinarian who exercised effortless and admirable control over everything and everyone in that ward, including any young doctor who stepped out of line. The only one she deferred to was Matron, a tiny, formidable figure who inspected everything once a week with a glance like a laser beam. And the whole place ran like highly polished, well-oiled clockwork.

There has often been talk of the relative merits of the old system of sister and matron compared to the modern manager set-up in the NHS. I have experienced both regimes.

A few years ago, I was in a Derby hospital for a short repair job. I received good care and attention, for which I remain duly grateful, yet there were aspects of the hygiene that would not have been tolerated for a second in the old days. I recall one meal arriving under a plastic cover that had a huge crack in it. Condensed steam dripped from the crack – which was obviously impossible to clean – onto the food below. I pointed this out, but the only reply I got was 'Don't you want it, then?' I asked the nurse to break the cover so that it could not be reused. She refused and put it back on the heated trolley for someone else. Sister would have broken hearts as well as plastic covers if that had happened on her beloved ward.

In some ways, though, she could be a bit of a tyrant, and as I slowly improved I countered the boredom by organising a resistance movement among the other service patients whenever she became too impossible. For instance, she had a strong aversion to moustaches – I've no idea why – and would loudly demand the removal of any incipient facial hair decoration from any patient attempting to grow one.

One of the RAF lads opposite to me was making a hooked wool rug for his occupational therapy, so one morning we passed round several strands of his black wool to each patient on the ward, each in a bundle neatly tied in the middle. This we combed out into a fair imitation of a handlebar moustache, and everyone stuck it under his nose. Then we lay there in silence, like a squadron of fighter pilots going on a suicide mission, awaiting Sister's arrival and trying hard not to giggle. Normally, she marched down the ward, saying good morning to each patient in turn, but this time she did the walk in total silence, her face a tight-lipped mask. She finally reached the door of her office, turned, and bellowed back down the ward, 'All right, you lot – now TAKE 'EM OFF!' But there was no more trouble over moustaches.

Her other great aversion was equally odd, because it was beer bellies, but the Great Beer Belly Battle was one that I did not win.

The occupational therapy lady came round with various hobbies to keep our minds and fingers busy, but none of the soft toys that were her stock-in-trade were to my liking. Squashy blue bunny rabbits and purple ducks were hardly me. Instead, I began to make a twelve-inch-high cloth doll of an RAF pilot officer. I made his body out of pink cloth, complete with handlebar moustache and blue eyes, and then gradually tailored a complete RAF uniform and cap, with wings and medals, beat-up peaked cap and leather shoes, and even a tiny leather wallet in the pocket containing miniature pound notes. I was very proud of its accuracy.

But in my quest for authenticity I over-stuffed the pink body to give him an appropriate beer belly, and for some reason this enraged Sister. Each morning she would grimly pound the doll's stomach flat with her fists, despite my vehement protests, and then march off, smiling happily, leaving me to plump the stomach back to its full glory. Sigmund Freud might have explained her fixation, I certainly couldn't.

But I wasn't the only one to suffer at the hands of the nursing staff. However much discomfort I felt from my continual jabs, it was as nothing compared to the crusty old groundstaff flight sergeant in the next bed.

Chiefy Frost had been in the Air Force, as the old joke has it, since Pontius was a pilot. He had been everywhere, done everything, and he possessed a stare like an open razor, guaranteed to cut young rookies down to a very small size.

One morning, a young nurse approached his bed with a poised syringe and a bright air.

'Right, Mr Frost, roll over, I'm going to give you an injection.'

He gave her a baleful glare, one that could get airmen quaking in their boots, wondering what they had done wrong. 'Oh, no, you're not', he snarled.

She hesitated a fraction. 'Now, come along, I've no time to waste. Over you go!'

'You', he growled, 'haven't ever given an injection before – have you!'

'Don't be silly,' said the nurse, colouring a gentle pink, 'I've done dozens of them.'

'Oh no, you haven't. I've been watching, and you ain't done one yet, not while I've been in here. Well, you ain't going to start on me.'

At this, the young nurse's nerve broke. 'Oh, go on!' she pleaded, 'Please! I've got to practise giving them as part of my training.'

'So go and practise on somebody else,' he told her,' and when you've learned how to do it properly you can come back and do mine. Not before.'

Her eyes grew watery. ' Oh please!'

They say women's tears melt good ideas. At the sight of her pleading face his resistance wavered, and eventually he growled reluctantly. 'Oh, orl right, then, just this once. But you'd better do it right, my girl, that's all. I shall be watching you like an 'awk.' Frankly, I didn't see how he could do that without eyes in the back of his head – or considerably lower than that – but with bad grace he bared a large pink buttock and resentfully propped himself up in bed on one arm.

His words had made the poor girl so nervous that she was shaking like a leaf, it was a wonder she didn't curdle the contents of the syringe. But screwing up her courage, she took a wild lunge at the pink flesh – and missed it by a mile. Instead, she speared him straight through his hand, pinning it firmly to the bed.

He howled like a wolf on heat. 'Kee – rist!'

The air turned purple with profanities and she fled down the ward in tears. She was brought back by Sister, who addressed Chiefy coldly. 'Mr Frost, you have a choice. You can either have this injection done by the nurse or by me. The way I feel at the moment about the lack of co-operation my staff is receiving, I strongly advise you to choose the nurse.'

Chiefy was no fool. He was an old hand at poker, and he knew when to hold 'em and when to fold 'em. He gave in as meekly as a lamb, and actually it wasn't too bad a jab, not for a first time. Well, all right, a second time.

Chiefy wasn't the only grump in there. There was a civilian at the opposite end of the ward – I never learned his name, but because of his sorrowful view of life in general I silently dubbed him Doom and Gloom. He had a long doleful face that badly needed ironing.

Soon after I came into the hospital he wandered down to the servicemen's end of the ward. I reckon his only reason for doing so was to try and find someone in a worse condition than himself, this giving him some small relief from his overall pessimism about how the world in general was rapidly going to the dogs.

He walked very stiff and upright, as if he was for ever attempting to maintain his balance in defiance of a malevolent force of gravity. This was because the whole of his head and shoulders were encased in a rigid plaster cast, with an oval cut out of the front to form a frame round his face. He shuffled up to my bed without preamble and stood looking down his nose at me. The imprisoning confines of his plaster prevented him from doing little else.

'What's this lot for, then?' he asked gloomily, indicating the wooden framework surrounding my bed.

'I was in an plane crash.'

He considered this carefully.

'Were you flying it?'

I said yes, I was – at least, until it crashed. After that, there might be some argument about the matter.

'What speed were you doing?' He seemed genuinely interested so I told him, around a hundred and thirty miles an hour when I hit the trees.

'And what exactly', he demanded moodily, 'did you do to yourself?'

'I got a broken thigh, a broken arm, a collapsed lung, and a few hundred cuts from broken perspex.'

A look of utter disgust spread across his mournful face, the look of a twelve-year-old lad who's been invited to kiss his old aunty when it wasn't even her birthday.

'Is that all?'

I felt a bit narked. After all, I had the most varied and the most fearsome combination of wounds in the whole ward.

'Isn't that enough?' I asked.

He turned to go, then he turned back and said accusingly, 'I fell off a step-ladder and broke me bleedin' neck. 'With that he shuffled off back down the ward to his bed. He never came again. He'd made his protest about the gross unfairness of the world, and that was that.

Of course, there were as many foul-ups in those days as there are today.

A fierce little woman in a white overall came charging down the ward one morning, pushing a large mobile X-ray machine, and stopped beside me.

'Bed twenty-three?' Yes, I said. 'Right!' She began to rig up her machine. 'I have to take a picture of your leg – see how it's getting on.'

That sounded eminently reasonable to me. I watched her plug in things and adjust other things, but I did intervene before she actually pressed the switch.

'Excuse me. You're taking a picture of my right leg?'

'That's right.'

'I broke my left leg.'

She looked annoyed. Not at her mistake, but at the impertinence of my interruption. 'Nonsense!' she answered tartly. 'It's the right one.'

I indicated the stainless steel spike hammered through my shinbone and the weights hanging from it. All on the left side, as, I pointed out, was the pain. And didn't she think I might be considered something of an authority on the matter? Grimly she checked her notes.

'This is bed twenty-three?' I couldn't deny it.

'Broken femur?' I had to admit that was true, too.

'There you are then, it's the right leg', she said in grim triumph, putting down her notes and preparing to take the shot.

I confess it. I'm not at my best when faced with earth-shattering, gold-plated, fireproof stupidity. I grabbed the switch and refused to let go until she checked with Sister.

She glared at me in scarlet fury, then turned on her heel and clacked away down to the ward office. When she returned she didn't say a word and she wouldn't look at me, but swiftly packed her machine and wheeled it back towards the door.

'Well?' I called after her. She threw me a look of pure hatred. 'Wrong ward!' she snapped, and disappeared.

Two strange RAF officers appeared one morning in Sister's office, and she came down to have a word before she'd let them through to my bed. Did I feel up to seeing them and answering a few of their questions?

It was the court of inquiry. I had been expecting them and I said I might as well get it over with.

After every accident such a court is convened, in order to determine the cause and to apportion blame. If they couldn't find any other reason for a crash they had a nasty habit of pronouncing it as due to 'pilot error', particularly if that unfortunate hadn't survived to contradict them. Not nice, and not always fair, but tidy. And they liked things to be tidy. It is usually held on an air base, with at least one of the officers an aircrew member, and they call witnesses and produce a report. I was proving awkward in being neither conveniently dead nor likely to be back to fitness for quite a time, so they had decided to convene a small informal session at my bedside.

They were both nice chaps, and the senior man, a squadron leader, handed me a gift of fruit from his wife before we began. They weren't looking for a scapegoat, the evidence they had found so far was enough to show the cause of the crash, and they already had the culprits, they just wanted to determine whether I could have done anything different that might be of future help to other aircrew.

The non-technical reader will have to forgive this short explanation of what had happened.

The aircraft had Merlin 113 engines. These did not have conventional carburettors but were fitted with the Stromberg fuel injection system, which pumped fuel directly into the eye of the supercharger. The amount supplied to the engine was controlled by a diaphragm that moved in response to the differential hydraulic pressure on each side of it. This hydraulic oil first passed through a filter to clean it of any dirt or harmful foreign bodies, and the filters required constant checking to make sure that they were clean. The filter on my starboard engine had not been checked and was full of scrapings and general gunge from the system. The result was that the diaphragm suddenly jammed into maximum position and flooded the engine with petrol – I had seen it spurting out of the exhaust – and I had suffered what was known as a rich cut.

I told them the rest of it, how the feathering mechanism on the propeller hadn't worked, but had unfeathered again, killing my speed, and how I had tried a second time, but did not have the time or the height required for it to operate.

Had I, in the turmoil of doing all these things on my own, accidentally feathered the other button the second time, so that I had lost power from both engines? Frankly I couldn't be certain, but I didn't think so, I had clipped the top of an elm tree at the bottom of my dive and I thought that this had force-feathered both props. They agreed that they found gear teeth missing in the feathering mechanism, which would tend to confirm this. So it was left at that, but from that moment on all feathering buttons on the twin-engined aircraft – which had been placed next to each other – were moved quite a distance apart, so that there was no possibility of it happening again. Which showed the value of a court of inquiry.

As a result of my crash, the airman who didn't check the filters and the corporal who didn't check the airman spent quite some time as guests in His Majesty's Glasshouse, paying for their sins. I sincerely hoped that Dismal Dan didn't catch any backlash from the incident, but I didn't dare ask in case I gave the officers any ideas.

And that was it. The two men thanked me and hoped I'd get well soon, and that was the last I saw of them.

However, their final report couldn't explain why that particular aircraft had been notorious for causing trouble for every squadron that it had been on. Some aircraft were like that: whatever you did to them seemed to make no difference. We used to call them 'Friday afternoon Mosquitoes' (assuming that they had been rushed out of the factory in time for the weekend), and we avoided them like the plague when we could.

Like most people, we assumed our Mosquitoes were all built to precise dimensions, but one rather tubby squadron pilot always asked for a certain aircraft 'because it had more room.' We laughed at the idea, and went out with a tape measure to prove he was being ridiculous, but he was right. The Mossies made by London Transport were two inches wider than those built by de Havilland. And two extra inches in a crowded cockpit on a four- or five-hour trip was luxury indeed.

Many of the squadron aircrew, from my navigator to Basil, my flight commander, came in to see me. Even the medical officer who had sorted me out after the crash called in at one time or another (but not the CO; I saw neither hide not hair of him). It was due to one of these visitors that I was the cause of Sister's loss of face with Matron.

One good-natured young navigator, Mike Trotman, arrived too late in the afternoon – visiting times were strict in those days – so I told him to come back in the evening. 'And bring some beer with you!' I called. It wasn't allowed, but I figured he could smuggle in the odd bottle, and it had been a long time since I tasted the stuff. But he didn't return; instead, a taxi-driver staggered into the ward late in the evening, clutching a gallon of light ale, and asking for Chalky White. Mike had had to go back to camp to do night-flying, but had sent the maximum amount of liquid refreshment that his taxi-driver could carry. The night nurse panicked in case it was discovered, so I carefully hid it behind my locker.

Next day was Matron's inspection, and as she passed my bed she pointed out that my locker was askew. Sister hurried to straighten it, and there was a loud crash as beer bottles fell in all directions.

'I think you dropped something, Sister!' said Matron icily, and swept out.

Once she calmed down, Sister was very sporting about it, and let me keep the beer, but securely hidden away inside the locker, so I was able to offer hospitality to my visitors.

I never saw Mike again. He was due for a rest, and went instructing up to Leeming in Yorkshire shortly afterwards. He was on board an old Anson aircraft when it hit another plane fairly low down. There were some visiting ATC cadets aboard, and there was too little time for everyone to clip on the loose parachute packs, though one of the crew heroically thrust his own chute at a cadet and pushed him out. Sadly, Mike was one of those who didn't make it. A lovely lad.

Yet despite Sister's iron regime, the nurses were a lively fun-loving bunch, not averse to playing a prank or two of their own. Larry, my navigator, and another mate, Johnny Wakefield, were regular callers to see me, and two of the nurses decided on a small prank. Although not normally allowed, they managed to rustle up a cup of tea for each of my visitors, and for a bit of fun they laced them with cascara. However, it seemed to have no effect on either of them, so on their next visit the nurses decided to double the dose in each cup. Larry drank his down gratefully, but Johnny had let his tea get cold while chatting and decided that he didn't fancy it. Whereon Larry, ever the gentleman, protested that it would appear churlish to leave it, and drank that one up as well, cold as it was.

That was four strong doses of cascara in all – and Larry had drunk the lot! It didn't help any that they then went back to a sergeants' mess dance where they supped liberally of the local ale. I heard later that, around two in the morning, Larry awoke with his stomach in turmoil, convinced that he was dying. For the next two hours he charged up and down the corridor frantically trying to reach the loo in time. Now it so happened that the next room was occupied by an old and rather bad-tempered ground-staff sergeant who hated jumped-up, noisy aircrew and all their ways. After suffering these nocturnal scamperings for half the night, he came charging out into the corridor in a flaming temper.

It was rather unfortunate that he happened to sleep in the nude, and even more unfortunate that he chose to sally forth on the one desperate run when Larry lost the race to get there in time. They say that the sergeant skidded halfway to the bathroom on his back, which was rather a waste, because he had to go back to collect his soap and towel, and he spent the remainder of the night soaping himself vigorously clean in a scalding hot bath.

From that moment on, for some reason, the two nurses responsible never seemed to be around during visiting hours.

Days ran into weeks and weeks into months, but though most of my injuries healed, the broken left leg stubbornly refused to knit properly. Initially the muscles had caused the broken bones to overlap and shorten the leg by a couple of inches – I would have had to spend the rest of my life living on the side of a steep hill. The weights were slowly succeeding in pulling the leg out straight again, but if left on for too long the knee could be permanently damaged. So they extracted the steel pin from the bone (with a pair of self-grips, a good heave, and a 'Yipe!' from me) and hoped the joint was strong enough to hold. It wasn't. It started to buckle, and the houseman tried packing the side of the splint to support it.

He didn't realise that he had caught some childish disease – from his young son and he was feeling very groggy. As a result he read the X-ray upside down, packed the splint on the wrong side, and bent the new join even further, making the leg more suitable for a greyhound. It would have to be reset.

Butcher Bill was furious. We heard the row going on in the office, and then he came down the ward and harrumped some unbelievable nonsense in my ear and I was sent for a second op.

Usually, they gave you a shot of Pentathol to relax you, followed by the main anaesthetic. Instead, halfway through the procedure, Butcher Bill decided not to use anaesthetic after all but rely solely on the Pentathol he had already given me. He would try a simpler way. So, although I was sufficiently under to be unable to protest, I was only too agonisingly aware of what was happening.

And what he was doing was putting his knee against the new join and pulling hard on each side to straighten the leg! Not exactly rocket science and very painful. Having got the overlap down to an inch he decided to settle for that, slapped on a plaster cast and returned me to the ward.

As I had had no follow-up anaesthetic to fully knock me out I was still strongly under the influence of the Pentathol, which, of course, is a truth drug. This makes you feel extremely happy with life in general, and you will gladly confess to starting World War Two with a little prompting. The other patients decided to have a little fun at my expense, taking evil delight in asking my opinion of the physical attributes of the various nurses on the ward – which I happily gave in embarrassing and noisy detail. I followed this up by singing a number of bawdy RAF songs at the top of my voice, and finally grabbed a startled probationer nurse who happened to be passing, hauling her across the bed in a fond bear hug – egged on by the cheers of my disreputable companions. Moments later we were unceremoniously prised apart by Sister's iron hand.

'That's quite enough of that, Mr White!' She had been listening discreetly but with great amusement behind a screen further along the ward. Now she calmly and decisively intervened.

Later I recalled very little of my bravura performance, but enough to blush hotly for days afterwards, especially in response to the giggles of some of the nurses as they passed, while others kept me waiting an agonisingly long time for a bottle when I needed one. In Pentathol Veritas!

So be warned, always take plenty of water with your Pentathol. Failing that, get the surgeon to stitch your mouth shut.

Larry was getting married to his girlfriend, Marian, in Harrogate, and despite being on crutches I was determined to be there. The two had first met, briefly, in her home town, whose hotels were used as a Holding Unit for aircrew returning from overseas. But despite their mutual attraction, when Larry moved on to Leeming to train on night-fighters he had got engaged to a cool, rather aloof girl in the WAAF there. The adoring Marian was heartbroken.

Training complete, Larry moved again, on to the squadron at Tangmere, where we met. We got on well, so when my navigator, Andy, left the RAF we crewed up together. But his engagement wasn't going smoothly due to their being so far apart and to her ambitious parents' ill-concealed disapproval.

Then a new pilot officer arrived fresh from Leeming, an amiable air-head who couldn't open his mouth without putting his foot in it and kicking his brains into touch. In friendly conversation Larry asked if he knew WAAF X there, giving his fiancee's name but not their relationship. The newcomer happily chortled that he knew here intimately, adding lurid details of her private anatomy while everyone sat in horrified and embarrased silence. The hoot of the NAAFI van, sounding like the rescue bugle of the United States 5th Cavalry, heralded the arrival of our tea and rock-cakes and we thankfully tumbled out, leaving Larry wondering whether the penalty for striking a superior officer was worth punching him on the nose.

It was almost certainly empty crewroom bragging, but it spelled the end of the rocky romance and a surprisingly relieved Larry took the train north to seek out his first love. But before they could set a wedding date Marian's dream-come-true almost turned to nightmare as Larry narrowly missed involvement in my crash. Twenty minutes longer on that plane would have put him in hospital beside me, or worse. But now the wedding was on and nothing could keep me away.

A warm if slightly crutch-impeded congratulatory handshake to my navigator, Larry Euesden, and his bride, Marian Smith, outside Christ Church after their wedding in Harrogate.

Photo courtesy of the *Harrogate Advertiser*

Getting on a train for a start wasn't easy, but I managed it by throwing my crutches aboard, then sitting on the carriage step and hauling myself upright by the window strap. I sat with my plastered leg sticking out into the aisle, hoping it wouldn't get kicked too many times. Helpful cabbies eased my journey between London stations, and eventually I reached Harrogate, though without any luggage, which was impossible to carry on crutches.

After the newly weds disappeared on honeymoon to a supposedly secret destination, we discovered the address of their hotel, and during the evening's party sent a string of telegrams to await their arrival. These were phrased in the specialised night-fighter code, devised during the war to hide any reference on air to radar. Who thought up this code we don't know, but we strongly suspected a certain Max Miller.

Here are some of the code calls with their meanings:

'Are you getting plenty of joy?' (Are you picking up any radar signals?)

'Flash your weapon.' (Switch on your radar set.)

'My weapon is bent.' (My radar set isn't working.)

'I have a bandit on my backward.' (There's a hostile aircraft close behind me on my rear radar.)

'Intercepting a bogey.' (Coming upon an unknown aircraft.)

'Increasing angels' meant you were climbing, and if you found yourself charging at another aircraft you were 'closing in a head-on', when you used 'a Whiting manoeuvre' to convert it to a 'rear interception'.

I'll leave it to readers' imagination as to the exact details of our messages. Suffice it to say that the telephone girls were in fits of giggles, and the happy couple were greeted by a hotel manager bearing a large grin and a fistful of embarrassing telegraphic advice.

The party went on long after they had left, and included our usual RAF songs and party routines. These last were songs with actions, varying from the doleful 'Plughole Song' ('Your baby has gorn dahn the plug 'ole!') and 'The miner's dream of home' to 'Framed in the window of the forty-first floor was a yewman face . . .' On this occasion our party pieces included 'The Revivalist Meeting', which goes something like this. A preacher harangues a congregation at a healing convention, imploring them to 'have faith in the Lord' to be cured. To cries of 'Halleluyah, brother!' a lame man was told to 'throw away his left crutch', which to loud acclaim he did. Then to 'throw away his right crutch', which he did. And everyone leaped to their feet, shouting 'Praise the Lord' at the miracle. All except the lame man. He fell flat on his face.

Well, there was I, actually on crutches – it was too good a chance to miss, and I did the routine for real. To great cheers I threw away my left crutch, and then as everyone roared encouragement I threw away my right crutch. And guess what – yes, I fell flat on my face. I'm glad Sister wasn't around to see it!

We ended with the Mossie song:

'Just an old-fashioned aircraft, with old-fashioned ways,
And an old-fashioned hole in the wing.
The old-fashioned engines have seen better days,
And they're tied on with old-fashioned string.
There's no tail on the back, and it's riddled with flak,
Still there's something that makes it divine,
It's so safe and sound – it can't get off the ground -
Not that old-fashioned Mossie of mine!'

These days, weddings aren't what they were.

Of course, we could have done 'Lancaster Bomber', but that routine was usually reserved for new crews in the mess, especially innocents fresh from an operational training unit who don't know any better.

It begins with the setting out of a 'cross' of chairs, about six in a row, with the one at the end facing backwards. Two or three chairs are placed on each side, forming the aircraft 'wings'.

Then the crew is selected.

The 'pilot' sits in the centre, with the 'bomb aimer' in front, the 'navigator' behind, and 'Tail-end Charlie', the rear gunner, sitting at the far end, facing backwards. Two newcomers are then invited to become the 'port and starboard engines', sitting on 'the wings'.

A mimed start-up and take-off on an operation is then begun, with 'the engines' making appropriate engine noises. At that point, one man comes riding into the mess on a bicycle. He is a 'German night-fighter', and he circles the 'Lancaster', making attacking swoops with 'ratatatat' sounds of gunfire, which are replied to by Tail-end Charlie with similar sounds.

Finally, the 'pilot' shouts, 'The starboard engine's on fire!' and the man representing that engine is encouraged to strike a match and hold it aloft. The cry is echoed by everybody watching. Then, 'The port engine's on fire!', and another match is scraped alight and held aloft.

'We must put the fires out!' yells the 'pilot', and, right on cue, all the watching mess members repeat the cry, slinging their beer over the unfortunate 'engines', to put out the burning matches!

But, as I said, we didn't do that one. You've got to have a bit of decorum at a wedding.

Back to hospital, and at long, long last, after almost ten weary months, I was being discharged. On crutches, with my left leg firmly set in plaster and still no more than an inch shorter, despite my wedding antics, I was on my way back to the squadron. Bert Bamberger gave me a lift up from the village station to the 'drome in his little three-wheeler Morgan with its tiny engine bolted on the front. I had to poke my unbending plastered limb out into the fresh air, resting it on the mudguard.

Like all 'dromes, there was a wooden barrier pole across the entrance that the service policeman on the gate would come out and raise, once he was satisfied with your credentials. Though not, of course, for Bert and his Morgan. Bert would belt up the road from the village at top speed, heave the steering-wheel round ninety degrees and charge at the pole.

Then at the last moment he would yell, 'Duck!' and you would crouch down behind the tiny windscreen as it scraped under the wood by a gnat's whisker, happily leaving us halfway to the sergeants' mess by the time the indignant 'Snoop' had come running out of his gate-house.

I was back!

CHAPTER TWENTY-EIGHT

The Last Op.

Down on the squadron nothing seemed to have changed much. Yet things were subtly different.

There was a new CO – the old one had moved on, and I hadn't seen or heard from him since I ended up in hospital – and there were one or two new crews down on the flight line. Like policemen, they seemed to be getting younger all the time.

The sleek Mosquitoes still stood in a menacing row in front of the huts at dispersal, with their eternal aircraft smell of hot oil on metal, cooling slowly, a click at a time.

But the once most beautiful and versatile aircraft ever built were now elderly ladies with odd little bumps on their smooth contours. This was a new era, the era of the jet, and they were due to be pensioned off and replaced with the NF II Meteor twin-jet night-fighters in a year or two's time.

But then, I myself had barely a year to go to the end of my service, and I still had to return to hospital each week for physiotherapy. So although at times I looked at the Mossies longingly, I would never climb into one again.

The dusty crew-room seemed unchanged. There were still the big faded old easy chairs and the row of wire-fronted wooden lockers, each with its individual chalk drawing on the door to identify the owner. That was the Order of the Cat Club – one of our little squadron giggles. Everyone identified his own individual locker by drawing a picture on the locker door in chalk. The drawing had to demonstrate a title that included the word 'CAT'. A drawing of a cat and a comb stood for the word CATACOMB, a cat with a kitten was KIT-E-KAT, with a capital R it became CATARRH, a cat leaning to one side became CATALYST, with a tree trunk it was a CATALOGUE, and so on. It was just one of the squadron conventions, like the Squadron Egg.

Except that the Squadron Egg was no more; it had met its end many months previously, down at Tangmere, and it was at my hands. Another squadron idiosyncrasy, it was allegedly a once-fresh egg from wartime days – legend had it that it was one of the special ration issued to operational aircrew, and its rightful owner had not returned from a night sortie over Germany to claim it.

If you were appointed Keeper of the Egg, you signed your name on it, kept it safe, and passed it on to someone else when you moved on. It was handed over to my care at Tangmere, and by then it was at least four years old. A bunch of us were in my room one night and I was telling the story of it to some squadron newcomers. In those days I wore a heavy gold signet ring, and as we talked I was absent-mindedly tapping the egg gently against it.

The tapping must have stirred some primeval form of life still lurking within the shell, because it suddenly exploded. A purple liquid shot out over the room and its occupants. The stench was incredible and took days to disperse. The ghost of that long-dead eggless pilot must have been chuckling far into the night at our discomfort.

The heavy gold signet ring that did the damage was a twenty-first birthday gift from my parents. But it had been stolen in hospital while I was still unconscious on the operating table. And although it bore my monogram, AGW, in a design of my own, and I reported its loss to the hospital authorities, the new National Health Service was just being set up and nobody knew who was responsible for such a loss. So I received neither rescued ring nor compensation.

But worse was to follow.

Back on the squadron once more, I found that most of my flying kit had also been stolen. Not that I had much use for it from now on, but I had to bribe the stores sergeant with a number of very large whiskies to write off the missing equipment on the quiet.

Worst of all, dear old Shambles, the Austin Seven that had carried me faithfully round England's shires since 1943, and through some remarkable escapades (not to mention some remarkable police stations and magistrates' courts), had been steadily robbed of its innards while I was in hospital. It now lay forlorn and impotent among the trees behind the sergeants' mess. It was the Last Post for my little car. Someone offered me eighteen pounds for what was left of the gutted vehicle, and with a sad heart I had little choice but to accept. I spent the money on my wife's twenty-first birthday party.

During the war, your property would have been sacrosanct. True, it was our habit when on operations to raid the kitbag of anyone who went missing, but this was an honourable custom. The kit was auctioned off cheaply to any of his pals who happened to be short of that particular piece of equipment. It saved that man from being put on a charge for losing RAF property, and the money collected went towards drinks all round in memory of the missing man.

This was different – the morals of the wide boy that had thrived underground in so many ration swindles during the war now seemed to have come out into the open and spread from civvie street into the peace-time service.

But the RAF's big problem now was what to do with me? I was like a spare brick at a builder's wedding. For a while they found me makeshift jobs, things like disciplinary NCO for the squadron (which was a case of poacher turned gamekeeper, if you like!). Deadly boring, at times I tried to enliven parades with a little humour. Instead of giving the age-old commands, 'Squadron! Stand at EASE, atten-SHUN, to the right dis-MISS!' I changed it on occasion to 'Stanley's KNEES . . . Artie SHAW . . . to the right, Dick SMITH!' but it didn't go down too well with the station warrant officer. Let's face it, putting airmen on a charge for not saluting or picking people for guard duty over Christmas because they had turned up late for parade was not a job I cared for.

For a while I ran the Link Trainer, a sort of cross between a Wendy House and a vacuum cleaner. It was like a big toy aircraft in which aircrew members practised instrument flying without leaving the ground, but it quickly degenerated into a surreptitious poker school, and when the CO noticed certain NCO aircrew suddenly volunteering for the Link Trainer he rightly became suspicious.

Finally, I got a job I liked. For a glorious three weeks I was given my first command of an RAF station! I was made commanding officer, no less, of RAF, Bradwell-Juxta-Mare, on the Essex coast.

Now in case you, or someone you know, ever served there during the war, and you remember Bradwell as a night-fighter base of some note, with intruder Mosquito aircraft operating under the command of wing commanders and the like, let me hurriedly disabuse you. I was a warrant officer in charge of one corporal, one cook, and four airmen, and all that remained of that once proud 'drome were a couple of huts and a radio.

The tiny unit was there to control the firing range on nearby Dengie Marshes. The warrant officer who normally ran it was on urgent leave, and I was sent in as a sort of locum. Various squadrons would fly over to practise air-to-ground firing at targets on the marshes and would call up – first for permission to start firing, and afterwards to ask us what, if anything, they had hit. Presumably, if they received no answer to their second call they had hit us.

Bradwell Waterside, the nearby village, consisted of a pub and a scattering of houses on the River Blackwater, a dark inlet where old hulks of steamships that were no longer wanted were moored out of harm's way to rust quietly to death. The whole place was like a graveyard full of ghosts.

On my first evening I set out to walk to the village pub, and after a few yards I heard the RAF lorry behind me, but when I looked round the driver – and apparently sole occupant – had stopped and was earnestly inspecting the bodywork. A few yards further on I heard it again, looked round, and this time he was studiously checking the tyres. The third time it happened I went back and found the whole group of them hiding in the back of the lorry. As I was a new incumbent they weren't sure how I'd take their illegal borrowing of the lorry for a night out, so they had slowly followed me until they could judge what my reaction would be. I laid down some new rules on the spot. First, I told them, they never borrowed the vehicle unless I said so, and I wasn't going to say so unless I came too. Second, I informed them of the price of my looking the other way – they would buy my first pint of the evening.

After that we got on famously, and spent many pleasant hours in the little tavern, where the locals ran a fierce cribbage school in the bar. On Sunday nights the lorry would meet me off the bus on my return from the weekend.

On the downside, it was a tedious journey to reach my new small kingdom from mid-Kent. It involved crossing the Thames on the Gravesend ferry and then travelling by train and country bus until you reached this tiny village at the end of the world.

But it was on the long, dull train section of the journey, from Gravesend to Burnham-on-Crouch, that I met up with the redoubtable 'Chopper'.

I never knew his real name, but I always thought of him as 'Chopper' because he was a dental mechanic. Yet he was a dental mechanic who had walked with giants, or rather, flown with them. He was that rare thing, a genuine IBM. And in case you're wondering, IBM didn't refer to Intercontinental Ballistic Missiles or International Business Machines, it was our sardonic name for Intrepid Bird Men.

You sometimes met them on long train journeys or in crowded pubs. As soon as they saw the wings on your chest they would start regaling you with tall tales about their time in the Royal Flying Corps in the First World War. A high proportion of them were phoneys, because there hadn't been that many pilots in the Royal Flying Corps. But you soon learned to sort out the sheep from the goats (or rather, the parrots from the eagles!) with a discreet question or two. The phoneys always made small mistakes. For example, they would claim to have been 'in' so-and-so squadron, whereas a real flyer would say he was 'on' that squadron. Or you'd drop in a technical term or two, and they wouldn't know their aileron from their elevator.

Chopper was sitting quietly in a corner of the railway carriage when I boarded the train for Burnham-on-Crouch, and on seeing my wings he began to chat about flying in true IBM style. But his claim to have started flying back in 1910 made me sit up sharply, because that was the very start of flying in this country. Apparently, a gang of enthusiasts used to fly their frail wood-and-wire contraptions from Pearl Beach on the Isle of Sheppey. But what made my eyebrows shoot up into my hairline were the names of the people in that gang. Chopper talked casually about 'Harry Hawker' and 'Geoff de Havilland' and 'A.V.R.' – Alliot Verdon Roe – and Oswald Short. They were people who had gone on to build great aircraft companies. I could scarcely believe him, yet when I tried to trip him up I couldn't. Instead he continued to amaze me as he chatted on.

'I remember old Noel Pemberton-Billing', he said reflectively, mentioning a name few had heard of. 'He was a naval officer who came down to see us fly. His brother had an old Blériot, and Noel said, 'Give us a go on your plane.' '—— off!' said his brother, 'You're not going to break my aircraft – you don't know how to fly.' So Noel said, 'Blow you, then, I'll build my own plane!' And he did, by seeing how the others were made. And after he'd built it, he got in and flew his first solo in it.'

From that astonishing beginning, Pemberton-Billing went on eventually to start the Pemberton-Billing Flying-Boat Company, but in 1914 when he entered

Meeting with 'Chopper' on the train

Parliament he sold it, and it became the Supermarine Aircraft Company, later builders of the Spitfire. So P.B. and Harry Hawker, between them, had been historically responsible for the two fighter aircraft that did most to save the Free World in the Battle of Britain in the Second World War!

Then Chopper asked me what aircraft I flew, and I said Mosquitoes. Ah yes, he said, one of old Geoff's planes – what armament did we carry? Four 20 mm cannon and four .303 machine-guns, I told him. 'Nice!' said Chopper, wistfully. He thought a bit, then added, 'Of course, in World War One all we had were darts.'

'Darts?'

'Oh yes, they were in metal canisters with paper across the bottom. We'd fly along the German trenches, hold out the canister and tear off the paper cover.'

What did the Germans do, stick a dartboard on the spike on their helmets, as protection? But Chopper didn't laugh. 'Oh, these darts were different, they'd go straight through a German helmet!' he said, 'In the end they were banned under the Geneva Convention.'

I asked what their planes had been like.

'They had wooden frames,' he said, 'and were covered in fabric for lightness. You had to paint the fabric with dope to tighten it over the frame. If we happened to run out of dope, we could always nip round to the cook-house for some sago.'

Sago! That could come in handy, I observed, if you crash-landed behind enemy lines – you could destroy your aircraft by eating it! 'Oh, it worked well.' He ignored my levity, his blue eyes misty with memories. 'But if it rained you were in trouble . . .'.

We were drawing into Burnham Station, where I got off, but I could have cheerfully stayed on all day, listening to his tales. Later, as the ramshackle old bus took me through Southminster and on to Bradwell, I thought about Chopper and that youthful gang flying their sago-stiffened crazy wood-and-fabric aircraft forty years before, in the golden afternoon of Empire. I imagined them exploring this new dimension, with the wind singing through the wires, tumbling down the blue skies and charging the snow-white castles of the clouds. That kind of flying, I decided, must have been sheer magic.

Of course, you sometimes came across Intrepid Bird Men in the service, as well. A warrant officer we once had on the squadron, John Whitehead, was one of that rare breed of engineering officer who wore wings – he had started out as a pilot many years before, and his brick-red complexion told of his service in India and the Gulf, between the wars.

He would regale us with tales about the frail wood-and-wire 'Stringbag' planes that they flew in the service long ago, and we used to tease him. 'Ah, but do you think you could have managed two engines at once, John!'

'I think so,' he answered calmly, 'I once managed six.'

'Six!' Got him this time, we thought! 'The RAF never had an aircraft with six engines!'

'Oh, yes, they did,' he said, 'the Short Sarafand. It was a big seaplane with six Rolls-Royce Buzzard engines.'

It was built by Short Brothers (Oswald Short had been another of Chopper's old gang!) in 1934, for the RAF. It was intended as an answer to the monstrous Dornier flying-boats of the Germans, when the future for communicating with a distant empire seemed to be in flying-boats. But although it was quite successful, they only ever built the one. Seaplanes fell out of favour – pilots tended to prefer their runways flat, and not with six-foot-high asphalt waves.

'We tested it off Lowestoft', John told us. 'Officially I was second dickey (second pilot), but my real job was as the cardboard-and-string man.'

We had to ask! What did he mean, cardboard-and-string man?

'Well, it was a big plane, and came in to land very fast. We didn't have flaps in those days, not like you sissies! The only way to slow it down for landing was for me to dash up to the upper gunner's position and hold out a big sheet of cardboard in the slipstream!'

And the string?

'We tested the aircraft on the bombing range. I lay in the nose, holding the end of a piece of string that went back through the fuselage and was tied round the pilot's ankle. When I judged we were over the target I pulled on the string and the pilot picked up a practice bomb and chucked it over the side.'

There was no answer to that, but somehow, it put into proper perspective today's casual circling of the globe in big aluminium tubes. Something seems to have gone out of flying when you surrender control to a tarted-up alarm clock that sends messages down miles of wiring and does all the flying for you without even bothering to ask you first.

Eventually the time came for my demob. I hadn't flown for two years, and I couldn't bear to be in the RAF and not fly. But I considered that they owed me something for my injuries. Like a disability pension, maybe? After all, it was their fault that I now felt more comfortable walking with one foot on the pavement and the other in the gutter. However, it seemed that they thought otherwise.

I went up to Stanmore, in London, where I was examined by a very unsympathetic RAF doctor (maybe he was having a bad air day). He seemed convinced that I was faking my short leg in some way to try and wangle an undeserved pension. Perhaps he'd just been to see Charlie Chaplin's latest film, *Limelight*, and this gave him the idea.

He covered my legs with so many ink dots that I looked like a drug addict who'd been injecting himself with a fountain pen. He then spent a long time measuring the distance between the dots, but try as he might, he couldn't get those on one side to match the ones on the other, so in the end he gave up trying. Whether he just threw my application in the bin I don't know, but I was never given any answer to my claim, they simply ignored my repeated requests for information and that was that. (More than fifty years later I was to reapply and be given a reasonable pension, but they refused me any back pay.)

I left the Air Force in November 1950, almost nine years to the day after I had entered it, and returned home to Derby to help run the family business. And despite everything that had happened, at the end of it all I wouldn't have changed a single moment of my time in the RAF for anything. What more could a man ask of life than he live through tremendous times with great companions?

And that should have been the end of my flying career. But it wasn't.

CHAPTER TWENTY-NINE

Return to the Sky

Certainly I never expected to fly again. Conventional wisdom at that time had it that after a serious crash you should get straight back into the air as soon as possible (not in the same aircraft, of course, you can't fly firewood!), or you would lose your nerve. All complete nonsense, of course, as amply demonstrated by our old friend, Tin-toes Bader et al.

Still, I was surprised when the Air Ministry invited me to rejoin them in 1951 for a few months. Why they sounded the trumpet call in my direction I'll never know. Maybe they had forgotten I hadn't flown since early 1948, and was liable to walk in circles when I closed my eyes. Or maybe it was all a cunning plot, and they thought I just might bust the other leg this time and level things up, saving them an awful lot of argument. (If they did this often enough, they would probably claim that I'd only been four feet tall in the first place.)

The reason for my recall to the Colours was that there was an emergency on. In the Cold War between the West and the new Soviet Empire things were hotting up. The Russian blockade of Berlin, which left the air corridor as the only route left open to supply the city, made the Government realise how much the RAF had been run down post war, and just how much they needed it right now. So a call went out for volunteers from the Reserve to train up to the latest standard.

And I had signed on for Four and Three, that is, four years' active service and three on the reserve, so I was pretty well committed to answering the call. What's more, they were offering a rather juicy bounty at the end of it all, and I was getting a bit bored with Civvie Street. The way I saw it, you've got a long sleep coming to you some time and the sole purpose of life is to build up a heap of dreams ready for it. So I jumped at the chance.

It was like starting all over again. We were sent to Oakington, near Cambridge, to fly on the Harvard advanced trainers that I had last flown in Arizona ten years before. No one mentioned my crash. Certainly I didn't, in case they had made a mistake. I was eager to get back in the air, and a few moments after my first take-off, everything fell into place. (Perhaps I could have phrased that better!) Anyway, I passed the initial course with ease and was awarded a White rating for instrument flying. My confidence flooded back.

But the next section was very different. We moved to North Luffenham, near what is now Rutland Water (in fact, very near – it's now underneath that water), and prepared to convert onto Vampire jets. This was a big step because none of us had flown jets before, and they were single-seat aircraft, so there'd be no instructor beside you in the cockpit – the first time you got in you flew it entirely on your own. Jets were fast, and you landed them differently from old-fashioned planes. So to break you in gently they first sent you up in a Spitfire.

Which was rather a daft thing to do, because, of course, they were single-seat planes too, so you still got in and flew the thing without anyone sitting beside you, showing you how to do it. But these aircraft were not Reginald Mitchell's beautiful little planes that won the Battle of Britain, they were Spitfire Mark XXIIs, with a far more powerful engine in them than the original Merlin.

But a Spitfire's a Spitfire, right? Wrong! A Spitfire XXII's engine was a Griffon, and it was a much bigger engine to shoe-horn into such a small plane. An awful lot of it was left dangling out over the front end. Three more feet of it to be precise, making it extremely nose-heavy. So much so that if you put both brakes on at the same time while taxiing out to take off you would tip on your nose, smashing the five-bladed propeller.

So I taxied out very carefully, using one brake at a time as we were told, stopped at the end of the runway and stuck my head in the cockpit to do my pre-flight check. And when I looked up again I was shocked to find the plane was creeping slowly forward onto the flight path and another plane was just coming in to land!

Sheer instinct took over. I banged both brakes on hard, the aircraft tilted forward onto its main wheels, and for a second hung balanced there, held by the pull of the prop, while I pushed desperately – and ludicrously – against the back of my seat to try and make it drop down again. To my great relief it fell heavily back onto its tail-wheel once more, but – although I didn't realise it – this action burst the tyre on the tailwheel.

Even at the best of times the Spitfire XXII took off like a drunken crab with piles, and now it persisted in trying to imitate a corkscrew. You saw almost nothing with that monstrous engine in your face, it was like steering a Formula One steamroller while wearing a blind-fold. Somehow I got it up there and down again in one piece and taxied back along the perimeter track to dispersal, little realising that I was sending out smoke signals ahead to the chief flying instructor. The friction of the burst tailwheel along the runway had set it alight, and it was burning merrily beneath me as I taxied in. He ran out and frantically guided me through a large puddle to put out the flames, but his own temper was still smouldering when I got out, and it soon flared into rage. There were a few heated words exchanged. The burst tailwheel explained the battle I'd had to keep straight on take-off. So, perhaps understandingly, I can't claim that the legendary Spitfire was my favourite aircraft, though I will admit to being a little biased.

After that, we moved thankfully on to the Vampire jets, and getting used to their tricycle undercarriage.

The tiny aircraft were a joy to fly, making our big jump to a totally new form of propulsion that much easier. There was no swing on take-off, the jet pushed you forward in an absolutely straight line. The only problem with a jet was on landing – while you had power on you had forward speed, and while you had forward speed you produced power. And there was a minimum engine speed to ensure you didn't get a flame-out. So where for years it had been drummed into you never to touch your brakes until you had almost stopped, you now had to do the precise opposite and slam on the brakes the moment you touched the runway or you'd keep rolling all the way up the Great North Road to Scotland.

Naturally, once we'd safely completed the course, the RAF hierarchy tried its usual sneaky tricks. Ah! – about the bounty we promised you, they said. It only applies to Class E reserve, not to Class G reserve – recall to the service is part of their contract. (There's no prize for guessing which reserve I was on!) Anyway, after furious argument they very grudgingly saved face by adding, 'Of course, you are entitled to termination leave, with pay!' So I ended up with about half of what had been promised.

Still, I'd have done it anyway, just to get in the air again, and the money came in handy to pay for my last big dream. Before finally settling down to a humdrum life in Civvie Street, I wanted to carry out one last big trip. Only this time it would be on the continent itself instead of several thousand feet above it.

I called it 'Operation Hooter-Scooter'.

It started when some World War One buff persuaded me to go with him round the First World War battlefields of northern France and Belgium. But then his wife hinted that there might be a much bigger battle right there in his own kitchen if he tried shooting off with a mate, leaving her at home on her own, so he pulled out at the last minute. Disappointed, I determined to go it alone, but I decided to change wars. I'd sooner see places that were connected with World War Two.

I'd always had this great curiosity to see some of the places that I had flown over so often in the darkness. Like Dunkirk, Arnhem, Brussels, the Ruhr, the River Rhine – such places had just been names on our flight plans, and up at several thousand feet they had seemed so remote. (And thank God they stayed that way!) Of course, such trips these days are commonplace. Youngsters think nothing of thumbing a lift to Khatmandu for a curry, or backpacking to places we've never heard of and they can't spell. But at that time, a week in Billy Butlin's at Skegness was more often the highlight of the post-war year.

Of course, once out of the Air Force I had to find my own means of transport. So I bought a Corgi from a chap in Wirksworth.

No, not one of those dogs with short legs and even shorter tempers that patriotically bite the Buckingham Palace postmen on the Queen's birthday, but a type of motor-scooter.

For those who've never heard of the machine, it was a crude ancestor of all those later Italian motor scooters like the Vespa. The Corgi started out in life as a fold-up, very basic means of transport – a sort of back-pocket motor bike – that paratroopers could take with them when they jumped out of aeroplanes. More scooter than motor, it did sterling work during the war, but I can't help thinking that its chief value lay in the fact that the enemy had little choice but to surrender on seeing them because they were helpless with laughter.

Imagine a lawn-mower bolted onto a petrol tank with two tiny wheels under it. At one end was a saddle stuck on the end of a long metal tube, while at the other end two more tubes formed the handlebars. It was more notable for what it didn't have than what it did. There was no springing other than the air in the tyres, no starter motor – you bump-started it – and just the one gear. There was a small hooter that sounded like a butterfly's fart and lights like a terminally ill firefly. It had a clutch like a concrete corset and a single front brake. And that was about it. Still, the man who sold it to me swore that it came up Cromford Hill without stopping, and that sounded good enough to me.

I strapped a grip full of clothes on the back carrier of my tiny vehicle and cheated on the first leg by taking it on the train as far as London. I planned that my first big test would be riding on it from the 'Smoke' to Folkestone, where I was to put up for the night with George, an old wartime navigator pal.

It was a nightmare ride. I was so low and out of view of other traffic that drivers took me for a jay-walker, and the vibration of the engine, combined with the lack of springing, caused almost every bolt to vibrate loose. The result was that everything that could fall off did fall off. My licence plate, my GB sign, my AA badge, my carrier, and my horn all took it in turn to work loose and drop off with a loud clatter, usually just past a traffic light, so that I was constantly surprised by lorries charging at me at right angles in the middle of trying to screw things on again. Added to all that, I managed to pick up some dirty petrol, which necessitated a periodic stripping of the carburettor and removal of the jet for cleaning by blowing through. This wasn't easy because I only carried two tools, a screwdriver and a pair of pliers.

I reached George's place late at night, completely shattered. However, a few beers and a good night's sleep and I was ready next morning for the real start of my Odyssey.

I rode to Lympne Airport and bought a single ticket to Boulogne on a Bristol Freighter car ferry. Stashed in there among the Rollers going to the Riviera and the Maseratis off to Mentone, my little scooter looked ridiculously like a Corgi on its way to Cleethorpes. But it was only half an hour's trip and then I was belting off east towards the Belgian border, to a chorus of curses from approaching drivers. They got very excited when they found me coming at them head-on. The trouble was that the minor roads I was travelling on had a small smooth bit in the centre but both sides were rough cobbles. I had had enough of things dropping off my machine, so I determined to commandeer this middle bit. Being French, they were equally determined that they weren't giving way to a small, badly built lawn-mower driven by an eccentric Englishman, so it became a constant battle of wills. (I remember thinking, rather cynically, that if only they'd shown half the aggression at Dunkirk it might have been a different war.) The road was a very minor one, and kept forgetting where it was supposed to be going, so I repeatedly ended up in a farmyard. But just occasionally I would pass a famous name from World War One, which kept the journey interesting until I finally crossed the border and ended up in Ostend. That was enough for one day, so where to stay? My system was simple: pick a clean hotel in a grubby street not far from a railway station. It always worked.

Next day I set off once more, this time for Brussels.

There was a motorway between Ostend and the capital, and I soon found myself hurtling along it (albeit at a very slow hurtle) in a sea of speeding cars.

They cut me up ruthlessly with a contemptuous blast of their horns, but it was the big lorries that were terrifying. These continental juggernauts not only charged past so close that I had to breathe in, but many of them towed one and sometimes two large trailers on the back. This third section swung to and fro like a bullwhip, coming within a hair's breadth of squashing me like a bug on a windscreen. How they ever stopped without jack-knifing was totally beyond me.

After a couple of hours of this wall-of-death stuff my engine suddenly spluttered and died. Time to clean the jet once more – I pulled out of the river of traffic, stripped the carburettor down with my screwdriver and pliers, blew through the jet and started to reassemble it. Unfortunately, in trying to make it vibration-proof I overtightened it – and the next second the tiny jet broke in half!

It was one of those moments when you began to question the whole meaning of life. I stood on the edge of the unheeding tide of traffic with the useless jet in my hand and wondered whether I'd ever see England again. It was the middle of the country, with not a building in sight, and none of this lot was going to stop for anything or anyone.

And then, in my darkest hour, my Guardian Angel curled off the road and drew

Seeking help at the roadside.

to a halt beside me He rode a motor bike with a big yellow box side-car and he looked like a man who had failed his trade test for the AA but had forgotten to hand back the uniform. He had a couple of days' growth of beard on his chin and a Gauloise dangled from a corner of his mouth. His greasy cap-band proclaimed that he was 'Touriste Secours', or 'Tourist Assistance'. There was just one trouble, he couldn't speak a word of English. So all right, there were two troubles, because I could only speak a fractured French that not even Froggy Freeman, the French master at Bemrose School, could understand, and he taught it to me.

I held up the broken jet between two fingers. 'J'ai trouble', I said.

He inspected it and gave a deeply insolent shrug that roughly translated from the French as 'Vous can blankety-blank say that encore, mon ami!'

But helpful advice came there none. Instead, he kept looking at his watch as if to hint that he really should be on his way to somewhere else.

I tried again. 'Ou est le premier garage?' (Where's the nearest garage? Froggy would have been very proud of me.) The shrug became a caricature of indifference. I tried the same phrase with 'village' replacing 'garage.' The shrug developed almost into an epileptic fit.

Fury gripped me, but I kept my voice calm and smiled winningly, just in case. He could offer me no advice so I offered him my own advice as to what he could do, anatomically speaking, with his motor bike and his side-car and the whole of his 'Touriste Secours' organisation. The effect was dramatic.

'Aha!' he exclaimed, and burrowed in his box, to reappear with a jet remarkably similar to my own. However the hole was much too large, so he rummaged again and produced a bit of electric cable from which he stripped some fine copper wire. He twisted the wires together and pushed them into the aperture, then screwed the jet back into my engine, trapping the wire in the thread to hold it steady. I couldn't believe it when the engine started at the first go, roaring with joy.

How much did I owe him? He held up three fingers (if he'd held up two I swear I'd have hit him): three francs. I offered him more, but he flatly refused, surely the first time in history that the French language had been used to turn down a tip. Then the grubby Sir Galahad swung back into his saddle and, Gauloise pointing lance-like at the sky, charged back into the stream of traffic and away.

I passed him again on my way back home, and gave him a cheery toot on my horn, but he just stared at me blankly. Maybe he couldn't tell one ex-RAF pilot on a modified lawn-mower from another. Or maybe he had finally worked out exactly what I told him before he managed his miracle.

In the meantime, I had other problems. The nearer I approached Kraut County (as we used to call Germany), the more apprehensive I became. I had driven for many years now, but that was in Shambles. The fact was, I only had a provisional licence for scooters and motor bikes. This was fine in France and Belgium, but Germany demanded a full licence. I rode up to the Border Control Post uncertain of whether I would be able to flannel my way through.

It was a large wooden hut set in a forest clearing, and half a dozen border guards watched in silence as I pulled up. They were large men in grey-green uniforms and they looked like bad-tempered Alsatians.

Then one of them strode up to me, beaming with delight and pointed to my small scooter. '*Ach zo! Der parafluger, ja*?' he chortled, and called his companions to come and see.

Apparently he had been in a German regiment at Arnhem, and he had last seen a vehicle like mine floating down from the sky at the end of a parachute. Papers forgotten, he gave them all a little lecture on the battle while his companions listened, transfixed. They asked me the cubic capacity of this wonderful little machine, and I couldn't say '98' in German, so I told them '*Ein hundert!*'

'*Ach, zo!*' they exclaimed in awe (Germans do a lot of *Ach, zo*ing). Then they clapped me on the back, and sent me on my way with their best wishes.

After a hard pounding along the autobahn I reached Cologne, a ruined shell of a city on the Rhine. Its cathedral lay miraculously untouched among the devastation of the bomb damage. I wandered round it, but found its fine architecture unmatched by the sparse interior.

But my money was running out fast, so I looked around for a cheap bed for the night. I found one in the shadow of the cathedral, and it only cost three marks. But it was like no hotel I had ever seen before. It looked as if a giant had dropped a vast cube of concrete into the square. There wasn't a single window in the place, just a dark hole of a door. Inside, the rooms seemed like square caves chiselled out of the main block.

It had once been an air-raid shelter, and all they had done was put a bed, a cheap dressing-table and a single light-bulb in each room. The light they put by the door and the bed as far away from it as possible, so that once you turned off the switch it was as if you had been struck blind. There wasn't a vestige of light to be seen, you groped your way to bed and if you woke during the night you didn't know if your eyes were open or shut. It was a terrifying feeling. Twice during the night, I fumbled my way to the door to check my watch in the cold empty corridor, lit with a single dingy light-bulb, that had all the charm of a Dartmoor Prison landing after a riot.

The next morning I sat on the banks of the Rhine and looked out over the river into Germany. I would have liked to go on, to places like Frankfurt, Nuremberg, even Munich, but I was beginning to worry about how long the temporary repair to my machine would last, and my money was going fast. I decided – very reluctantly – that I had to turn back.

To save repeating the long dreary part of the autobahn between Cologne and the frontier, I took the train to Liège, in Belgium, with the Corgi tucked safely in the guard's van. It was a fatal mistake. No problem, said the Germans jovially, and waved me helpfully through into Belgium.

The Belgian Customs thought differently. At Liège they acted like policemen with piles, an unbending pain in the backside.

Where was my licence to import a motor vehicle into Belgium?

A motor vehicle – what, my little scooter! You'd get more power out of an electric shaver. I explained that I had already been through their country once and out again to Germany by road.

In that case, where was my licence to export a vehicle from Belgium? What really bugged them was that I had gone out by road and come back in by train. That came under two different departments, throwing their civil service files into chaos, and this they could not tolerate. I would pay dearly for my unfriendly action.

My little scooter was impounded and taken on to Brussels, where it was removed in a lorry to the Customs House in the city centre. I had to pay both the extra train fare and the cost of the lorry, but I myself had to walk there from the station, to sort things out.

All afternoon I sat in a small hallway, fuming at a closed window while they took a vindictive delight in pretending that no-one spoke a word of English, nor understood a word of my French.

Eventually, my being there stopped them from closing up and going home. I refused to move without my scooter and got my own back by pretending I knew no French, which wasn't all that far from the truth. Surprise, surprise – they suddenly discovered that one of them spoke fluent English after all! I was fined a small amount for breaking some archaic regulation and let go. I left with the distinct impression that nobody had told them the war was over. No, I'm not talking about World War Two, or even World War One, they were still trying to get revenge for Waterloo. God help this country of ours if we ever come under any regime centred on Brussels.

A day later, on my final lap to the Channel ports, the last rivet holding the chain sprocket to the back wheel sheered. I was – where else! – in Dunkirk. Cobbles had finally triumphed over cogwheel, and I was well short of the airfield at Boulogne. In any case, I had no return ticket to board the Freighter, as I hadn't known the date of my return. I had changed what little money I had left at the Belgian border, it was getting close to the time of the last flight and I couldn't afford an overnight stay as well as my air ticket.

I tried a small bicycle repair shop in town – could they help? They considered drilling and fitting a set of spokes, but finally abandoned the idea as impractical. In dark despair I went in the café next door and spent my last loose change on a coffee, wondering how I could get in touch with the AA. I had joined them at the last minute before my trip, as a precaution, but had lost the emergency number. I finally decided, without much hope, that I would somehow have to try and make myself understood on the unsympathetic Frog phone system.

I turned to the chap at the next table. '*Ou est le telephone, M'sieur*?' I asked. He smiled at my awful accent. 'Try English, old boy!' he advised.

By sheer chance I had sat down next to another Briton. What's more, he had his French wife with him – they were on their way to see his in-laws and, again by chance, had called in this very café on the way, for a drink. In no time at all, she sorted out a stroppy phone operator and the AA, and persuaded the ferry people to hold the plane as long as they could. Then the husband treated me to another coffee and said goodbye. I haven't the slightest doubt that the next time I meet them will be at the Pearly Gates, where he and his wife will probably talk St Peter into letting me through without a proper halo.

At the last possible moment a large Frenchman turned up at the café in a Citroen with a trailer on the back. He slung my Corgi on it, and drove like a bat out of hell for Boulogne. The Bristol Freighter stood impatiently with engines idling, and I was rushed aboard. The waiting Roller drivers and Maserati men, fresh back from the Riviera, looked at me with a wary respect, wondering at the identity of the apparently anonymous chap they had been kept waiting for. And that odd little machine he had – surely King's Messengers hadn't been reduced to riding those things in the latest economy cuts? Had James Bond been around in those days they would no doubt have suspected me of being Agent Double Oh One Point Five.

For my part, I just dropped thankfully into my seat, recalling one of my mother's favourite sayings: 'Better to be born lucky than rich!'

We landed at Lympne just before dusk. The AA put my scooter on the train to Derby for me and I caught a bus to Folkestone and a bed at George's.

While on the bus I decided that I had had my fill of foreigners – with the honourable exceptions of a 'Touriste Secours' man and a friendly French lady who had had the good sense to marry an Englishman. My wanderlust, I decided, would in future be confined to the back garden. I was safely back home, so pull up the draw-bridge. These days, I would probably have added, 'And while you're about it, get Rentokil to stop up that rat-hole of a tunnel under the Channel.'

So I finally settled down.

All of this happened such a very long time ago, between fifty and sixty years, yet I remember it as if it was yesterday. My trouble is remembering yesterday.

But of one thing I am very sure. Once you have flown, especially in the small hours of the night, you can never be quite the same person again. Because you can never forget that tremendous feeling of freedom, and awe at the immensity of the universe. It stays with you for the remainder of your life.

'To tumble, helter-skelter, down great avenues of air,
And charge the snowy ramparts of a battlemented sky,
To storm to breathless worlds beneath a savage sun's cold stare,
To fly – to fly!'

CHAPTER THIRTY

Laughter in the Clouds

It can't be all that long now until the final take-off.

Many of the squadron are already up there, circling, waiting for the rest of us to join the formation.

Nobody's quite sure what our target will be – some say we'll go to one place and some say to another. (There are those who reckon it's the same place anyway. With all that psalm singing and all those plucking harps on damp clouds, what was heaven for the righteous would be absolute hell for the wicked.) And there's some argument as to the best way to get there. But I've no doubt we'll make it all right. We've already been more than halfway to both places.

There have been days when we broke through the dark cloudtops into a bright new ocean of blue sky, where we chased our happy tails in the dazzling sun, and felt we were pretty close to heaven.

And there have been nights of crippling cold in a black sky laced with flak and fire, and ablaze with laser-like searchlight beams that could bleach the courage from you, while a town burned in the darkness below. And you've felt as if you were within a roasting eyeball's distance of hell.

Most of us are hoping for an easy trip, but we'll just take things as they come. So long as it's not one of those heavens where grizzled old warriors are awarded seventy virgins apiece. At our age, a thing like that could kill you.

And, of course, it could turn out to be very different from what we expected. We could end up on some Planet Valhalla in a strange new universe, where long-forgotten friends and long-forgiven foes wassail together while they yarn away eternity. I'd settle for that. Who knows, with a bit of luck we could even end up back on the same calm, contented and dignified planet where we lived when we were young. Because we most surely aren't on it any longer.

But wherever we end up – be it in Hull, hell, or Heddon-on-the-Wall – I know that I shall be in splendid company. And there'll be lots of laughter in the clouds.

CHAPTER THIRTY-ONE

The Mosquito

This is as much the story of a superb flying machine as it is of the people who flew it.

The Mosquito was the brainchild of the de Havilland Aircraft Company. The DH 98 (its official title) was an all-wood midwing monoplane powered by two Rolls-Royce Merlin engines. Conceived and produced within a year, the prototype's first flight was made on 25 November 1940, soon after the Battle of Britain, from a meadow behind Salisbury Hall, where it was built. This building now houses the Mosquito Aircraft Museum, where the prototype, W.4050, can still be seen.

It was produced in forty-three different versions, ranging through fighter-bomber, bomber, night-fighter, photo-reconnaissance, trainer and even target tower. Originally spurned by the RAF because it was constructed of plywood in an age of metal aircraft, it was nicknamed 'Freeman's Folly', after Air Chief Marshal Freeman, the one top RAF officer who encouraged it. It was built as a private venture and became known as 'the wooden wonder', one of the finest and fastest aircraft in the

The author and his navigator, Warran Officer Larry Euesden, flying a Mosquito Mark 36 in formation during a Battle-of-Britain flypast over London in September 1946. This mark was too late for the war – the prototype flew in May 1945 – but it was a development of the Mark 30, generally considered to be the best night-fighter in the conflict. Both were fitted with Merlin 113 high-altitude engines (but no pressure cabin!). The bulky nose, spoiling the clean lines of the original aircraft, housed the latest American Mk.10 radar but the twin receiving aerials on each wing-tip were standard on night-fighters from the Mark 2 Mosquito and the Mark 4 radar onwards. (See chapter twenty).

The hexagon logo on the nose was the badge of 85 Squadron.

Second World War. It could carry the same bomb load as an eleven-man Flying Fortress, with a crew of only two in a tiny cramped cockpit. As a long-range night-fighter and low-level intruder it destroyed the *Luftwaffe*'s night defensive forces and reduced RAF bomber losses by up to eighty per cent. It made pinpoint precision target attacks on Amiens prison and various Gestapo buildings to release prisoners or destroy vital files. It was variously fitted with a six-pounder cannon and depth charges. There was almost nothing that it couldn't do in air warfare. It even flew, unarmed, to Sweden for vital ball bearings and delivered (in a flimsy hammock in the hold) members of the Diplomatic Corps.

It was not an easy or a forgiving plane for beginners to fly, any more than a thoroughbred is an easy ride for an amateur jockey. But to those who learned to

War and Peace 1

A group of 239 Squadron aircrew outside their crew-room at West Raynham in 1944, at the height of the bomber offensive. (The C.O., W/Cdr Walter Gibb, is on the far left, the author on the far right). All but one of this particular group survived, but the final Squadron casualties were near thirty per cent.

handle it successfully it was the ultimate air fighting machine. Tremendously fast – the original aircraft was faster than a Spitfire – and carrying remarkable loads, it started with an all-up weight of 15,000 lb and went on to a weight of 25,000 lb in the final night-fighter version. It could range as far afield as Czechoslovakia. A total of almost eight thousand were built, and the plane was used by the RAF as a night-fighter until 1950. Today, there are few left, and only one still in flying condition, that being in the United States, in the Confederate Air Force.

War and Peace 2
Compare this picture of 85 Squadron pilots in 1947, after the war. Of this group the two Flying Officers on the right, F/O Platt and F/O Maxwell, were later killed. Myself (back row, far left), F/Lt Stan Durrant (front row, 3rd from left) and W/O Dicky Colbourne (back row, 3rd from left) all suffered serious injuries – Dicky was awarded the George Cross for dragging his navigator from a burning plane – while Sgt Bob Collins (back row 2nd left) had a minor ground prang (See chapter fourteen). Only the Flight Commander and the C.O. (front left) survived unscathed. It seems that in peace-time flying the difference was you risked death from cock-ups instead of cannon fire.

Index